From the
BATTLE OF
BRITAIN
to the
KOREAN
WAR

From the
BATTLE OF
BRITAIN
to the
KOREAN
WAR

SERVING IN THE WOMEN'S VOLUNTARY SERVICE
AND AUXILIARY AIR FORCE, 1940–1954

To Nanny + Marc

love from Steve

STEPHEN WADE

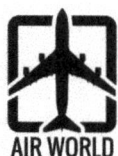

AIR WORLD

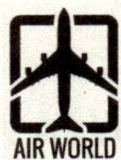

AIR WORLD

FROM THE BATTLE OF BRITAIN TO THE KOREAN WAR
Serving in the Women's Voluntary Service and Auxiliary Air Force, 1940–1954

First published in Great Britain in 2023 by
Air World
An imprint of
Pen & Sword Books Ltd
Yorkshire – Philadelphia

ISBN 978 1 39904 088 4

Typeset by SJmagic DESIGN SERVICES, India.

Printed and bound in the UK by CPI Group (UK) Ltd.

Pen & Sword Books Limited incorporates the imprints of After the Battle, Atlas, Archaeology, Aviation, Discovery, Family History, Fiction, History, Maritime, Military, Military Classics, Politics, Select, Transport, True Crime, Air World, Frontline Publishing, Leo Cooper, Remember When, Seaforth Publishing, The Praetorian Press, Wharncliffe Local History, Wharncliffe Transport, Wharncliffe True Crime and White Owl.

For a complete list of Pen & Sword titles please contact

PEN & SWORD BOOKS LIMITED
George House, Units 12 & 13, Beevor Street, Off Pontefract Road,
Barnsley, South Yorkshire, S71 1HN, England
E-mail: enquiries@pen-and-sword.co.uk
Website: www.pen-and-sword.co.uk

or

PEN AND SWORD BOOKS
1950 Lawrence Rd, Havertown, PA 19083, USA
E-mail: uspen-and-sword@casematepublishers.com
Website: www.penandswordbooks.com

MIX
Paper | Supporting
responsible forestry
FSC® C013604

Contents

Introduction

The Archive

I have been a writer for many years, and in that time my projects have been created for markets, often commissioned. A compelling story had not come to me, insisting that it must be written: that this life must be told. But then, a few years ago, such a story came. Rescued from a residential home where the last of three Cleethorpes sisters had died, a massive archive came my way. One of my students told me about it, and that it was about to go to the tip. Did I want it? Oh yes.

What I didn't know was just how massive the archive was. This eldest sister, Ruby (but known as Chris or Christine), had kept every single scrap from her life and the life of her sister, Beryl. There had been three sisters, all precious stones: the third was Illyrine (known as Rene).

There were five large boxes of letters; three boxes of slides, three photo albums and enough ephemera to fill a parish chest. From all this came Beryl, who was born in 1914 and died in 2005. She had served in the Second World War as a WAAF (Women's Auxiliary Air Force); then in Korea with the WVS (Women's Voluntary Service), followed by the Middle East, then to matron in an orphanage, and so on, until she retired into part-time work. Beryl never married but had at least three proposals of marriage.

I had to tell her story. She looks at me now from her picture, which rests on my bookshelf. But I also chose this project for the opportunity to engage in the search for my mother's life in the war. She was yet another dressmaker, like Beryl, and I never wrote down her life either. She died in 2011, aged 83, and she was making clothes on the day before she passed away.

If ever we need to look for a woman from the past whose life is an inspiration, then we need to look at a dressmaker from Cleethorpes who went to war – in fact, to several wars. They were not some marginal scraps on the edge of things. We're talking about the Second World War, the Korean War and the Middle East when it was breaking up, yet again, in the late 1950s.

I am trying to trace an extraordinary life: the woman in question is Beryl Baxter, one of three Cleethorpes sisters who all went to war, going their different ways. One Baxter sister, Chris, married Denys Peek, later the author of a best-selling war memoir; another, Rene, served in the forces, and as for Beryl – she went to war. Beryl died in December 2005, after a long and eventful career that included, in the post-Korean War years, working as a Matron at the Kent School in Germany (for forces families) and later working at various schools and orphanages. My book will recount her life from joining the WAAF in 1940 through to WVS work in Pusan and Inchon during the Korean War, and finally in Habbaniya, Iraq.

Beryl and her sister, Chris, saved everything from their lives, and this book emerged from their massive archive; material including everything from pictures of Hitler's bunker to Eisenhower's D-Day message to the forces, and from Beryl's entry to a beauty contest to her countless journeys across the globe by sea and air.

At the heart of the story are her letters home: thousands of them to her sisters, mother, friends and workmates. As I read these, gradually, I came to know Beryl like a close friend, following her through landscapes of war and into a succession of emotional entanglements in her progress through an adventurous life.

The Story

What to do about Beryl? She is a girlfriend. She is an inspiration. She has been in my life for three years, begging to have her life-story written down. Now the time has come to do that for her. Although she has been dead for some years now, so much evidence of her life survives that she is more real than a living person, in some ways at least. As I am a writer, I deal in stories; when I was a teacher, I was enmeshed in people's stories, and when I later worked as a writer in prisons – with both men and women – I had more stories. Before I acquired the archive of her life I lived innocently, with no notion of just how problematic an *excess* of material on a life might be. I was far more accustomed to the writer's struggle to handle too little material.

But now, as my little writing den gradually filled up with paper all relating to Beryl and her sisters, the time to start writing this story became more pressing. She had become my Muse I think: perhaps a Muse with an accusing tone about her. *Get on with it. I did. Roll up your sleeves and write my damned story, you slacker.*

Beryl Baxter looks at me from the shelf in my office. There are two photos, and on one, taken for a passport in 1938, there is a beautiful young woman aged 32. She wears a tight blouse with short sleeves, very much how we might imagine an office worker or a receptionist from those pre-war days. The other shows her just a year before, looking at the camera with a serious, resolute face. She is, by any standard, stunningly attractive, and on the back of the photo is a small entry-form, cut from the *Grimsby Telegraph*. It is for their 'Beauty Tourney' and Beryl has described herself on the form: she was then a dressmaker, single, living in Grimsby, and her full name was Beryl May Baxter. The paper was 'on a quest for a girl of beauty, charm and grace to become the Cleethorpes Carnival Queen.'

For over a year now I have been in love with this woman. She died in December 2005, but to me she is alive, charismatic, and yes of course, she is every inch a 'Carnival Queen' and would have done her town proud. In fact, she did her country proud and that is why I am writing this now.

INTRODUCTION

The WAAF

Beryl Baxter's life of service began when she joined the WAAF in 1939, and from there, working in at least four different bases around the country. She was to travel the world, and become, in many ways, the sister, girlfriend and mum of hundreds or even thousands of service personnel across the world. On the one occasion when the press took notice of her, she was profiled in a magazine and the writer summed up the essential nature of the girl from Cleethorpes:

'Seeing her, those soldiers' mothers would be the first to say, "Mind you bring that nice girl home to tea."'

The eldest of three sisters, Beryl lived with her family until the war came. She stopped dressmaking for villagers, to become a WAAF clerk. Then, as a plotter, she was engaged in air-sea rescue work; later she was posted to Malaya, demobbed, and joined the WVS in England.

One of her passports says it all: stamps and visas from Germany, Switzerland, Malaya, Singapore, Japan, Iraq, Libya and many more places. In her archive she has torn fragments showing that she travelled on ships and planes across the world, regularly; she was even on board the famous *Empire Windrush* after it had brought the first West Indians to Britain, and just before it was burned and lost on its final, fatal voyage. She was, I soon discovered, usually close by as a witness to many of the great events of her time. I feel that she was always near, ready with tea and sympathy, but more creatively, with a smile and a joke.

Beryl wrote endlessly to everyone she met and kept all their letters; she was mother to countless orphans and children at boarding school. Most of all, she will become, as the reader follows her story, someone known as vividly as a family member. Why? Because she loved and accepted love. She worked and saw the virtues of work.

Beryl was, in the finest sense, both everywoman and also Beryl, a unique woman. She is still watching me from that shelf, telling me to get on and tell her tale. But first, how and why did this begin? It started in a place she herself adored – a classroom.

It was in a classroom at Hull University where I first heard of 'three sisters who travelled the world'. My class was in creative writing and we had reached the topic of 'research'. Of course this is usually a dull aspect of the work, but in this case, a dry account of archives and sources was halted by a student in the group who mentioned a massive archive, which was destined for the waste disposal site if no one claimed it. She mentioned the three Cleethorpes sisters whose letters were in the material, and she knew that in their lives, letters had been generated in hundreds, and possibly in thousands, written between c.1938 and 2000.

How could I, a confirmed lover of past times and their alluring ephemera, resist this invitation to claim such treasure? Time is so greedy and it would soon claim this apparently chaotic heap of refuse from past years, covering everything from shop receipts to train tickets. The result was a trip to a suburb of Hull one Saturday morning. I expected to find perhaps a few folders or maybe a box or two of letters. What I took home was a mass of material, ranging from tin boxes of slides to hundreds of photos (large and small), and from multiple packs of letters all rubber-banded with scribbled words on scraps of paper, such as 'Korea' or 'Singapore', to theatre programmes and postcards.

The Sisters

Here were the remains of three lives, sisters, in a rich abundance of paper and card, with a photographic documentary element to accompany it. At first the story within that sheer uncatalogued mountain of memories seemed elusive, almost impossible to access. There would have to be weeks of reading, sorting, listing and logging of all the material. This would have to be done with a tiring process of selection and rejection, as some of the ephemera was of no value as social history or as something that would enlighten a reader about the life in question. At the heart of this story there were sisters – Chris Illyrene (known as Rene) and Beryl: three gems indeed in their mother's loving eyes. There was also a mysterious other sister – Miriam, who was swarthy, sturdy and somehow Mediterranean, exotic, among the array of pale Brits. She remained a mystery for some time.

The sorting was finally complete. The lives pieced together and the letters all arranged in date order. The story was there, awaiting its storyteller. I have had to restrict the timeline to the years c.1939 to 1955, as Beryl's experiences as a plotter for the RAF (Royal Air Force) and then in the theatre of war in Korea provide more than enough for two volumes.

Occasionally, she made it into the limelight. One or two magazine features from the 1940s and early 1950s give us a profile of exactly what she did with her life up to 1950 when she left for Korea. This, for instance, from her local paper:

Eldest of three sisters, Beryl Baxter lived with her family in the country till war came. She stopped dressmaking for villagers to become a WAAF clerk. Then, as a plotter, she was engaged in air-sea rescue work; later she was posted to Malaya. Demobbed, she joined the WVS in England when she heard they ran an overseas branch. Her training included motoring with meals on wheels, airing invalids and helping to run clubs for old people. Then she set off for three years' voluntary service in Germany.

The dressmaker had gone to war, with sewing-machine and determination to be of service. The same profile makes much of that fact: '... a trail of tacking threads followed Beryl Baxter and her sewing machine through the NAAFI clubs of Bad Oeynhausen, Luneburg, Buxtehude, Berlin and Bielefeld to Hamburg... Off duty, besides dressmaking, she went "walking round, seeing how the rest of the world lives".' On duty, she ran libraries and dances; helped reunite families and welcomed soldiers' wives at airports and railway stations. The reporter was impressed during the interview with this country lass, summing her up in these words: 'As organizer in charge of eight women at Hamburg House, she was one of the youngest to hold such a position. She hid her blue eyes behind spectacles in an attempt to look suitably dignified.'

There is the photo on the shelf then: that beautiful woman as she was when a succession of young servicemen were smitten with her and saw her as either wife material or as some kind of goddess of the war zone. She would have hated any fuss, let alone any idolization. With Beryl, it was hands-on, old school, job done, involvement in life.

Another photo in her archive introduces Beryl. This is the young WAAF recruit of 1939 answering the call to defend her homeland as the bomber raids began and the fighter pilots were being trained. She looks at the camera with a smile tinged with toughness and endurance; swaddled in the RAF greatcoat there is a young woman of 25, with that firm lipstick and flattened hair (with a little bow atop) characteristic of her time. Under the coat there is a white shirt and dark tie. She is uniformed in an age when almost everyone had some kind of identifying clothing, some mark of who they were and what they were about. What she was about was training, and she was on her way to RAF Silloth in what is now Cumbria.

Just as I have come to know Beryl, so I have deepened my understanding of my mother, Joyce's world too; they shared so much, from the stitching and hemming up to their loves and affiliations, their dreams and their aspirations. At 14, Joyce was doing as she was told in a man's world. Over the fireplace in the family terrace in Beeston there was granddad Joe's thick brown belt. This was the focus of discipline: through threat and fear. At her sweat-shop, she did as she was told. There was no union. You produced the goods and you survived. Later in life she had worked for others and then for herself.

She could look at a woman and then make a dress to fit her; she could look at a man and then make him a perfect made-to-measure suit. This has given me a special insight into Beryl's life. She made and mended clothes all through her life, as my mother did.

Beryl and her Generation

The most learned social and cultural historian, looking for the origins of that desire to make a difference, to contribute to the general pool of contentment, that emerged, as Beatrice Webb put it, towards the end of the nineteenth century when 'the idea of service was transferred from God to man', would struggle to explain the relentless need to achieve something worthwhile in the generations between c.1914 and the late 1930s. Of course, in the way of all this was the advent of totalitarianism. Set against this need to serve one's less fortunate fellow people was the wave of belief in strength, domination and control. But Beryl and her peers came from a society that was 'on the march' to show that it was bent on making things better in the struggling world that followed the death of Queen Victoria.

Film clips of the Edwardian period, along with countless memoirs and surveys of social history, show a society whose members wanted to be joiners: to be members of clubs, societies, social crusades, professional groups, and friendly societies. Beryl's family's contribution to this was their participation in the work of the Salvation Army in Grimsby and Cleethorpes. But beyond that was the implicit belief in self-improvement. After all, the last quarter of the nineteenth century had seen the burgeoning of the lower middle classes, most easily observed in the growth of the commuter class, whose desire for education is seen from one angle at least, by E.M. Forster in *Howard's End*, in the character of Leonard Bast, who reads the works of Ruskin, attends classical music concerts and enjoys debate and discussion about contemporary issues. In fact, that summary could almost apply to Beryl Baxter. She learned German, she read widely, she showed in her letters that she reflected on contemporary issues and trends, and above all else, she wanted to 'make something of herself' – a cry from the heart of many working class people who were no longer trapped inside their own niche in the social hierarchy after the education acts of 1870 and 1902.

The depth of feeling related to the idea of public service, together with hard work and earning money, is evident in Beryl's life before she became a servicewoman. In 1934, her parents wanted her to leave school before the statutory age of 14, but the County Council of Parts of Lindsey wrote to say that the girl would have to stay at school, stating that 'she is under obligation to attend school regularly until the close of the school term during which she reaches the age of 14 years...'

But within four years of leaving school, when war was imminent, Beryl had eleven shillings in the Penny Savings Bank at Weelsby Street Council School; she had also gained her second class certificate in dressmaking of the City and Guilds Institute, and in 1938 she passed the exam in German run by the Union of Educational Institutions. The year following, just before she joined up in the WAAF she also took her certificate in first aid from the St John's Ambulance Association. It was a time, in the late 1930s, that the entire family was preparing for war by gathering all the skills they could. Her sisters took certificates in air raid precautions. Beryl herself had invoices printed for 'Miss B.M. Baxter, dressmaker and costumier.' Her aunt had shown her a way, as she was Miss Gladys Driver, 'dressmaker and milliner' with a business address at 113 Weelsby Street. The Baxters and the Drivers, through the interwar years, were burning to swing into action, to be qualified and to contribute to society.

Exploring and recounting Beryl's life and in looking again at my mother's life, which was only ever passed on to me in scraps and fragments, I have come to see that as time goes by and the ranks of the veterans in the parades continue to shrink, the real comprehension of 1939–1955 fades away into that foreign land where they do things differently. It slips into the nostalgia magazines and the young only know it through the schoolroom, in textbooks and in old films.

I'm hoping that those young people read this, so they will learn as I have done. I am a child of the 1940s, born just after the desperately savage winter of 1947 when Beryl's generation had fought the wars and come home exhausted to see again the Home Front exhausted too. The 1950s were to bring a hunger for tranquil family life, for peace and harmony, and most of all fun. Beryl worked hard for that, and found it.

I see now how deep was the silence of those who had fought in the momentous wars of the twentieth century. I understand their reluctance to tell their stories. There were glimpses from uncles and aunts, grandparents and parents, but these were merely beams of light through chinks in the curtain of the past, never the full, dazzling sun of truth and reality. Uncle Bill had been there to see Mussolini and his woman strung up by the mob; another Uncle Bill had been a Chindit in Burma; Aunt Grace had battered her face against a post while walking in the black-out, and my mother had run home from the pictures when the siren sounded for the bomber-warning. But still, arching over all this, there was the general silence. Folk wanted to get on with life; they hungered for family stability, for normality. In contrast, for Beryl, her family were destined to touch a grander, more arching narrative of the Far East, for as well as Beryl's wartime in Korea, there was her sister, Chris's, marriage to Denys Peek, later to be a celebrated author related to the literature of the PoWs of Japan.

As I write this in late 2022, Denys Peek is still alive. He was born in 1921. His book, *One Fourteenth of an Elephant* (2005) dealt with the horrendous period he spent, along with his brother, as a prisoner of the Japanese after the fall of Singapore in 1942. He was at Wampo camp, Tonchan, Kanyu and Hintok. The book is arguably a modern classic of war writing. One review expresses its strength: 'Told with clarity, passion and an incredible eye for detail and description, this is an utterly enthralling story...'

As Beryl's brother-in-law, he was often in touch with her, and with Chris, of course. Finally, when married, he became a harbour master. Life with Chris did not work out well. They were divorced, and in the 1960s Denys went to Australia. He and other people from Singapore and Hong Kong figure in Beryl's letters from time to time, and it is clear that she liked him.

From my point of view – as a child of the 1940s I can now place Beryl's cultural life in a broader, more meaningful context. Looming over the following narrative is the sobering reflection that VJ Day came after the dropping of a nuclear bomb; Beryl's generation knew, at the back of their minds, that fate and circumstances could easily have brought the bomb into the armoury of the fascist states, and the world could have been very different. Reading Beryl's thousands of letters, it becomes evident that she became gradually aware of the wider questions embedded in international politics, and one of the most impressive aspects of her correspondence is that the letters open up the nature of sensitive, hardworking service men and women, who had to live in the minutiae of routine and disciplined life, while at the same time, keeping an eye on the distant threats to their civilized order and everything in life that they loved and valued.

The 1950s Context

An editorial in *Down Your Way* magazine summed up the decade of the Korean War by referring to the general feature that 'We were more respectful, disciplined and law-abiding...We were a nation of small shopkeepers; Woolworth's was our only convenience store for the cheap and cheerful.... Our only recreational 'drug' was recreation: kicking, hitting or throwing a ball around...' That might be a shade too cheerful and dreamy, but the essence of truth is there. Beryl went to Singapore and Korea at that time when there was a simplicity imposed on life mainly caused by the privations and aftermath of a society, which had been bombed and had lost a considerable slice of its population.

This book, after the wartime chapters, concentrates on that society, a time when people who had survived the threat of invasion and a profound threat to all they held dear now faced an uncertain future, but a future that was, nonetheless, optimistic though on a small scale. My own parents, who were working class, had aspirations which were typical of many and, like Beryl, my mother was a machinist who wanted a small business. My father, ex-navy, believed in fate and in work and play to the extremes. He cared little for possessions. His love of a family was at the heart of everything he thought and did.

To sum up then: introducing Beryl Baxter to my readers means that they are about to meet a woman who, on the surface, was typical of her times, but who, in her spirit and in her aspirations, was a very modern woman, keen on fulfilling all her dreams, and she saw work and service to her compatriots as the way to succeed. As my quotes from her letters will show, there was always a shadow over her – a mystery illness. Her two sisters were also to find that their physiological nature and general health would stand in the way of their plans in life, but all three donned their uniforms, and illness, chronic or otherwise, never kept them back.

Chapter 1

The WAAF
Training in Wartime

Beryl Baxter never planned anything. She just volunteered, along with thousands of her contemporaries. But nonetheless, as we look at the war period with the knowledge of hindsight, we discern a pattern: that there was a massive, embracing narrative arching over everyone, as the consequences of totalitarian action swung into place, and some individuals were embroiled in all kinds of large-scale events, while others saw little. The popularity of *Dad's Army* and our tendency to laugh at amateurism casts a dark cloud over the efforts of ordinary Brits as they began to see the magnitude of Hitler's threat – notably after Dunkirk. In the case of Beryl the dressmaker, she was destined to be involved in more than one theatre of war, and at the outset of her own war, there is no doubt that she bravely went wherever fate took her, and such is the profound story of those people of our island who worked whenever and wherever they were needed. One way of understanding Beryl and her generation is to check on some of the sources of the twentieth century development of the unmarried woman who trained for any one of thousands of possible occupations.

In 1909, the popular journal *The Englishwoman's Review*, contained an essay by Dora Jones, expressing this radical change, full of possibilities for women, even before the impact of the First World War, when women did many traditionally male jobs. Jones wrote: '... the average schoolgirl at the end of her course appears to have the choice of between thirty and forty avocations. She may be a teacher of the elementary school type. A nurse, a journalist, a chemist, a doctor, a bookkeeper, a teacher of ju-jitsu, a laundry manager, a rent-collector, a hairdresser....' Charlotte Brontë, writing fifty years before Jones, said something much closer to a definition of Beryl Baxter: '... there is no more respectable character on this earth than an unmarried woman who makes her own way through life quietly, perseveringly – without support of husband or brother, and who – having attained the age of 45 – retains in her possession a well-regulated mind, a disposition to enjoy simple pleasures, fortitude to support inevitable pains, sympathy with the sufferings of others and a willingness to relieve want...'

When she entered the war, the initial 'Phoney War' and the Battle of Britain had run their course, in terms of London and the first aerial threat of any consequence, but her training began when the next phase was imminent. There was much more bombing still to come in the shires, and a more general fear of invasion as the world waited to see what Hitler would do after his advance on Russia. Beryl and her sisters had a feeling that there was 'total war' across most of the world, but they fixed their attention on the immediate. They had no other choice.

Her sisters had joined up as well: Rene into the clerical side of the RAF and Chris as a WAAF teleprinter operator from 1940 to 1947. Beryl was the one who was most accurately described as being close to the front line in her war career. They all experienced a great deal of variety and a string of challenges, but it was Beryl who most profoundly developed the need to be involved with the armed forces.

The context of her world as she writes her first letters is in sharp contrast to the diarists and creative writers who had lived through the Blitz in London. More typical of the period between c.1939–1942 is perhaps in James Lees-Milnes' reflections: 'I went to bed soon after eleven in our cellar. At 12.15 a bomb fell with great noise. Our basement was filled with fumes, so I guessed the bomb had been pretty close. Got out of bed, put on gumboots and walked into the road.' Beryl, by 1941, is in distant Carlisle, and although she is aware of bombing raids, her first duties and concerns are with daily routine and the commands from above.

With this in mind, it is clear that from Beryl and others like her we have a less common perspective on the war. Little details such as her habit of knitting during a concert, or how she worries over her sisters and their illnesses; at the end of the first phase of the Battle of Britain, she joined the fight at the very epicentre, and in her time in Silloth she had not neglected the first demands of wartime for a service-person: that of understanding the reasons for every hierarchy. When someone 'throws their weight around' as she sometimes comments, it might be for a good reason. In other words, she becomes empathic and looks to understand motivations in the established tier of command.

The switch from civilian to WAAF tyro was no great ordeal for her, as she was accustomed to following orders, working in a team, and coping with any demands made on her mental and physical strength. From her hundreds of letters written in the years c.1940–1944, we learn that there was a longing for fun and escape from duty in her generation, but that longing was as strong as the general determination to join a struggle for survival. Beryl's letters show a notable restraint when compared to some wartime literature. If we glance at Joan Wyndham's journal, for instance, we find this as a typical entry for events in 1941: 'The station dance. Great excitement, everyone hoping to get off with a pilot... The hut was small and crowded, boiling hot and smelling of Brylcreem and sweat.'

She entered a war that had created a very special and unique atmosphere. The indefatigable writer and traveller, H.V. Morton, writing in 1943 looked back on that peculiar time just before Beryl joined up, evoking the social world in which she was to move around from base to base and from leave visit to various towns and homes: 'At this fateful moment in history... I took my gas mask in its virgin cardboard box and a small, dramatic first-aid outfit I had bought before... Gone was the careless, easy-to-see England that had been technically at peace for so long. It was another England I should see, technically at war.'

The life of service she embraced, coming from an attitude to life, society, family and others, was to create her own testimony to the culture she knew at a time of profound crisis, and like thousands of other women at the time, she was to make an immense contribution to a society in extreme need. The literature of these women – who gave willingly and wholly to others – keeps on growing as more research is done. Karen Farrington, for instance, in 2022 published an account of *The Angels of Engelmere Wood* telling the story of Lady Peyton's house, opened up to evacuated girls, and in particular the life of Doris Bailey who was the matron. This kind of contribution happened right across the country. A typical one such initiative was in Newark, for example, where Mary Collis and Madeleine Curry opened a home and workshop specifically for girls working in the factories.

For the first chapters in her Story, Beryl has to be linked to the Women's Auxiliary Air Force (the WAAF), which had been formed in 1939. She was there at the beginning of the Battle of Britain, when the German bombers were smashing British cities in what is now referred to simply as The Blitz.

In the first of the three passports I acquired in Beryl's archive, dated 1938, the photograph shows her aged 24, and states that she was a welfare worker from Grimsby. By the date of the passport being cancelled, the visa stamps total eighty-three, spanning visits to and from Japan, Holland, Germany, Hong Kong, Cyprus, Burma, Singapore, Aden, Jordan and Libya. Beryl Baxter was always on the move, as were her sisters. They came from a family whose lives were devoted to public service and to their country, from the First World War to the sisters' last work before retirement, in nursing, charity work and the caring professions generally.

In the Edwardian years, just on the eve of the First World War, there was a widespread acceptance of the nature of serving others. Being 'social' and community conscious, was central and fundamental to British identity. In addition to absorbing this ethos, the Baxters and Drivers were also involved in the good work being done by the Salvation Army, and of course, when 1914 came along, and young people were asked to respond to the call for conscription and go to fight or serve in another capacity at 'The Front' against Germany in France and Belgium, then the urge to contribute was as strong as ever. That ethos could be summed up by some key phrases: *Keep busy; do your bit; make a contribution; volunteer to help others; be patriotic and caring.*

Beryl's Grimsby family – the Drivers and the Baxters – were involved in the coal delivery service, dressmaking and in military service. Many of her relatives went off to war in 1914, and some never returned. But for Beryl, starting work around 1930, she would have been fully aware that she was one of many, and that they all thought the same way about what life was for. Her sister, Chris, for instance began her war by studying typing and French, while working as a shop assistant; she then served in the WAAF as a teleprinter operator, later moving to work in RAF Signals until 1946. She then worked in a transit hostel in the Far East, in Singapore later transferring to work with the Nederland Line, Royal Dutch Mail service.

Beryl's life echoed this. Apart from her WVS (Women's Voluntary Service) career she was an airwoman between June 1941 and June 1949. The assessment written on her discharge sheet by her commanding officer describes the woman revealed in the thousands of letters home – letters I use in this biography: 'During the period of three months she has been at this unit, she has proved herself to be a hard-working, capable girl, always cheerful and co-operative. She is very keen on social welfare work and should be successful in civil life especially if engaged in work of this nature.'

The Women's Auxiliary Air Force was formed in 1939, and enlistment was steady and numerous; pilots in the air command were in a separate group – the Air Transport Auxiliary, and so the

WAAF were dispersed across the whole establishment of the RAF during the Battle of Britain. The range of their work was impressive, going from simple packaging to radar, transport, and in the control of aircraft, mapping and plotting in many operations rooms, giving us the familiar image of uniformed female staff around a massive table, moving models around and responding to orders by the minute.

Beryl's training involved short stints at a number of locations around Britain. By June 1941, she arrived in Silloth, Cumberland. The aerodrome there had been opened in April 1939, and was basically a maintenance unit. A year after opening, it became Operational Training Unit No.1, working with Lockheed Ansons and Hudsons. When Beryl started her training, the place had been further developed, not only with new runways but with ASAF (Army Strategic Air Force) Liberator bombers based there too.

Beryl wrote home as soon as she arrived. Her letter opens up the truth of travel around the country at that time:

> Dear Mother,
> I know you will have seen by the postcards I sent that I arrived. Safely, but the latter part of the journey was quite eventful. The Newcastle to Carlisle train was an hour late so I missed the last one to Silloth. In the same boat as me was another WAAF from Coningsby... we were accompanied by two civilian men, students, who were also stranded en route to Dumfries. The four of us set about finding shelter for the night... we were soon joined by a Canadian soldier who carried our bags and took us along to the Toc H which proved to be closed for the night. Nothing daunted, we tried the Girls' Friendly Society which was very obliging, giving us a bed and food. Two old ladies, sisters and Catholics, were in charge.

After that, Beryl's trials were still not over, but she made it for breakfast the next day, and she notes that she received 'a hilarious welcome from the girls who were wondering what had happened to me...' But within a day, there was more drama, when an escaped prisoner was brought in about to be tried at a court-martial. Beryl wrote, 'She had got as far as the camp gates by the sea, and a soldier sentry recognised her... our Flight Officer made her empty her pockets, which after a struggle in which we all joined in, she did so.'

In the summer of 1941 Beryl was so much inside a routine that she could produce a commentary on the Carlisle weather. She was 'settled here nicely' and she loved it. But regarding the weather, she wrote, '... the mountains disperse the cloud into showers... one advantage however, is that the daylight lasts much longer.' The real excitement that August, though, was a party. She explained that at the WAAF party, 'Each has a short duty and I am at the refreshments bar. Our tickets allow each WAAF to take an airman so we are going to see among the many of them who want alterations done today.' There is evidence of Beryl's relentless quest to have a fully rounded education, and she wanted to learn something about music, and on that occasion, she had a chance to try out the bagpipes. In fact, there was a busy social round, with regular RAF dances and all kinds of social celebrations.

Beryl at this time shows why and how she was later, in her WVS career, to be involved in entertainments:

> The army was there: Polish, Canadian, Australian, New Zealand and of course all the WAAFs that could be spared from duties. The Central Hall, Silloth, was beautifully decorated by WAAF with flags and wings. I was detailed for refreshment duty from 10.15 to 11.15... All our officers were present, male and female, even the dentist. One of our sergeants crooned into the mike, for dancing, and we had several amusing competitions among the dancers...

Beryl was at work doing clothes alterations by Christmas, after such a challenging and busy initiation into life in camp. It is clear from the letters home that life was all about travel, self-help and coping with any task that came along. Many letters are about her sewing and about parcels being sent home or received from home. Her references give a vivid insight into camp life: 'I thought perhaps your parcel had lost its way as you will know by the second epistle I wrote I am writing this at work, after dinner, whilst Margaret is at the dentist's and Bill is altering a tunic...'

The immediate aim of the recruits was to attain the rank of Leading Aircraftwoman (LACW) after gaining their first status of Aircraftswoman 1st Class, and in December, Beryl wrote to her mother: 'Margaret, Bill, Ben the Jewish tailor and myself all went down to Witteringham, Northamptonshire. We stayed till Thursday... we girls had passed out ACW1 and the men LAC [that is to wear propellers on their sleeves]. We two girls are to sit for our LACW's in January.'

In early 1942 Beryl had some leave. Her Silloth Christmas had been very happy, and she notes that the party was 'a hilarious affair for even the M.O. got tight', and she went to see a film, accompanied by a corporal of the police with whom she had been to the Christmas party. Then, in February that year, there is a reference to something that recurs in the story of Beryl's life. She had a chronic illness. She went to see a new sick bay, and in discussing illness, she explained to her mother: 'You know things do not improve and there is a lot of uneasiness about the usual worry. I wish I could see a clear path to the root of *the trouble*. You know by this letter that I am very worried and I wish that you could help me. Anyway, just keep praying for me. I need it.'

Everyday life carried on, whatever the illness was, and Beryl collected coupons, bought flannelling and had her fortune told. She was still learning, growing intellectually, and taking all available opportunities to improve herself. She was having German lessons from a sergeant in the intelligence corps, and she also managed to have a short visit to Wordsworth country, and to Threlkeld, by the beautiful mountain of Blencathra. Beneath all this, she was instinctively following the attitude expressed by writer James Agate in his diary for 1940: 'A good wartime maxim – no day without its laugh!'

That summer she also thought about her future, and she was beginning to long for a change of work and location; she reported in a letter about an interview with her Flight Officer 'about my remustering' and apparently, though she had filled in an application form, papers had been lost. She summed up her situation stoically with the words, 'So the decision of the Air Ministry Records is what I await now.'

Life in training was rich and full, with time to sit by the River Eden to watch a cricket match, and go to the picture house to watch films. By July 1942, Beryl is still in Silloth, and she was working as a tailoress. There is something of the atmosphere conveyed in a letter home in July: 'We had two new tailoresses posted to us last week... Mary is Scotch and comes from Dunfermline. She is a very bonny blonde lassie. The other one is an equally bonny brunette who comes from Grimsby. They both came from a Scottish drome. They do not like it here at all.' But there was plenty to do. Security films were shown regularly, such as *The Next of Kin*, which, as Beryl noted, 'everyone here has been obliged to see.'

(It is interesting to note that even the word 'clerkess' was used on documents at the time.)

There were men, of course, and most of these trainees and conscripts met the WAAF women. In the memoirs of the men at this time, we have another view of Beryl's world in her year of initial training. Keith Waterhouse, for instance, was recruited into the RAF and he recalled: 'While Wythall seemed small beer compared to Malaya, a compact former balloon station with comfortable quarters in marked contrast to the Nissen hut wilderness of North Yorkshire, it had two advantages. One was the presence of a large quantity of WAAFs, the first female company encountered in six months. He later adds something that Beryl never really mentions: 'The course finished with a jolly NAAFI [Navy, Army and Air Force Institutes] dance followed by a mass exodus to the nearby allotments where all who retained their virginity lost it...'

But by the late summer of 1942, Beryl was restless. She wrote home, 'I am so determined to change my job.' She referred to others who were posted away, such as one girl who was sent to 'a Scottish isle off the coast of Argyllshire' Beryl explained that 'According to a letter we got from her today she likes it and everyone is very kind and hospitable. The inhabitants only speak Gaelic and there are no trees.' Beryl comments that 'We WAAFs don't half get about' and she is restless, interspersing her reports of activities with some general notes, such as 'The war seems to get a bigger mess than ever, doesn't it?'

There is much to be learned from the documentation in the war culture. A plethora of information booklets is in evidence whenever we review the social history of the WAAF lives. For instance, Group Captain Selway produced a booklet of 'Notes for new arrivals' aimed at WAAF recruits. Selway covers mail, travel, welfare, medical issues, sports, education, legal aid, church and library. An insight into Beryl's activities is found in Selway's list of entertainments. He includes a station cinema, open every night except Wednesday; a show from ENSA (Entertainments National Service Association) every other Wednesday; dances and whist drives, and performances by the Station Voluntary Band. The NAAFI was open for a mere three and a half hours a day.

Beryl had become used to the officialdom and protocol in a fighting outfit. In her cache of materials that were preserved from that time, the modern reader finds as much social history as details of daily military duties, and in fact that is a fair reflection of the life on the Home Front when fear of immediate invasion had faded. By the time Beryl settled into a new life in Watford, fully qualified and by then proficient in all the basic skills and knowledge of her place in the scheme of things, most activity was related to sorting out the ruins and worrying about overseas theatres of war, where so many loved ones were caught up in what was to be one of the major wars in world history.

Chapter 2

In the Operations Room

After the Battle of Britain, which tapered off in late 1940, there was an aftermath, with two years of various bombings of different methods and objectives, and so by 1942, when Beryl's training was complete, she still experienced bombing, but she was at work at the hub of the gradual switch from defensive to offensive action between the German bombing campaigns after 1940, and D-Day.

She travelled south from Silloth at the time when the triumphs of the 'fighter boys' and also Hitler's tactical errors in the wider context had meant that the magnitude of British successes could begin to be understood. Historians have since assessed the significance of the Battle of Britain successes in cosmopolitan terms. John Ray, for instance, in his detailed account of the war of the fighters and the Blitz lists several significant outcomes, and principally perhaps is this: 'By fighting on without surrender, Britain gave hope to many nations in Europe which were conquered and occupied during the war years. Millions of the territories which fell under German domination regarded Britain as a beacon of light and hope amid the darkness and oppression.' Beryl came into the very heart of the British fightback at the very time when the air success and the failure of any German invasion had opened up new possibilities. Not the least of these was the entry of the USA into the war.

From her lowly place at the end of the chain of command, Beryl saw and commented on the multi-national unity and effort. She met Americans and also had glimpses of the higher command. Her correspondence between 1942 and 1945 gives both a panoramic view and a close-up on the social life under the threat of destruction.

By October, Beryl was on the move to Middlesex. She was about to experience a huge transformation in her life, and in particular, in her experience of the war. From the wilds of Cumbria where she was mending clothing and organising parties, she went to the very hub of RAF activity in the Battle of Britain. By mid 1942, when she arrived at RAF Uxbridge, the base had been at the heart of the action. It had been a government estate since 1915, and by the outbreak of war it was the HQ of No.11 Group RAF, responsible for supervising and protecting London in the years of bombing. Beryl Baxter, dressmaker from Grimsby, found herself in the No. 11 Group, and living at 'The White House' from where she wrote home. Her base was to be known as the Battle of Britain Bunker. Not only had the Operations Room played a part in the Dunkirk events, but it was to feature in D-Day, and in fact, Beryl kept her copy of the circular from Eisenhower telling his force that he had 'full confidence in your courage devotion to duty and skill in battle'.

Not long after arriving in Watford, Beryl wrote home, and she had plenty to report. It must have been an exciting place to be. Records show that there was an area in the bunker where the royals could observe; also, visits from Charles de Gaulle and Lord Mountbatten are recorded, and she may even have met the actor Rex Harrison, who was stationed with Bomber Command.

A letter home in November 1942, gives us a comprehensive sample of activities done and experiences logged; she went to see *Mrs Miniver* 'a very lovely film of this war' and to the theatre to see Jack Hulbert and Ciceley Courtnedge in *Full Swing*. Still hungry for entertainment, she went to a gramophone recital in the recreation room. Work followed: she wrote, 'I am now going to supper and then on duty at midnight until 7 a.m. Ugh! It's cold for night watch here tonight.' She did one night watch in every three nights, and in the midst of all this, she told her mother, 'Still, I do like this job!' She took all the simple pleasures she could in her free time, even cycling to Denham with her friends to see the British Film Studios.

She reported for her mother: 'We had our tea at the loveliest Tudor style cafe – hot scones and butter, jam and sponge cakes and tea from a willow-pattern tea-service.'

In early 1943 we learn from the many letters home that education takes a front seat. 'I found that I had to have a week's course of lectures beginning on Monday morning so I did not get a break.' The subjects of the lectures are not specified, but this reference hints at something quite demanding: 'Never in my life before did I hear in so short a period, the words scaffold and execution, and I hope not to repeat it.'

What begins to emerge as a major characteristic of wartime correspondence is the sheer diversity and demands of travel across the land. Beryl and her peers moved around, on leave and in finding activities in their spare time, using buses and trains, but more often hitching lifts and sharing various vehicles. It seems to be a very dangerous occupation, a woman often travelling alone and taking lifts from strangers, but she took the risks.

Still, time off the shifts meant that she got to know London well:

> *I... went up to London... next morning I went for a walk in St James's Park, which today is a picture all yellow and white tulips, lilac, mauve and white and yellow roses, and of course the multi-coloured ducks on the lake... Of course the sparrows and fluffy baby ducks came too. I had that Long-deferred visit to the Tower, and all the gruesome spots to be seen there. The Beefeater who showed us around had a lurid imagination and an Irish brogue.*

Adventurous travel, by hitching, was common and Beryl notes that when her mother found out that she had hitched from Watford to Gorleston (Suffolk) 'she worried herself very much' Beryl explained what had happened: 'Joan herself and another Joan, another friend of hers, hitched up, the same day together. I was supposed to be with them but went alone as I knew we would never get far if all three were together.' A particularly interesting note follows in the same letter: 'One amusing part of their hitching was when a convoy of black American soldiers insisted on giving them a lift but they were a little nervous of accepting.'

One truly epic level adventure in internal travel occurred in August, 1943. Beryl tells the tale:

> *Last week on break I went to Oxford with Joan Hall. We hitched the 30 or so miles. It is from here. The first lift we got was from a Wing Commander with a very nice car, who took us as far as Denham. Soon after this an American army transport came along and took us all the rest of the way. The boys in it gave us sweets, chewing-gum and apples, took us out to a super lunch in Oxford. They wanted us to go right through to Newport in Wales, and we surely would have done if we had not promised to meet Joan's boyfriend in Oxford. We could have got back in time from Wales the next day...*

It is clear from this that there was an unwritten code of mutual help and respect for fellow service personnel on the road. The long trip ended when they caught a bus in Abingdon and made it home.

January 1944 began for Beryl with the usual routine of darning, knitting and reading in her free time, but there is now a German class. Since her teens, Beryl had taken an interest in learning German, and of course, knowledge of the language was a decided advantage in her current work. She had gained a basic certificate in her early teens and now joined an evening class. The students were keen: 'Peggy has insisted that he [the teacher] comes up to the house to teach us now, so that may have something to do with... everyone is as keen as mustard about the class and the rivalry is amusing.'

The pleasures were taken and enjoyed to the full, but the dismal events of the war impinged on all Beryl's communications. Writing to her mother in April 1943, she notes: 'I'm very sorry to hear about the ATS [Auxiliary Territorial Service] girls; one of our girls has just lost her home through bombs. It happened whilst she was in hospital for an operation.' Beryl herself as she wrote had a painful blister, a dose of hay fever and of course, homesick blues.

The fun was always there, though, and always taken seriously. A Wings for Victory Week was held in April. 'It ended with... a smashing dance at which there was an auction of things such as a bottle of whisky, a kiss from a pilot officer, a box of Turkish cigarettes, a dozen eggs and a cake.' It is also worth noting that criminal trials were also accepted as part of the available public entertainment, because Beryl went to the Old Bailey to see 'how English justice works'. It turned out that the case she saw was a divorce. She was rather disappointed: 'The participants were all farm people from Devonshire. The speech was mostly in broad dialect and very amusing, and so were the judge and K.C.s... I must go to a juicy murder trial some time, I think.'

She also used her spare time for reading. In one letter she wrote: 'I've read some good books lately. *Blood Relations* by Philip Gibbs is the best of this week's batch. *Cross of Peace* by the same author I am reading now. I am also half-way through *Memoirs of a British Agent* by Bruce Lockhart.'

She was now working under the threat of Hitler's V-1 – the so-called 'Doodlebug' rocket bomb. As its German name states ('weapon of reprisal') this was an instrument of terror, meant to hit targets in common life and so inflict fear and panic on civilian populations. In the summer of 1944 the first ones arrived, and the very first hit killed several people in London.

That summer Beryl wrote to her family: 'As you will see by this, I am still alive and kicking, despite the doodlebugs. I am rather unpopular with my room-mates about these things, as every time a low-flying aircraft comes over, I wonder aloud if it's a doodlebug.' Then, later on, she gave a more detailed account of the fear these monster bombs created:

> One night... they [her workmates] were all asleep and I was late to bed, sitting on my bed doing my hair. I heard the alert but did not take much notice till I heard a low-flying aircraft (I thought) then the engine stopped running just as I was wishing one of the girls was awake to identify it with me. One was, but as a great crash shook the place, she sat up in bed and said sleepily, 'My dear, that time is was a doodlebug and you never thought to mention it...'

A month later there was another close shave: 'A doodlebug is certainly something I shall miss when I am on leave... one decided to be really spiteful, and blew out the windows of our mess, but mercifully, it was just in that morning interval when it had been cleaned but it was half an hour early for the serving of lunch. We were on duty in Watford so that was better still.'

Life at Cassiobury Drive, Watford was always busy, and in between worrying about doodlebugs, there was plenty of distraction and interesting leisure. Writing in mid 1944 she notes that 'Ruby is up to her eyes in romance', but Beryl herself was always on the move. She enjoyed the country around Berkhamstead, which was 'gently sloping country' but also never ignored entertainment to send home, such as this snippet of royal activity:

> I heard a good story today. Not long ago it appears, the King and Queen paid a visit to Portsmouth, and visited one or two of the ordinary folk. The King wore naval uniform, and the Queen knocked at a door, which was

opened by a raggy urchin. She asked politely, 'Is your
mother at home, sonny?' To which he replied, 'No ma'am
but she said that if any sailors and girls called, the use of
the back room is half a crown.' I should love to have seen
their faces...

It was not only the bombing that caused a stir in the mess: the mice were another irritation. One of her mess-mates was terrified of mice, and Beryl wrote: 'We have a family of field mice living in our room. One night when I went in about ten p.m. during a raid...she was marooned on her bed and dare not get off it as mice were running over the floor. She wanted to get under the bed away from the flying glass but still couldn't make up her mind...'

The esprit de corps was very rich, and it is clear from the letters home that Beryl was well liked. So much so that she was the subject of some badinage, and even a friendly poem, in which she was described:

She always wears the same old dress.
Poor girl it's just her luck.
To wear initials on her breast
But it isn't Donald Duck.
She's square of chin and light of hair.
Her dress well made of cotton.
All night long rests on a chair.
God bless her little...'

At Watford, Beryl still had the time to cultivate her theatrical interests, and in one letter she described her work with the Unity Theatre, which had been formed in 1936, at first in Somerstown; it emerged from the growth of the Workers' Theatre Movement, which aimed at opening up social issues and concerns specifically for working class people. In this it was entirely in keeping with the boom in documentary writing and the many small magazines that were interested in expanding readership of literary forms and political writing to wider audiences. At its heart it had a Brechtian basis, an agitprop aim. They even included air raid shelters and other public spaces in their drama locations. Several notable writers of the 1930s and 1940s had been involved in some way, including Lionel Bart, Christopher Isherwood, Ted Willis and several famous actors.

Beryl went to see their production, *All Change Here* in July 1944. She was far more than a spectator, however:

> *A show that is still running is All Change Here given by Unity Theatre, of which I am a member. I saw it last night and had a talk to some of the cast. One tried to recruit me as an actress, but I think I must sort out that idea a little more before I accept... At present I just help in the wardrobe department when I have time.*

The D-Day landings took place on 6 June, and Beryl, along with everyone else, was full of interest in this. Her copy of the circular from Eisenhower is preserved in pristine condition in her archive. She was also doing her bit, as usual.

In one of her last letters from Watford, before she was moved, her test for a promotion to LACW (Leading Aircraftwoman) was imminent. But she still found time to help out in the local Orthopaedic Hospital. She wrote, 'I'm no good of course at skilled nursing but I can char generally. The cases in there are chiefly spinal cases from Normandy battles. They are a happy lot, however, and are employed doing the loveliest toy-making and tapestry embroidery.' She had even thought about trying to get out to France and join in the assaults and advances. She notes that for anything like that she 'may have to learn to cook, or anything domestic'. Some of the girls from her station had gone to France, and she was keen to join them.

At this time she was applying for a number of new posts, and even considering transferring to use her special skills: 'I have just put in for a course as a dressmaking instructress' and she was having problems doing that basic work, noting that patterns were hard to find and were consequently very dear. Yet she was working hard knitting to make up for the lack of sewing equipment. She told her mum that she was 'getting through compiling a civvy wardrobe... it would be quicker if I had a machine here...'

Although she never realised it, she was also a witness, over the years of her time in the home counties, to a transition that the writer and traveller H.V. Morton summarised when he wrote a preface (in the 1960s) to a book he had published before the war: 'The countryside was still largely hand-tended: the tremendous mechanization of agriculture, which occurred during the Second World War, had not taken place and the plough team jingling home was still a characteristic sound in many villages.' Somerset Maugham, doing the same update for his *Writer's Notebook*, gave the opposite picture: 'The war had destroyed much: there had been a grave loss of life but there was no longer the unemployment the fear of which had hung, a black cloud, over the lives of my friends.'

By early the next year she was bound for RAF Aston Down, near Stroud. She arrived just a few days before VE Day, and in a letter home written in late May she was clearly busy wondering what the future would bring now that there was no more active service in the war. She wrote, 'Of course, I suppose we shall all be drafted to other jobs soon like helping with demobilization etc. I have put in for an interpreter's job in Western Europe, as anyone who has knowledge of German and could be fluent on a three-month course... can apply.' She explains the major reshuffling in her life as well, in a broader context: 'Most of the Watford girls are now being sent back to the R.A.F. as R.O.C. has now closed down.' This group, the Royal Observer Corps, was always a temporary measure. But her letters evoke the spirit of the time, with such

19

important details of social history as the re-establishment of the iconic Eros:

> *London shows lots of signs of returning to peace... Now*
> *I saw that yesterday the Eros statue is coming out of its*
> *wartime dress of protective hoardings which encourage*
> *one, in large letters, to save.*

Beryl in May 1945 was at a major turning-point in her wartime life. She was frustrated when she learned that she failed her test for LACW by only six points. That time was one of transition, but the aftermath of the doodlebugs was still in everyone's minds. Beryl recalled a friend: '... it worked out to losing her brother and father in a doodlebug raid, which is not so happy a thing to happen to anyone.' There was exhaustion in the air that summer. She comments, '... everyone is getting so tired out at present. The M.O. says we are very tired and low in resistance through our type of work and hours of duty.

But at the heart of these summer months was VE Day and her own celebrations, as she was pondering the fact that she had to sign on for two years in order to get into the occupation army in Germany. The celebrations began, and Beryl gives a lengthy account of this, following a lecture on being demobbed and resettled, the party began:

> *Two of our sergeants have come in properly tiddly.*
> *They are celebrating already. I wish you could see them*
> *standing on the window sill demanding unconditional*
> *surrender from two other N.C.O.s standing below on*
> *the path, who have a bottle of whisky. We are waiting for*
> *our share of it when they've finished parleying. I have*
> *arranged to go with a boy friend to Cheltenham tomorrow*
> *to a philharmonic concert in the town hall.*

The celebrations there got out of hand. While bonfires were being lit, and the whole camp was singing and drinking, there was an accident: 'Three of our girls and several of our officers were in a car crash during the afternoon. The driver was very drunk but on-one realised it until too late. Today everyone seems to have a hangover.'

Just after this they had to smarten up, as they had a visit from a VIP Beryl reported, 'Whilst I write this, I can look up and see Mr Herbert Morrison, Minister of Home Security, who is paying us a visit today.' But in between the pubic events and duties, Beryl was continuing with a hobby she had been cultivating for some time. She had become interested in palm-reading, and she was perturbed by this at the time, when there was still much suffering around: 'I'm getting a little scared now of telling people's futures, as so much works out as I say. But as I have a penchant for telling the pessimistic side of things you can see what I mean. One lady who works in the canteen greatly believes in me, but as I told her of coming events which worked out...'

It was a worrying time as well as a jubilant one for Britain. Winston Churchill had been seriously ill not long before VE Day, suffering from pneumonia, and a little later, there were some who thought he had dementia. Henry Channon, in his journal, also noted that there was a bus strike on VE Day but that didn't stop Beryl from travelling, of course. Channon was in London for the celebrations, writing that on the day he woke up in the Ritz and then 'Everyone kissed me... The streets were empty of cars... singing people but no rowdiness.'

In August she was moved again, and this time it was to the accounts section at RAF Merryfield near Olminster, Somerset. This base had been prominent in the D-Day preparations, as it was the centre for 1,500 American troops in May 1944. On the big day, the base contributed to the formation of the huge force of aircraft going over to Normandy; later it was used for the squadrons working on evacuation, and by the time Beryl arrived, Transport Command, specifically for No. 53 Squadron. In early 1944 the American forces' engineers had worked on the base, in preparation for the bombers, which were to operate from there later.

For Beryl it was a period of transition, and really her career was in a hiatus. Clearly, she was at a crossroads and longing to be in Europe. But as she arrived there, the news of VJ Day arrived and she wrote: 'Everyone on camp seems to have been put off the stroke so far as work is concerned, by the wonderful news from the Far East. I spend my odd moments trying to imagine what this means for the many prisoners of war who were taken at Singapore.'

But everyday life still had its pleasures and distractions. For most of her life of service, Beryl had boyfriends, and indeed she was to have several proposals of marriage from servicemen in later years. But in Somerset at this time, she had attentions from one young man that were not really welcome: 'I travelled back from London to Taunton with one of the corporals from Merryfield. I am afraid, however, he has attached himself to me which is promising to be a bit of a nuisance. We have been cycling together... him trying to show me the lovely odd spots of beauty... the air is like wine, and I have already lost most of my cold.'

Here we have Beryl's nature encapsulated in the juxtaposition of what was potentially romance with everyday maladies. In her life there was always something urgent, either duty or deadlines, and somewhere close by, there were possibilities of relationships and ties of emotions. However, there was very little time for anything but work in late 1945. She was swamped with office work. 'I spend a lot of my time dealing with release papers. One of our boys goes tomorrow on occupation duties in the Far East – lucky devil, I wish I were him.' But the reader has the impression that she never slept. When she was not on official duty she was still sewing: 'We had a concert here and in company with the tailor, I helped with the costumes. It was a great success and afterwards we had a lovely supper party.'

Social life was dizzying and demanding; on one occasion she notes that she was having a coffee supper at 12.30 a.m. and that 'after that there was crackers, a bonfire and eventually a dance... we got to bed by 3.30 a.m.'

In 1946 Beryl was moved again, now serving out her time in the WAAFs and thinking of her uncertain future. While in transition, she was briefly based at Milton Ernest Hall, which was the centre for the Special Operations Executive, in Bedford. It was for a while the base for the US 8th Air Force. For Beryl, it was a busy, sometimes confusing place, but she did plenty of dressmaking and witnessed lots of activity, such as a bunch of officers shooting game birds, but she had more time to write home and catch up with things there. One officer was clearly dishing out plenty of onerous work, as Beryl wrote, 'Brenda is Barbara's buddy now so she leaves me alone except for such things as making me duty airwoman this week so I couldn't go away. Thank God she has gone away though, till Tuesday...'

Things were about to change, and radically, as she moved to the South East Asia Command headquarters.

Chapter 3

Away to the Far East and Back

The first trip out to Singapore was momentous. Not only did Beryl have her first taste of the Occident: she also met and stayed with her sister, Chris, who was serving there. When Chris left the service she worked for a Dutch shipping line, and it was around this time that she met her future husband, Denys Peek. But in 1946 she still had a few years to serve in the WAAF, leaving service in June 1949. Beryl was now with the South East Asia Command, and after VJ Day, there was plenty to do in all areas of the Far East. In March 1946 Singapore became a Crown Colony. The place Beryl was to experience was teeming with people of all races and backgrounds. She was to arrive in a tumultuous world.

Part of this world in transition was, of course, the massing of prisoners-of-war of the Japanese. From late 1945, Singapore had been the headquarters of the British Military Administration, commanded by Mountbatten. There were widespread social problems for a while after the end of the war with Japan; these were partly owing to the confusion in the shipping administration, and there were food shortages. Not until a year or so after Beryl's arrival in the autumn of 1946 was there any sign of improvement. There had been criminal activity on a high level too, and there were the usual accompaniments of post-war slumps – malnutrition and no real welfare provision.

Yet at the time of Beryl's arrival, at least education had been attended to, and measures were taken in this respect, notably in the reopening of schools. By March 1946, 62,000 children had been put into the school system.

There had been a useful contribution by the Foreign Office in 1945. There were some loose ends regarding the political situation involving Malaya, and some still thought that Singapore should be included in that confederation, but guerrilla fighters and others who had fought Japan were involved in peace preparations and in forming new alliances.

The problems facing the thousands of service people such as Beryl, going out there to help wherever they could, naturally included the assistance required for the prisoners of the Japanese – those who had worked on the railways and others who had been in the tough camps. The issues faced were primarily those of malnutrition and tropical diseases. The consequences of malnutrition had to be dealt with in terms of 'syndromes', so that, for instance, specific illness such as dysentery, malaria and cholera had to be treated. There was also, naturally, what we today call PTSD (post-traumatic stress disorder). It has been estimated that this was evident in a third of the prisoners from the Far East theatres of war.

Christine (Ruby) was waiting for Beryl in the summer of 1946; she was with the WAAF Singapore Signals Centre, and she wrote to her sister several times before Beryl boarded the ship in Liverpool. Chris gives glimpses of this new Singapore. Much of what she notes is entirely cultural, and so we have a brighter side of life in a post-war society, such as the visit of The Anglo-Polish Ballet, or her going to the cinema to see *The Barretts of Wimpole Street* with Roger Livesey. She had a friend called Alan and went for dinner at his bungalow where he lived 'with three other naval officers at HMS Round the Bend – a delightful spot about fifteen minutes drive from Tanglin'. She also made full use of the more classy side of life there, going to the notorious Phoenix Club for a dinner and dance. Then there was the esprit de corps as in a visit out to Jurong on the west of the island where 'The RAF were great fun and gave us a lovely time, even packing us with sandwiches for the night watch.' Jurong-Krangi was a fall-back defence line position.

On the more unpleasant side of post-war life, there was the notorious Changi Jail: 'We spent a day up at Changi but I didn't see Dora. I wonder if we'll like it when we move up there. Changi Jail looks a sinister spot. Did I tell you that one of the war criminals was shot there recently. I haven't fancied the beach since.' Still, Chris always loved to report on the high life and on living conditions. She loved to inform Beryl about domestic arrangements, the price of fabric and food, and on cultural activities. Bungalows were a favourite topic: 'By the way, bungalows here are two-storey affairs often. Servants' quarters at the back downstairs, open balcony lounge and dining room upstairs. Very pleasant. Their boys served a lovely five-course dinner....' She relished the culture of the days of empire, of course.

In June, Chris sent a letter with a detailed plan of the flats where she was living. It shows a degree of luxury she always loved, from the bathroom 'complete with hot water and cold showers' along with French doors leading onto a grand balcony, lots of large windows, and beds for six people. She noted that it was 'rather like a hospital'. The pleasures of life were also available at the NAAFI lido where there was, '...a huge swimming pool beside the sea, with stretches of grass to sunbathe on... a wonderful view over the harbour to the waterfront buildings, a large clubhouse... I'm going to a party there tonight.'

There could be no sharper contrast than the letters from the two sisters. Beryl's words were all about work, practicalities and social conditions; her sister was keen to stress the good things and to largely ignore the tough realities of the post-war world.

Then, on 22 September 1946, Beryl set sail for Singapore, on board the *Empress of Australia*. There was an element of foreboding in the journey because, earlier that year, the ship had been in trouble at Liverpool when its anchor was tangled with that of a cargo liner, the *Debrett*, and it had taken seven tugs to extricate the vessels.

Still, nothing could spoil Beryl Baxter's sheer delight in going on that journey. Her letters home show a woman living in absolute bliss as she progresses through the Mediterranean, Suez and the Indian Ocean; she loved every minute of that journey. She also acquired a word that would become one of her favourites. She was just 30 years old, embarking on a new adventure, and everything was 'wizard'. Before she sailed, she wrote to say, 'The girls are a wizard lot, eight of them on my draft and another eight in the hut next door... the tropical kit is wizard. We are thrilled to bits with it. I wish you could see me in a khaki drill suit with a large-brimmed felt bush hat, turned up one side like the Aussies wear. We've had a very busy week, visiting M.O's and dentist... I had a broken tooth repaired... we had an x-ray taken of our lungs...' She had spent some time packing as well – 'what a panic... thirteen pairs of knickers, blue khaki and white, and bags of stockings for protection against mosquitos.'

From Burtonwood, Beryl had written and made sure that she asked for essentials from home, although some items were for sheer style, such as snakeskin shoes. She enjoyed Burtonwood, 'a lovely camp' and there she had fried egg, peas and spuds, bread and jam, with home-made currant buns. But the place was to be the last of England for some time, and she had her essential vaccinations that didn't affect her 'except to bring on the usual again' whatever that was.

On 24 September she was out at sea 'on the foaming brine' looking at Cape Finisterre, after leaving Liverpool, '*The Empress of Scotland* coming in as we came out, and greeted us on the siren. The first day meant that fifteen WAAF girls were seasick but when recovered, Beryl reported as if she was a child full of joy at a party: '... we even get China tea... at the shop on board we can get Turkish delight and biscuits, soap, and all sorts of things unrationed. At breakfast we always get fruit...' In the evenings, they all wore their full-dress uniforms 'while the civvies come out in all manner of creations'.

The accommodation was eight in a cabin designed for ten, and Beryl was pleased with the wash bowls, mirrors and wardrobes; she relished people-watching and commented on '...quite a lot of the Chinese navy with officers on board... never saw so many lovely kiddies before, lots are Chinese and Eurasian... so many harassed mummies, so we look after offspring while mummy gets a bite to eat.'

The ship had plenty of servicemen bound for the East as well: 'A lot of RAF boys from the PDC [Personnel Dispatch Centre] are here, bound for Japan, and the missionaries and priests aboard are all for Hong Kong.' The RAF boys had been on a leave of eight weeks, and in fact some were for Singapore. Beryl begins to use the word 'Singy' for Singapore as the trip progresses.

There was also the practical and important question of sea-sickness. She managed to cope with this after some initial difficulties, noting that, 'One soon learns how to walk with a sway and get along, but in makes me giggle when in the dining-room walking sedately down the middle, one's feet suddenly seem not to know their way. It's like having had one over the eight.'

She was rapturous and always looking for words with the right level of joy in them to describe her situation. At one time she wrote:

> To say I'm enjoying this trip is a gross understatement. It is lovely just pleasing oneself and drinking in the ozone. I'm hoping to sew on deck tomorrow in the sun... this is the last letter today... We are the only servicewomen aboard except an ATS girl... You can imagine, we nearly fall over male escorts wherever we go, as most of the civvy women are mummies with bags of little darlings...

By mid-October the ship was in the Red Sea. Beryl told her mother that, 'Whilst I write the water keeps running off me in rivers, and yet it is queer, I never felt fitter.' She noted an unusual situation: 'One of our girls who can't perspire is being worked on in sick bay, with first ice-cold baths followed by very hot ones to make her sweat. She is suffering from heat exhaustion.' Another girl fell asleep under the shower. As to general behaviour, the order of the day was nudity. She says that 'Nudity as far as possible is the mode for all ages.'

As happens so many times in Beryl's international life, there is a man who likes her company, and she wants to be left in peace. She explains, 'I've got a bookish Flight Lieutenant trailing me like a pet lamb. He is very nice but believe it or not a little shy. I get loads of fun out of him. Men are so numerous and women fewer that really one gets a little tired of their attentions.' She liked her own company, and although she was sociable and warm, Beryl was self-sufficient. In fact, one of the most meaningful insights into her at this time, in her early thirties and starting out for an exciting adventure, is in this brief image: 'I am sitting under an awning now with a monsoon raging around me. It is lovely and cool, however, and I've just sighted some sharks and dolphins.'

She was barely sleeping with the excitement of the journey. Close to Colombo, where her letters would be posted, she described her day as starting at 6.00 a.m. 'to get to the cooler morning air and see if any new land has loomed up in the night'. Darkness fell at seven and was 'just like a curtain being drawn'. Colombo meant that 'the boys will be rushing off the ship to get a drink, as this is a *dry* ship. In Colombo she had a 'wizard' time bartering down prices when she went to buy clothes. After a 'wizard' omelette and chips, Beryl and friends did a tour of the town. They were just four days away from Singapore now.

Chris was waiting at the harbour, and soon they were all at Changi camp. She wrote home: 'Nice having a sister here... we can pool our dresses and thereby ring the changes.' Shoes, she noted, could be made by the Chinese into any style required. At the camp she saw one of the more obvious results of the victory against Japan:

> *Japs POWs do all really filthy and heavy work... Nasty looking efforts these Sons of Nippon are, when you read in the Straits Times of the atrocities mentioned in the Singapore War Crimes trials it makes one's hair stand on end, and one yearns to whip them along the road or hang them. The infamous Changi Jail near here is full of them,*

the big noise Japs. Some of the boys I met on the boat are
in charge of them.

The billet consisted of large rooms with wooden screens at intervals, and there were wooden beds or charpoys with string mesh and 'three biscuits on top and a nice soft pillow'. Beryl the dressmaker was struck by the materials and the embroidery there but dress patterns were unobtainable. She was thrilled at the sight of the locals at work: 'The Chinese are great sewers and in the village one can see young and old machining and cutting, night and day.'

If a modern reader wanted to learn about the social and living conditions for people at this time and place, then Beryl supplies the sense of material reality. In plain terms, this means surviving in everything the heat has to threaten one's peace of mind. First there is life with the insects:

Sleeping inside a mosquito net is cool and gives one
a little privacy. I've only seen one "mossie" yet and
I swatted it. The flying tiny ants like midges have had a
meal off my plump legs, fresh from England, a nice and
juicy morsel I suppose they think.

The war trials continued to make news during the first weeks in the new atmosphere, but repeatedly, the necessity to have lots of clothes and provisions took up most of the thinking time. She always paints a profile of herself while writing to ask for clothes to be found and sent from home, such as this insight into her domestic life: 'I am sitting up in bed writing, having retired early after a glorious day in the sunshine. I went with Penny, a WAAF friend, and the five males she is friendly with, for a boating trip to one of the largest islands...'

One of the most interesting aspects of the socialising and conversations that filled the early days is the overshadowing presence of the horrendous wartime experience so many of the men Beryl met had experienced. So when a picnic was organised, this happens: 'Joe showed us a book of poems he had written, full of grim, graphic descriptions of life under the Japs. The YMCA in Singapore was the H.Q. of the Jap Kempetai, or Gestapo.'

So 1946 ended with a Christmas/New Year lunch, which was a 'wizard' affair, and it was just in time to invite more new arrivals, this time from the *Empress of Scotland*, along with twenty WAAF ladies from Hong Kong.

Beryl settled into her new routine and time passed. As 1947 progressed, her long letters give plenty of details about life in her Changi quarters, including a regime of nuisance behaviour from various dogs and monkeys around the compound. Yet she always includes information of some importance for the military history of her interesting times, such as, 'This afternoon we went down to the airfield to see the Gloster Meteor on its tropical trials. It was a lovely machine and a superb display... about four of us girls had a snap taken in front of it and it should be a glamour photo if it comes out okay...'

This was a jet fighter that flew first in 1943, and when Beryl saw this trial the jet had seen plenty of service already with 616 Squadron. The plane set a record for the first official jet aircraft in late 1945. Beryl was always keen to see and to monitor anything going on around her that was, or would be, of significant interest, and this experience was exactly the kind of event she would never miss. She also took every short leave to see the wider area, as in a trip to Penang.

In October 1947 she went home for some official leave and Chris kept her updated, including a degree of worry: she had heard of some infection affecting one of the troop ships. But all was well for Beryl as she sailed on the *MS Kota Baroe* in mid-October. After so long away from home, and so many letters to her mother documenting her air force life, now she was heading for Grimsby. She wrote 'Our first port of call is Aden, for fresh water, and after that Port Said.... We shall of course run into the heat again.... We have pilsner beer, cigarettes, books etc. and of course strong coffee, the Dutch drink.' We have some idea of the scale of the operation when Beryl notes that there were 1,200 British troops aboard, along with thirty officers. She was being looked after, as before: 'They have given us the best accommodation on board and go out of their way to make us comfortable.'

The leave marked a turning point in Beryl's service life, as she was obviously considering a change. Chris, writing from Changi, wrote 'I feel sure you will come back' but Beryl was considering Germany. It is tempting to infer that there was no real challenge for her in Singapore. One feature of her personality is the need to have a challenge, and one senses that there was more potential for that in post-war Germany. She had learned German when in her teens, doing a basic course. This had been followed up when she was in Watford, with regular German lessons being provided. There is no doubt that her imagination was drawn to German music and culture, and she preserved in her archive materials from innumerable concerts and cultural trips.

But before this happened, she was still committed to a few more months in Singapore, and in early 1948, as Chris was switching to civilian life, working now for the Nederland Line Royal Dutch Mail as a typist, Beryl came back out east, and in April 1948, Chris wrote home to bring together comments on all three sisters for the benefit of their mother: 'Beryl handed over £1 to me at the weekend, from some money which you sent her... Beryl is anxious that I mention health insurance to you and thinks it would be best to keep it up for when I come home.' Beryl, big sister to the others, was always being sensible and dutiful, and considering all the practicalities of life across the great world of war and post-war.

By September, Beryl was planning her return home, and she noted on the 10 September that she was booked onto the now famous *Empire Windrush* and that she would be home for Christmas. That great vessel was being patched up: '... two days ago it went into the

Johore Straits, to Seletar docks for repairs. It is scheduled to leave here on the 21st September if its boiler is replaced in time.' There was a rumour that the sailing would be delayed, and Beryl was giving her mother lots of instructions regarding her paperwork and records wanted at Somerset House.

Although the sisters wrote long and factual letters about the everyday affairs, there was always a sense of the nearby aftermath of the war. Beryl was aware of this in August 1948 when her application for some leave in Hong Kong was cancelled. She wrote home that 'The terrorism situation is under control. The Inniskillings from Hong Kong, with the Seaforths and the Malay regiments combined with the police are taking care of the whole sordid business.' She added that 'In Singapore Island the terrorism seldom raises its head... just odd incidents such as the discovery of seditious literature, or odd people around carrying arms without a licence. For this latter offence, the penalty is death.'

Chris kept in regular touch with her sisters through the year, and in early October she asked Beryl, 'What happened at PDC and where are you posted? Any hope of Germany yet?'

By November, when Beryl reached home, Chris in Singapore had met her future husband, Denys. She was, as usual, enjoying the social life and spending a lot of time talking about clothes and parties, but she was doing what she always did – working very hard and living life to the full. Meanwhile, Beryl was evaluating her life.

The *Empire Windrush* was fit for sailing in time for Beryl's booking home. This now iconic ship, with its famous connections to the arrival in Britain of West Indian immigrants in 1948 before going out to Singapore, began its life on the sea in 1930, when it was a passenger liner. Her first name was the *Monte Rosa*, and during the Second World War the Germans had used her for troop transports. She was converted into a troopship for British use in 1946 and became the *Empire Windrush* shortly before Beryl sailed in her, taking the name in early 1947. She ran the Southampton to Hong Kong route, and

Beryl was to see it again later, when it sailed to Kure in Japan, where she was to be based.

Beryl gives her readers at home (and posterity) one of the most comprehensive descriptions of the ship at the time that we have, from a passenger's point of view:

> *This is a lovely ship, fifteen thousand tons and an original 'German through joy' ship. Bits of the language still survive in different spots on board, and the dining room silver plate is definitely Germanic. It is so heavy that it is wrist-breaking to lift it...We have cabins for two... they are very compact, with hot and cold water, large wardrobe and mirror. Even a ladder for the top bunk. The ship has larger decks and better facilities than any I have known...*

In the German reference, Beryl means *Gemeinschaft durch Freude –* strength through joy, which was a phrase created by the propaganda outfit, the German Labour Front formed in 1933.

She noted that they were covering around 350 miles a day, and comments that 'this is very good going, as this ship took a fortnight at Seletar to have its boilers patched up.' She had everything needed for comfort, including a large library and plenty of wool for knitting. The food was excellent: 'We get four courses for lunch and dinner, and three for breakfast. We also get early morning tea in bed. Six members of the Highland regiment in full dress piped us aboard this ship, a quite impromptu performance...' She was ashore in Aden for several hours, and had time to buy some souvenirs; but she was shocked by some things, such as in this comment: 'I saw for the first time women heavily veiled, reminiscent of the Dark Ages rather.' There was also the usual attention from the men around the place. She noted at one point that 'we have acquired a sugar daddy apiece'. But as usual, Beryl kept plenty of time for herself and for chilling out; she sat in a swim-suit for hours, reading, knitting or sleeping. With customary humour, she observed the knitting culture: 'I think 78% of the people on board knit, with all the lovely wool available. Yesterday I saw a Wing-Commander crotcheting a beret. I propose to borrow that crochet book...'

There was always a glimpse of the after effects of war, however, as when she saw three ships packed with displaced persons on their way to Australia – 'all nationalities and hues'. It is not difficult to imagine her feelings on that trip: there she was, with time to reflect, in an atmosphere that must have seemed heavenly, with good food, time for recreation, plenty of friendship and new sights to see. But at the same time, she was in a time of transition. She had been at the very heart of the war on the Home Front; then she had been across the world to see at first hand the context of a massive conflict and its effects on so many nations. For a young dressmaker from Grimsby, this was the stuff of dreams. But she did reflect and examine her inner thoughts and aspirations. Chris, writing in April 1949, wrote, 'Mother told me that you were thinking of signing on for four years. I do hope not as I think you have a marvellous chance with the Emergency Training Scheme for Teachers...'

Clearly, she was considering all possible options. Beryl was always open to adventure, and if there was travel involved, then the temptation was irresistible. But on arriving home, after some time away from thoughts of the Far East or teaching schemes, there was the temptation to be in Germany, where the demands of occupation were intense, and the state of the country was chaotic and in many ways very dangerous. She had one brief respite, in Plymouth, before she was demobbed in June. She was based at RAF Mount Batten, and in February 1949, she was still in a pensive, inactive state, enjoying the scenery and the change in atmosphere: 'There are magnificent cliffs surrounding the harbour... wherever one looks from this camp there is a lovely view especially from the rear view of the billet where there is a panoramic view of Plymouth... the water here in the billet is always hot and the rooms warm.'

There were people who advised her about her future, seeing that she was at a turning-point, and we have a glimpse of the situation concerning the WAAFs here: 'The WAAF officer in charge here gave me a good welcome and did her best to try and persuade me to join this new, permanent WAAF, doing all in all up to 22 years with a 33 shillings a week pension at the end of it.'

In the summer of that year she was in turmoil, thinking of life's possibilities. She confided that 'the WAAF officer is still waiting for me to sign on, and so is the squadron leader for whom I work, as once I told him I would. Everyone who signs on is a feather in their cap, and believe it or not, five shillings apiece in their pockets.' Then, as she sat down to update the letter before posting, there was a step forward: 'I've had another telephone call from the WVS and the same optimistic tone was in it. Apparently my references were excellent. Whatever date I am demobbed I will have to stay in this district for it.'

Before being demobbed, she managed to fit in another theatre visit and this time, the play was written by one of the corporals at her base; the play was put on at the Plymouth Art Centre. So, she had twenty-eight days of leave, paid, and managed to go home for that time before the next significant move. She could still have signed on for the WAAF as her commander was keen for her to do so, but soon the decision was made. She was ready for something very different.

She still felt the call of Germany and its culture. Her archive gives evidence of this in her sensibility: wherever she found printed German she kept a souvenir. Other pieces of reagalia in her preserved materials hint at her deep interest in language in all its forms, and she took more than a passing interest in Russian and Japanese. Wherever she was posted, the aim to know at least a minimal functional level of the relevant language was always in her thoughts. She saw theatre in German and she travelled whenever she could to see almost every region of the country. Her destiny for a few years was to be the British Army of the Rhine.

Chapter 4

A German Interlude

Sometimes, fiction gives the reader a better insight into life at a specific past time, and in the case of post-war Germany, Philip Kerr's novel, *The One from the Other* does exactly that: 'I ran out of the office, jumped on a tram, then hurried across Nussbaum gardens to the Women's Clinic on Maistrasse. Half of it looked like a building site; the other half looked like a ruin. I walked through a gauntlet of cement-mixers, round a redoubt of new bricks and timber...' The girl from Grimsby was about to tread those streets, flattened by a Blitzkrieg from the RAF.

All her life, Beryl was a Germanophile. She gained a basic knowledge of German even before she was recruited into the WAAF, and her life during the war led her to learn more of the German language and culture. Her fascination extended to drama, opera, film and popular literature. She was probably unaware of a considerable interest in Germany in the ranks of the Anglo-German Fellowship in England, founded in 1935, and of course, suspended when war broke out. It was not outright Nazi, and, as writer Charles Spicer wrote in *Coffee with Hitler,* it was created to go along with a trade mission. For Beryl, it was a case of being drawn to the cultural attractions and the landscape. She used all available leave time to see the country, from Hamburg to Bavaria.

She was about to become part of the massive establishment of the British Army of the Rhine, which had been re-formed (the first having been active between 1919 and 1929) in August 1945. After D-Day and the advance of the army into Europe, the Brits settled in northern Germany, and after the momentous Yalta Conference of 1945 the partitions and responsibilities were defined, with the British zone spanning a large chunk of the north-west of the land, above the smaller French zone, with the US and Russians zones to the east.

The next time a letter arrived in Grimsby from Beryl it had come from Germany. She was at Spey Barracks, the home of the 1st Battalion Yorkshire and Lancashire Regiment, in Buxtehude. This was in February 1950, and there she was, now 36 and a member of the Women's Voluntary Service, which had been formed in 1938, conceived and created by Stella Isaacs, Lady Reading, after consultations with the then Home Secretary, Sir Samuel Hoare, and Wilfred Eady. The panel that planned and developed the notion of having a massive resource of women workers, primarily attached to the Air Raid Precautions (ARP), had several aims. Mainly, the scheme was to provide additional workforce in the duties of ARP, and to help to inform women about family help in the context of bombing.

However, the reach and work of the WVS became much more than this. By 1943 there were over a million members of the organisation, as their website notes, working 'from the collection of salvage to knitting socks and gloves for seamen'. When Beryl joined, it was mostly about every possible aspect of social care. Although many popular photos of WVS women at work consist of serving tea and staffing supply rooms, in fact, in the post-war world they played an important role in being ancillary whenever and wherever they were needed.

Lady Reading (1894–1971) impressed everyone she met. One profile of her even gave the opinion that 'had she been a man she would have become Prime Minister'. She was once the wife of a former US ambassador, served on a number of committees, and was the first woman to have a seat in the House of Lords, in 1958. Her WVS women were recruited from every corner of the land, and in the world at war, along with the post-war clearing and problems in the 1950s the recruitment to the service was focussed on making the WVS seem like a fulfilling career. We can see what tempted Beryl.

One leaflet stated: 'Members serve in NAAFI clubs and canteens for the British force in Germany, the Middle East, Austria, South East Asia, Japan and Korea... Army welfare work takes them to Trieste and to the Gurkha Brigade in the Far East.' That paragraph would have offered exactly what she wanted and needed when she left the WAAF on 3 June 1949. Her little green card that was her WVS uniform permit was issued in July 1949, so she wasted very little time wondering what path to take in life.

The information about what the WVS gave is compact and precise: if a woman was between 25 and 45 years of age, and did not have children under 15 years of age, she was eligible to apply. The contract was for 18 months and annual leave was usually 28 days in the year. Candidates should expect to serve anywhere where they were needed, and living expenses were met, along with a small amount for personal expenses.

In the recruitment campaign for the WVS in 1949 the conditions of service were very clear: the age of candidates was to be 25 to 45 years; two references were needed; the average length of service was 18 months, and regarding subsistence the explanation was: 'Living expense will be met and in addition, a small weekly allowance is made to cover out of pocket expenses. Annual leave varies according to the area but is generally 28 days per year.'

Beryl applied and she had to face a selection board in London. The leaflets distributed noted that 'a high standard of physical fitness is required'. There was one important stipulation: 'women with children under 14 years of age cannot be accepted'.

Beryl would have attended a preliminary selection board at her Regional Office, and if passed, she would have a medical examination in London. She then had a probationary period, and she would have had a series of inoculations, and a month was needed to do the basic training. Leaflets for recruitment from the 1950s show troops relaxing with WVS women in a lounge; people choosing records in a recreation room, and soldiers choosing books in a library. The WVS Bulletin for

November 1953 shows three women, and the caption reads: 'This attractive picture of three generations of one family has appeared on posters throughout the country in a big recruiting drive for WVS. They are the Centre Organiser for Sutton, Surrey, with her mother and daughter. All have worked in the WVS since 1939.'

That first letter home thanks her mother for a parcel, and asks for help arranging a proxy vote for the forthcoming election, but Beryl was already deep in the work and responsibilities of being a social facilitator, as we might call her today:

> *Next week we two are going to a very special cocktail party in Hamburg, so now I am up to the eyes in trying to organise an evening dress. The big people in WVS and Rhine Army will be there, so I must look my best, especially as a favourite Brigadeer [sic] will be there. It will be held in the WVS mess over Hamburg House, the large NAAFI club. I went to the Valentine Dance at the CWL Ritchie Club in Buxtehude. All the married families of all ranks attended in full force... I was more or less danced off my feet...*

She had a boyfriend ringing her every day, and notes that life is continually amusing, in spite of a persistent cold, and in between dancing and relaxing, there was discussion about what would happen if Churchill won the election at home, and whether or not there would be war with Russia.

The occupation of Germany certainly raised discussion. In the popular press at the time there were strong opinions on this, such as in a feature in *The Reader's Digest* written by 'A member of the RAF' that expressed one of the strong opinions: 'It is high time we realized that the whole stupid medieval of occupation is totally out of tune with modern ideas' and that 'Total disarmament must be completed. Every weapon from a peashooter to a cruiser must be taken away.'

Beryl was there, part of an army of occupation, and her comments and reports become increasingly packed with references to the situation. In August she has moved again, but is still in Buxtehude, and at the head of her letter she wrote 'please tell me your impressions of Germany's and my future'. Her letter came from a social situation in which there are terrible threats and deprivations, but she still manages to travel along the Rhine and elsewhere. She was in a place where the black market expanded, and many commentators dealt with the question about whether or not the Germans were starving. One writer, Adolf Guggenbuhl, commented that in 1948, 'The prevailing impression is not of poverty but of the grotesque vision called up by ruins of a vanished world.' He also wrote that it was a total surprise to him to find how orderly and law-abiding everyone remains, despite the chaos.

By the time Beryl was settled there, the worst of all this had passed. As Thomas Harding writes, in his family memoir of Berlin: 'By the Spring of 1949, almost a year after the Soviets had cut off supplies to Berlin, it became clear that the Allies were winning the blockade... The Allies had run over 275,000 flights, providing more than 2.3 million tons of food, coal and medical supplies to the population of West Berlin.' As Harding also notes, the winter of 1948 had been very severe, with snowstorms and temperatures twenty below zero.

Yet she still saw plenty of the Germany ruined by the war. One journey out from the billet prompted these reflections:

The train took us through desolation in such places as Hamm, Detmold, Minden and finally Bielefeld. It has to be seen to be believed. Everywhere the dust from the ruins rises in clouds and going out in toeless sandals is fatal to clean feet. The hostility and resentment of the people in this latter town in particular is like a perspex curtain between us and them. We (eight of us) stayed in Bielefeld for two days in transit at a very comfy hotel...

This really defines her situation. The billets were safe retreats from the harsh reality, but she made a special effort to see as much as possible. She photographed everything of possible interest, including the Hitler bunker. She increasingly saw the importance of knowing German. She noted after the Bielefeld visit: 'One just couldn't use English anywhere there, as 99% just didn't understand it or want to... they don't after four years of occupation by us.' Beryl worked hard to improve her German, even cultivating friendships in order to speak the language: 'I get my language practice from a Fraulein who works in the club, where she sits and sews on stripes etc. She speaks no English and always uses Deutsch on me as she found I can manage.'

Beryl reported on everything around her as time went on: 'The radio over here is full of anti-British and American propaganda, alternating promises or threats to the Germans. One of their latest is that when Russia is in full control of Germany any person who worked for the Allies will get five years forced labour in Siberia...' Yet much of her time, in the first six months, was fixed on thoughts of her future, and at that time she reflected that 'We may as well face up to the very real possibility of service life once more.'

Life in 1949 was a constant round of duties, visits and friendships with various young men. Occasionally the friendships grew close, as in the case of a young man called Richard. She wrote: 'He comes specially looking for me... he advertises his affection for me fondly and everyone is getting to tease me about it.' There was more to these events than simple friendship, though. A woman serving in the WVS had to fulfil several roles. It would not be going too far to say that they had to be sister, mother and girlfriend in their roles, which all formed elements on their main duties of running the library, dealing with entertainments, comforting the lonely, and seeing that there was food as well as attentive listening always on offer. She explains to her mother: 'One of our "duties" is to take it in turns to accompany the boys on trips to Celle or Hannover speedway. Another duty (most essential) is to make all shy boys feel at home, and to listen to their troubles, judging by the juvenile National Service types we collect as an admiring retinue...'

Writing to Beryl from Singapore in the early months of 1949, Chris wrote as though Beryl had not made a decision about life quite at that point. She wrote in February, 'I'm quite intrigued by your romance – he sounds awfully nice. Are you like me? Wondering if you can manage a husband and a career?' In another, she is responding to something Beryl had said at a moment of uncertainty: 'You sound as if you are in Waltham [Grimsby] for good. Any more prospect of getting a house or has it died down again?' These remarks hint at a period of doubt and confusion for Beryl in that interim period between leaving the WAAF and joining the WVS. All remarks made after June that year suggest that the right decisions had been made – probably all down to those WVS leaflets.

Judging from the letters home and from letters written to Beryl, she had made the right decision, going on the WVS route in her career rather than signing on in the RAF for four years. Mostly, her workmates were helpful and co-operative, but occasionally there was friction – something that happens in most workplaces. But in late 1949 there was a new organiser (the manager of the WVS section) and there was unpleasantness. Beryl explains that the new boss was 'about forty, small and mouse-like in appearance, and the same in nature. I am sorry to say she loathes me and I do her, so it is just as well I am to leave Berlin soon. The woman is inefficient herself, and old-maidish, fussy, and a snob.'

Towards the end of the year, her thoughts were turning towards possible changes in direction, and she was considering something totally different. She opens up to her sister about this: 'One of the British European Airways stewardesses came in the club and discussed her job with me... she is on the service which operates between Northolt, Hamburg, Berlin and Munich. BEA are in need of German speaking stewardesses...' It seems that Beryl had learned that passengers on the line mostly spoke only German and the staff on the planes knew little German. But there was 'an age snag'. She was getting on, in terms of the nature and demands of the job. Her friends were marrying and settling down, and here was Beryl, at 35, switching from job to job, having a wonderful time in between the war demands, without any sense of a real career. But for the airline job (clearly for younger women) she wrote, 'Perhaps my appearance will help me over the age problem.'

She was about to leave Berlin for Buxtehude in late 1949, but before she left, she paid a visit to Minden, which she described as having '... no English folks, only CCG and a small unit of army and is therefore quite German'. In this letter she faces up to her habit of travelling anywhere despite obvious risks: 'One can feel very insecure here in Germany, in a bombed-out place, however brave one is. The trouble with me is that I get right into this danger before I really become aware of it. I'm beginning to understand at last why drink is so easy to get and why so many people are taking to it.'

As 1950 began, Beryl was in Buxtehude. She was based at the Spey Barracks, which was to exist under British rule until 1956. Between 1948 and 1950 the 1st Battalion York and Lancaster Regiment was there, along with the 1st Battalion Royal Welch Fusiliers.

Beryl had plenty of advice from friends who knew Germany well. One correspondent expressed opinions on the politics that Beryl must have heard every day but did not repeat to bore her mother in Grimsby. A typical comment in these letters from others is, 'What do you think of the election and the way Germany is rising up again? You will notice that Hamburg is full of displaced persons... even the Intelligence cannot keep a check on them. It is disgusting that a fallen or so-called fallen country like Germany can de-ration all, including petrol. England is worse than any place I know of...'

She had been busy on relief duties at a number of places between the end of 1949 and January 1950. She reported on this conveying a dizzying sense of confusion and hectic social change: 'I arrived here after all my frequent moves... after my month relieving in Gütersloh

RAF camp, I was glad to return to Bad "O" [Bad Oeynhausen] for a well-earned rest, so I thought, but had only been back two days when I was asked to go to Luneburg to relieve for a fortnight.'

Then there she was at Buxtehude, and she liked it. She relished educating her mother and others at home with local information: 'This town of Buxtehude is one of the oldest in Germany, and we live just on the edge of it. We are only an hour by car from Hamburg where we go at least twice per week.' The famous *Staatsoper* had been recently re-opened, and this was a mecca for Beryl, the classical music fan. She saw productions of *Il Trovatore*, *The Magic Flute* and *Rigoletto* during her time there. Still, there was no let-up in her status as the honey-pot for the troops, and one night she heard two soldiers outside the canteen arguing loudly about who would escort her back to her room. She was, naturally, insulted by this, writing, '... I had not been consulted, oh no! That is typical of this regiment, which has been turned out of more cities in Germany than it is policy to recall.' Of course, she arrived at New Year, so it was inevitable that she would be kissed under the mistletoe, and her celebrations were probably the most entertaining ones so far in her world travels. She recalled for the benefit of the family, a hilarious encounter:

> *an ancient lady came forward to serve me, complete with outsize ear-trumpets and a hairdo a la Pompadour. The next five minutes were the funniest I have ever lived through, shouting my imperfect knowledge of her language down that trumpet was not very easy to do with a straight face, believe me. But our conversation went thus:*

> Me: *I want some views of the city.*
> She: *Awful weather, ja.*
> Me: *Half dozen please. Beautiful city... must have some pictures of it.*
> She: *I think it will snow soon again, nicht wahr?*

45

In March, she wrote one of her longest letters to Chris in Singapore. There had been another raucous celebration for everyone, but also her birthday was on the 7 May. Her news though, was mostly about escorting the regiment to Brunswick on special duties related to social unrest by the steelworks there. She explained: '... this regiment for whom we work are about to move en bloc to Brunswick and we two WVS here have been spoken for to go with them... the danger comes in the fact of the riots there... almost daily over the dismantling of the Hermann Goering Steelworks. The regiment is going in full battle kit to deal with it.' In fact, this was a major confrontation, relating to the Salzgitter plant. In the war there had been widespread use of slave labour there, but after the war, imported labour had kept the plant going, producing pig iron. The Buxtehude regiment sent there had to settle for a stand-off and finally, the local labour and the plant had a stay of reprieve, but not for long.

After this emergency, it was back to the routine of working in the club, visiting other clubs, and providing books, music and company for the troops. Beryl used all local transport in order to see the wider area. She took the suburban tube railway, the *Untergrundbahn*, and managed a break by the sea. There were parties and celebrations, as there was a strong emphasis on the various sections of the base liaising. She contributed to the provision of a bring-and-buy sale, and enjoyed the parties, but she couldn't resist recalling an evening with a drunk: '... myself and a NAAFI colleague had to commandeer a cart to bring her home. She had been drinking before she came... probably she was giving herself Dutch courage but whatever the reason for it, she certainly let down the WVS and her officer status...'

After more than a year serving with the WVS, Beryl had become proud and fulfilled, and happy to be a member. She has no time for slackers and for the officious and snobby: 'At Hamburg House are several ex-service WVS girls, who like myself are tired of fussy old-fashioned folk who don't even try to understand the boys, but like someone I work with, treat them like children.'

Her last months in Buxtehude, before a posting to Berlin, were crammed with trying to maximise her resources, the chief one being her sewing machine, wool and other accoutrements. She invested in a conversion, so that she could use a hand-electric model. It was 'a rather expensive do' but she loved it. There were difficulties with what might be called job politics, as the coming and going of WVS staff meant that the others did not get on well with Beryl. Moreover, Beryl had other social options. In leisure time, she could avoid the staff that did not match her well. She even had clubs to go to outside the base: 'We found an old ruined *Schloss* in one secluded corner of the bank. We were two WVS in our party, with two RAF sergeants, two army corporals and a NAAFI manager.' There was also 'a very nice club in Hamburg run by the NAAFI'.

She was working in a context of universal social change, and opinions on the German situation varied. James Agate, writing the ninth volume of his autobiography, attended a talk on Germany by Dr Freddy Renner, who expressed an opinion, which had some foundation in the documentation Beryl supplied. He argued that 'The Germans are wholly preoccupied with how to get food, cigarettes and chocolate. Insofar as they have a mind for anything else they have no guilt-consciousness. The average German knew nothing about the atrocities and neither did Hitler.' It was the kind of opinion meant to provoke, and in Beryl's world the same opinions were expressed. She must have listened to political discussions in awe of such perspectives on international politics. But it was all a part of her self-education – something she took very seriously.

The end of 1950 brought a sense of settlement and familiarity to her life. This is seen in her accounts of social life and friendships, such as the help she had when she had yet another severe cold: 'An admirer of mine, an elderly Scottish bachelor, brought me over half a bottle of rum, as he is worried over me. He is the manager of the NAAFI shop near where I work. I'm trying not to make him a habit...' With men in general in her mind, and in a Christmas mood, she confessed to Chris that her old flame Michael was 'the one'. 'After going out with older men recently, I'm now sure I prefer Michael and his youth. Ah me! I would have been his mistress long ago, but he preferred marriage.'

She summed up her year with one of the best memories, when she was travelling again: 'We have had a day out in the lovely university town of Göttingen on the borders of the Russian zone. We stayed overnight... The outskirts of the town are hilly and wooded and it was here that we discovered the cottage of Bismarck during his student days...'

1951 brought plenty of variety. Chris was still in Singapore. She wrote to apologise for forgetting Beryl's birthday. Chris was married and very much concerned with domestic matters such as furnishing and house-boys. She wanted Beryl to take some leave, but nothing was decided by August.

Beryl was far too busy. Not only did the work involve duties with current charges, but letters came to her asking for help, from men she had known in the past, such as this request:

> *Dear Miss Baxter,*
> *Just a line to let you know how everything is. I don't know if you remember asking me to write but anyway here I am writing. I am in the guard room for losing my temper and hitting a sergeant. I suppose you can imagine what it's like in the wilds, locked up all day. It's murder. Could you do us a favour and send us something to read? It will be invaluable out here... how about letting me know your Christian name...*

This was to be a pattern for all her WVS working life – requests for all kinds of things from former charges, ranging from cigarettes to hats.

The year's work began in Berlin, where she wrote home from the base of the District Supervisor at Summit House, attached to the

NAAFI. Chris wrote from Singapore that there had been serious riots, noting that 'heaps of Europeans have suddenly become interested in firearms' and that 'lethargic members of volunteer constabulary have started to attend the range when requested'. In contrast, Beryl's sense of danger came in her account of visiting the *Staatsoper* in the Russian sector again, and it was a risky affair: 'One has to go by underground to this place, as it is dangerous to take our car and driver. The fact is that the Russians often pinch the car and the driver. They return the car but often the driver may not be seen again...'

For recreation there were cultural events and parties. Beryl experienced the *Fasching* – the carnival week – and she comments that 'fancy dress was the main topic for a week'. In between the fun, the Russians still irritated: 'They are very fond of moving our sentry-boxes from one side of the road to the other. Our boys move them back again, now quite patiently, but one day one of them will get trigger-happy.' Her underground trips presented Beryl with the propaganda: anti-American posters every inch of the way through tunnels.

She was in Berlin for six months, and generally she enjoyed it, in spite of the Russian tricks. Sometimes she was in trouble, as when she boarded a train alone:

> *... One is never quite sure at what stage to see Russians board the train. One night I was approached by one of the famed People's Police, armed to the teeth, seven feet of heel-clicking Prussian... in a hurry I was, mark you, and I asked the way in carefully picked German. He looked me up and down for what seemed like an age, then softening visibly, he replied in worse German than mine. The truth dawned on me that he was a Russian officer who maybe trained thugs I have seen... short Russian stocky figures in the same uniform, patrolling the streets and stations in pairs.*

As the year advanced, Beryl was keen to enjoy everything on offer. She wrote to Chris that 'Life in Berlin is just one *alarum* after another, from our Red neighbours. All police and troops are on the alert from the evening of April 30th for the great May Day parades and on the 21st for Stalin's birthday, on this latter date, even the married families had a 9 p.m. curfew.'

Nothing kept Beryl from her theatre. On one occasion she went to see a production of *Rusland and Ludmilla* at the *Staatsoper* and she had a shock: 'The place was packed to the ceiling, and a large proportion of the people present were Russian military and their attachment.' She was still looking ahead, as 1952 would be the end of her contract. She thought again of the possibility of becoming a stewardess on the airlines. She saw a major obstacle, though: 'I cannot cook, and I would have to prepare snacks for the passengers.' But she had to do some cooking when she was at Hamburg, as she mentions being housemother, where she winged it and somehow succeeded, confiding to Chris, 'Of course it would never do to let the staff know that I've never cooked a dinner in my life.'

At the end of the year Beryl was moved to Hamburg, based at Hamburg House NAAFI. The situation could still be described as 'love among the ruins' as she reports on activities: 'Mrs W.E. and I went out shopping. I managed to buy a lovely soft coney coat. It was only fifteen and a half guineas... I wish you could see the house these German friends have. There was till recently a half of a half of a house through bomb damage. Now it is almost rebuilt in time for Christmas.' By the end of the year, the WVS staff lost the use of their allotted car, and that cramped her style somewhat. But there was a car available if required for something special, and she reports that the driver, Kurt, 'has been driving me to work and anyone can see that he is in seventh heaven...'.

Beryl was very much in a role that was in contradistinction to the greater world and its values. She was a fiercely independent woman, revered and respected, and in 1951, in a context still of rationing back home, and of male centrality in work and the home, she was a rebel, or at least a square peg. In J.B. Priestley's play, *The Linden Tree*, set in 1947, the professor, being pressed to retire, says 'A man stays where his work is and the woman stays with the man'. Beryl, now in her later thirties, was not caught in that bundle of old values, and neither was she the spinster of popular culture.

She was feeling, once again, that her current life was about to go, when she reflected, 'I would very much like to stay here and live "German" or go to Japan... however, some of the WVS who have tried to get to Japan have ended up in the Middle East.' But she was always busy, even giving some German lessons, and also entertaining members of the Danish Liaison Service. In fact, she was too busy to do the routine things, complaining to Chris that she never did any sewing at that time.

Before the end of the year, she visited Bavaria and was glad of a break from Berlin which, as she confessed to her mum, 'was very wearing, and there always seems to be a kind of tension with the Russians'. In Bavaria, though, she used her time well, to enlarge her knowledge and satisfy curiosity, going to Berchtesgarten: 'I visited the ruins here of Hitler's famous redoubt. It is very high up in the Obersalzburg, overlooking the town, which by the way is in the American zone.' Munich she saw also, and commented, 'it shows a good deal of bomb damage'. She then had a trip to Salzburg, and of course, she visited the Mozart Museum. The last stop was a ferry ride to Ludwig II's Chiemsee and Lake Herreninsel.

As the year closed, a letter from Chris gave Beryl get another account of life in the Far East, and her sister's letters gave so much detail that surely this all played a part in bringing thoughts of going to Korea and Hong Kong into Beryl's mind. Chris gave some startling details, such as this, on her father-in-law: 'Pop is such a demon for work... He is energy personified, and that after three years in a Japanese internment camp when he went down to about 6 stones. He must surely retire soon we think.'

The year ended with a striking letter from Lady Reading to all WVS workers. She sent them a poetic tribute, and asked them to imagine three gifts for 1952: 'All my three gifts are worth untold gold. They are not for sale and they cannot be stolen. The first is for you to spend on others, the second is for you to make your own, and the third is for you to share with all, and men know them by the names of SYMPATHY – COURAGE – and HOPE.'

Before she left Germany, Beryl wrote a very long letter home, reporting that the new German army was being trained at a rapid rate, and that she had heard that her building was to be their new HQ. Despite the fact that 'there has not been any exciting love life for me for about a year' as she wrote, there were the usual Beryl adventures, including plenty of violence among the British troops. One was particularly nasty when one man provoked trouble: 'He said the wrong thing to a couple of that famous Scots Black Watch and they, living up to their reputation as "ladies from Hell" started kicking him to death. He is always looking for a fight usually but he got more than he bargained for...'

She had been dizzy with mixed feelings and aspirations before signing on for Korea, and in fact, her first enquiry was a rebuff:

I applied for a posting in Trieste when I was in U.K. and H.Q. promised to keep me in mind for the next vacancy, actually I applied for Korea but I was told bluntly that I had "the wrong sort of face" for Korea. They want people who are forty and over and look it. Four WVS are already out there, three of which I have already met.

In her last month in Germany she was always suffering from colds and feeling run down. A workmate had a severe flu. She was also busier than ever, perhaps tying up loose ends before she left. Obviously, she had been given a Korea posting, so the information she had was not entirely true. In spite of that advice, in which it must have seemed that only motherly types, advanced in years, were wanted. That was not at all true. She had been dropping hints for some time, as she refers to a while ago when she was aware that 'Miss Marsden, the administrator here, has accepted the fact that I am agitating for a change of theatre.'

She managed some more European trips during her leave before she moved out permanently, and some officers took Beryl and friends out to Hamburg for a night of celebration: '... they took the WVS down the famous Reeperbahn, the nightclub locale.' The last thing she appears to have done was send some books out to ships' commanders, on vessels that were due to dock in Harwich.

Before going home to prepare for Korea, there was a last note of advice from sister, Chris:

> *Personally, I think Korea is much safer than Malaya... We have not been over the Causeway since 1948 except by air to Penang. They say that things will be very much better soon. Perhaps after a year in Korea you would be able to come to Malaya in comparative safety. You probably scorn danger etc. but you know I am not a scared cat and we feel very much safer in Singapore than any folk in the Federation... A girl in the office with a husband in Korea tells me that the food is very good indeed according to high officers who have lectured here passing through from Korea.*

She very nearly took a different course at the last minute, because after her failure to follow up on a BEA post, she was recommended for another job. The boss from the airport rang her regarding work as a traffic reception hostess, as she spoke German:

> *I went in one of our best Opel-Blitz cars, and took my best WVS member with me. The chappie who interviewed me was a nice, sensible north country married man – a honey to do business with, and I know it would have been a joy*

to work for him. He interviewed me in German, which in itself could have given me an attack of nerves... He was very impressed with me altogether, and seemed surprised that in such a responsible position as mine, I would want to work for him. However, when he told me I would be needed in a week, that was a very big snag, as I have to give a month's notice.

Korea it was to be then, but Beryl's wanderlust couldn't keep her at home in the leave period: she went to Denmark and Sweden before packing her bags and checking on all required paperwork. A new adventure awaited. It takes no special insight to know that the new adventure was totally unlike anything she had seen so far, but Beryl was accustomed to a challenge, and she knew that confidence and knowledge were the best armour against the unknown.

Chapter 5

The WVS

First Year in Korea

In the course of explaining the importance of a roof-tile from South Korea, dating from the eighth century, Neil MacGregor points out that moveable metal type was invented in Korea, coming from a culture that value technology and fabrication; he also explains the richness and success of the city of Kyongju, in the heart of what was then Silla, an advanced, sophisticated city with the well-earned status of being backed by China. Then MacGregor adds a comment that highlights a deep and fundamental division in this now still divided land: 'Not least among many questions at issue between North and South Korea today is what was really going on 1,300 years ago. As so often, how you read history depends on where you're reading it from.'

That last sentence runs deep, and in the case of Korea, as deep as it can get. Words such as 'partisan' or 'nationalist' hardly do justice to this ancient culture, argued about, fought for and split for so long. One of the most vivid and shocking accounts of the two Koreas featured in The *National Geographic Magazine* in 2003; the feature presented some very telling images of the DMZ – the Demilitarised Zone – which was formed and confirmed in 1953 when Beryl ended her time there, and still exists now. In a sense, the Korean War never ended. Pictures in the magazine include one in which 'soldiers come routinely eye to eye with their enemies' and the author, Tom O'Neill, explains 'Just getting to the DMZ is a challenge. To join the South Korean pre-dawn patrol I had to pass through several military checkpoints... The troops, known as the United Nations Command Security Battalion, also serve as a thin first line of defence against a North Korean attack.'

In other words, when Beryl finished her stint in the two major centres of administration on the island and in Japan, she left something unfinished, something that is at the moment as unfinished as the famous Schumann symphony. But what 'finish' means outside any concept of peace is anyone's guess. Then, to deepen the complexity, as Beryl saw and as still exists now, in the midst of all this there are Koreans who somehow continue with their lives and occupations, like men who harvest oysters on Baengnyong Island in the Yellow Sea. Beryl's photographic record of her time there shows dozens of Koreans simply trying to do their everyday labours.

She also landed in the midst of a war that had very high casualty rates, and in which a high proportion of the combatants in the British forces were young National Service personnel. Her work at Pusan in particular, gives ample evidence that she and the other WVS staff, along with the NAAFI people too, gave invaluable comfort and support to men who had come for some time off, out of a vicious, deadly and relentlessly demanding battle-front. Yet strangely, in several books surveying that war, there is practically no mention of the WVS. In historical surveys such as Bruce Cumings's history of the war, there is no mention at all of the WVS, and in Stephen Kelly's *British Soldiers of the Korean War*, which presents the war through the words of the soldiers themselves, there is no mention of the WVS either.

The first phase of the war, called by some Americans 'Operation Yo Yo' because it was a case of US and North Korean forces going north and south across the shaky lines of demarcation. The world's press reports, a year before Beryl arrived, saw a clear-cut confrontation, and the words were aggressive, tabloid and often extreme. In early 1951, for instance, *Life* magazine headed a feature on the war 'Reds shove fist into the big debate' and the Reds were winning: 'A British officer said, "I saw a column of our tanks coming back, carrying piles of dead and wounded with blood running down the side of the tanks.'" The photos from the war showed exhausted troops lined along a bank on a roadside, and troops walking along dusty roads, grimaces on their faces. But the report was realistic, if extremely hard and unfeeling: 'If killing Chinese in Korea could solve the whole problem, the present opportunity seemed spectacular. But China's Reds could expend lives almost endlessly and their offensive showed that they were willing to do just that.'

The war was depicted in that way, and Beryl sometimes adopted similar language. She used words such as 'gooks' and 'Japs' and thought of the Chinese, as in this report, as being merely hordes of fighters all exactly the same – a massive manpower machine against the more restrained and tactical West. She later saw things very differently.

The Korean War is often called 'the forgotten war' but it could be argued that in that conflict, the WVS are the forgotten force, and what they did was attend to every need and demand that was put to them, from keeping up a reading room to listening to soldiers going through loss and bereavement.

Officially, the war is given in the reference works as extending from 1950 to 1953, but it covers far more than that if we include the preliminary events and manoeuvres, which then embrace Hong Kong, and also some developments in Japan. For Beryl, doing her preparations as she made ready to switch from Germany in a post-war context to an actual theatre of war, in her mind, the priority was travel and the journey ahead of her. A map issued by the BOAC (British Overseas Airways Corporation) at the time gives a clear view of what her journeys were to be. Her route was to be via Singapore, Hong Kong and to Tokyo. En route were Cairo, Iraq and the Persian Gulf. When she arrived in Japan she was based at Kure, and from there she would sail to Pusan at the extreme south of Korea.

Beryl was now to go to a distant venue in order to do much the same work as she had done in Germany, but images at home in Britain of her profession were not always those of war. Part of the remit for the work was time spent in Hong Kong and Singapore, either en route or in leave time. *The Sunday Express* in late 1952 gave those at home the impression that serving in Korea was like having a summer holiday. It ran a feature headed 'One Woman – Alone Among 600 Men' and gave a profile of Elizabeth Hutchinson: she was shown having a cuppa on a sunny beach, sharing a table with several men, all drinking plenty of beer, and also on her bike, riding under a palm tree. The words ran: 'The island is called Gan. It lies 600 miles south of Ceylon. It is an important re-fuelling stop for RAF planes. Miss Hutchinson's task is to run the camp shop, to broadcast over the island's radio and to bring a feminine and motherly touch to island life.'

In contrast, the WVS Bulletin, the official magazine of the organisation, included, in an issue from 1953, a feature on returning PoWs from Korea, and a report on Korean war graves and how flowers from relatives could be obtained and placed on graves. Beryl was soon to find that her WVS experience was to be in another galaxy in comparison to the work done by Elizabeth Hutchinson. The contrast is easily grasped if we glance at one of dozens of letters she received from servicemen thanking her, written from places across the globe: 'Dear Beryl, just a few lines to thank you and Mavis for the best leave I have ever had. We have just finished building a road and I'm feeling a wee bit tired... I hope you will be able to understand my writing, as I'm writing by candle-light.'

In her transition period, before heading for the east in mid 1952 she explained to Chris: 'I would like to come east again with WVS and I must resign first in Germany and then come home, and start afresh.' She was about to go into a war that since it began in 1951, had taken a massive toll of dead and injured, and had escalated gradually, as forces from the United Nations, China, the British Commonwealth and the United States joined in the conflict.

In 1948 Russia had worked to create a Communist state in Korea, led by Kim Il-Sung, in the north; in the south, where the Americans settled after the first confrontations, Syngman Rhea led the Republic of Korea. The sequence of actions and invasions from the beginning was: the south was invaded by a joint enterprise of North Korean and Russian fighters; then a United Nations and American force went north and held land until further changes with supporting allies. It has been estimated that in November 1950, a total of 350,000 troops of the joint North Korean and Chinese were in the field. Then by spring, 1951, the opposing allied forces reached around 240,000 men.

North Korea gained an early advantage in mid 1950, but then American and Republican forces thrust north and won large tracts of land. Eventually, across the 38th Parallel, opposing positions settled by mid 1951; the great division was around 45km north of Seoul. When Beryl arrived, after some time in Kure, Japan, she was based at Pusan, (Busan today) at the very south of that defended area. Since late 1950, what became known as the Pusan Perimeter was held and strengthened. After a desperate and fully strengthened attack on the perimeter, known as the Great Naktong Offensive, the aggressors eventually turned back north. There had also been a major confrontation at Inchon, and many of Beryl's charges at the base had been in that battle. It lasted five days in September 1950, and finally led to the fighters of the Korean republican soldiers taking command of the area in and around Seoul.

When Beryl arrived, she was to meet men who had been in the thick of it, some being from the earlier conflicts before divisions were settled in a stalemate. A typical action in all this was at the Imjin River in April 1951, where Lieutenant Curtis won a Victoria Cross. Philip Curtis was just 25, and in the Duke of Cornwall's Light Infantry when he and his men were caught facing a line of enemy troops with a machine gun position directly opposing them. Although he was injured, and supposed to be waiting for the Medical Officer, Lieutenant Curtis set about shifting or destroying that machine gun. Anthony Farrar-Hockley describes what happened: 'But Phil has gone; gone to the wire, gone towards the bunker. And suddenly it seems as if, for a few breathless moments, the whole of the field of battle is still and silent, watching... the lone figure that runs so painfully forward... one tiny figure, throwing grenades, firing a pistol set to take Castle Hill.'

Before Korea there was time in Singapore and Hong Kong. She didn't think so at the time, but she was due to stay in Korea and Japan until mid 1954. Earlier than that, there was the journey, and we know that she went via Rangoon and Hong Kong for night stops. Her plane called at Rome, Damascus, Bahrain, Karachi, Delhi, Calcutta, Rangoon and Hong Kong before arriving in Tokyo.

Lady Reading wrote a welcoming letter: 'I do assure you how tremendously I appreciate the unselfish spirit of service which you are showing in volunteering to go to this posting. While I know that all our members feel that the work in Korea is perhaps more rewarding than any other area, it still is the most demanding assignment, both from the physical and morale point of view.' This was very accurate, as Beryl was soon to find out. But she had received some induction activities. Lady Reading wrote again: 'We shall want you to come to Headquarters for two days prior to your departure so that you can get the special items of uniform necessary for Korea from NAAFI and also tie up the various passport formalities.'

Eventually, Beryl was on her way, and at Hong Kong she planned to send a letter home, but had to wait and complete it on arrival. She enjoyed telling the family about her location:

> *I am sitting in a lovely bedroom in the Peninsula Hotel in Hong Kong. It is "the" Hotel, and it is like the Dorchester in London. I have my own bath, telephone, radio, Lavatory and sitting-room, with lots of soft-footed Chinamen ready to do my Bidding when I ring the bell... I've enjoyed the trip... but over the Alps before Rome, I wasn't well, with a cold, and the aircraft flew through a snow-storm.*

She had arrived at Kai Tak airport and then gone by ferry to the centre of the city. Her description was precise: 'The town is built on a series of hillsides facing a lovely bay with isles in it... it's crawling with expensive cars.'

Beryl was learning about the coming tasks as well, and she reports her findings: 'There are six WVS in Korea: four at Pusan and two at Inchon'. Then, she continues her letter after she has arrived, 'We've travelled the whole way [since arriving in Korea] with an officer who is going to the front-line. He has offered to take me out to see the town.'

Before leaving, there had even been messages from well-wishers, one of whom had royal connections:

The lady I work for is a relation by marriage to H.R.H. the Princess Royal. You see her daughter married the Hon. Gerald Lascelles last year. You may remember reading about the wedding. Now they are awaiting their first child. Lady Fox and Sir John Fox are the people I work for. Well my friend, take jolly good care of yourself and let's hope we will soon be seeing you... From what you told us at the Lyons Corner House you will do your very best. Lady Fox wishes me to send you her best wishes for a safe journey and says how courageous she thinks you are your colleagues are.

We now know quite a lot more about what exactly the WVS women provided; in spite of the paucity of detail or even general reference in many of the printed material, we have oral history and anecdotal evidence about the core duties that Beryl provided. One of the best summaries of this comes from an officer who, in interview, gave this information:

I first came across the WVS ladies at Norton Manor Camp, Taunton. I was very wet behind the ears – a boy of 16. WVS were amazing ladies who ran a centre in the barracks lounge with free tea and buns, books and papers, games room and a separate writing room. They always had a stamp for a letter when one was broke (most of the time). They were always older ladies, something of a grandmother complex for us youngsters. Next meeting with WVS was Detmold in Germany. Here they were very much younger ladies, all looking for husbands from the officers. That was not to say that they did not do a good job. Same centres as above but they organised days out to see more of Germany and to learn some of the language and customs. Also seem to remember film nights. In Germany the WVS was an official part of the British Army Of the Rhine and were protected by the Geneva Convention as non-combatants.

This is a very comprehensive account of the *raison d'etre* of the organisation, and is in line with Beryl's memoirs and letters. Arriving in Korea and Hong Kong, she would have been aware of the general tasks that would have been familiar to her, but on a larger scale. The same officer as reported above was fully aware of a deeper level of commitment and activity: '...for young soldiers with personal problems, normally focused on a pregnant girlfriend (no idea how that happened, Sir) the WVS was there to help. They were particularly adept at liaison with UK based welfare organisations and more comfortable in dealing with them than the army was.'

On arrival, with the year's end not too far away, Beryl wrote home from Tokyo and gave a swift sketch of the new country, a fresh and invigorating experience: 'Japan, with its lovely dwarf trees and pagoda buildings was a fairyland in a mantle of snow. The city itself is a fine modern one with lots of western firms represented there.' She wasted no time, before being taken to Korea across the water, in seeing the local theatre. In the Imperial Theatre she saw '... a *Takaraska* show, which was a musical comedy, and native Jap dancing, given by an all-girl cast. *Takaraska* is always so – girls taking the male parts... the opposite to the *Kabuki*.'

Her sister, Chris, wrote to respond to Beryl's new phase of life, and she missed nothing: 'The Marchioness of Reading and the Countess of Limerick are around these parts. The former I think is WVS and on her way to *youse folks* in Korea. I hope you are suitably impressed.' There was talk of peace in March 1953 and when Chris wrote again she gave the view from Singapore: 'Denys is very chary of peace in Korea. He has predicted for a long time that a peace treaty there would only mean the Reds would be turning their attention to the rest of S.E. Asia, and it would seem to be the case with recent events in Laos...' It seems that Denys was right.

Beryl also had warnings and advice about her destination, as in this from a friend in Cowes: 'My husband spent nearly 18 months in Korea serving with the RASC (Royal Army Service Corps) He was there from October 1950 and in charge of the first batch of five men who went out to set the NAAFI up. He had to make some very hazardous and dangerous journeys up the country, with goods, cigs and beer to our men in the front line.'

As one might expect, Beryl was keen to learn Korean, and she had maids around who knew no English, so she even worked at a smattering of Japanese. She wrote, 'I am learning Korean slowly from an army phrase book.' Soon she was in Kure, towards the end of 1952, when at home there had been horrendous smog, a crime wave of robberies at corner shops, and on top of this, there was still rationing. 'Kure is on the inland sea; there is also the small town of Shikito, and before the war, Kure was a hush-hush port where submarines were built. The inhabitants were not allowed to leave the base.'

This was now the NAAFI centre, and she soon had her first taste of her home for the next stage in her cycle of homes as a WVS worker. Early on, she formed the opinion that the Koreans were peace-loving people, dignified and approachable. But she soon saw that

America was 'literally financing South Korea. They do everything well, even to importing their own railway engines. Everywhere one can see Koreans in oddments of American army clothes.' She lamented the lack of sanitary towels and wondered how the Korean ladies managed, and also, there was a shortage of cotton (Sylko in particular) and so sewing activity was limited. She asked for all kinds of small provisions from home.

Beryl ended her first letter home with the news that Lady Reading was soon to make an appearance in Japan and Korea. In fact, Beryl noted that they 'constantly had official visitors', and one thing she couldn't fail to notice was something in the harbour, and this informs the reader about something very significant: 'From our windows we can see Danish and Swedish hospital ships, on one of which there are two female nurses. We met two Italian lady Red Cross nurses and two Americans came in from the Pusan base last week.'

It was a busy start to the new life, but every word she wrote in letters home indicates that she was excited and keen to make a contribution. The real challenges were soon to come. There were, of course, dark shadows over the year now receding, not the least of which had been the death of the King George VI. Frances Partridge, writing in her diary for that time, wrote, on seeing the funeral crowds: 'I saw a horde of human beings advancing towards me. The procession must have just passed their faces distinctly showing traces of a cathartic experience, like blackboards after a teacher had wiped them.' That was in February. In October, Britain exploded its first atomic bomb at the Monte Bello Islands, Australia. Agatha Christie's play *The Mousetrap*, began its extremely long run.

There was a mix of tragedy, light entertainment and general sadness as the old year died, but for Beryl, it was a case of concentrating her mind on a new phase of her adventurous life. She had gone from raw recruit to being part of an efficient and dependable team of organisers, and the word 'organiser' covers only a minute element in her job description. One has to be impressed by the central features of her first year out east; after a slow preparation in Singapore, she went first to Japan and met an utterly foreign way of life, with which she was engrossed and fascinated; from there she was pitched into both Inchon and Pusan and saw, every day, the troops returning wounded from the front line, and other troops setting out, wondering if their death was near. In that uneasy transit, for so many lives, she and her peers stood, reminders of British values: of caring and concern; of a mindset of support and service, and most of all, they represented the humanity, which was fundamental to their view of the world and of mankind. The burden on the shoulders of the WVS women was heavy indeed. Beryl had weathered the storm and every day had been a learning experience.

Chapter 6

The Momentous Year
1953

This was the year that Queen Elizabeth II ascended the British throne. It was also the year rationing ended. Cause for optimism had been impressed on the people of this island, with the Empire Exhibition still somehow insisting that, in spite of grievous losses and defeats, the country had triumphed over aggressive fascism and we islanders of this 'blessed plot' were still free. American culture was beginning to seep into our consciousness, but there was still a very British breed of ordinary working folk, desperate for family happiness and for the comfort of regular work and money for a good Sunday lunch and a few weeks by the sea in summer.

Yet as all this was happening, the warm-up to the Cold War was going on across the globe. Trouble was stirring in places such as Aden, the Middle East, Malaya, and in a small island north of Japan that nobody seemed to have heard of when the papers were discussed over a morning cuppa. In the Edwardian school text books the place was called 'corea' and was given a paragraph of explanation. What was to become the Korean War happened out on the fringes of what was the known world to readers of the Sunday papers, whose minds were absorbed in scandals, horrible murder and the doings of politicians of lax virtue. Yet that war was to draw in large numbers of young British men, doing their National Service, and of course, all the supporting personnel. However great and momentous the historical occasion, there are those without uniforms who do the essential work. Even in Samarcand, someone has to empty the bins and clean the drains.

Her first impressions were pleasant. She sent home a report that would have done well as a feedback from a foreign correspondent, as she went from Tokyo to Kure: 'There are everywhere around us lovely high hills. On the sea itself are steamers and quaint fishing junks. Honestly, it is all so charming... Kure itself is a very big port, used by the United Nations as a base for supplying Korea. No-one who lived here was allowed to leave it...' She began her vast correspondence with a balance that was soon to be expected for family at home – a mix of visual reporting and impressions, along with strong opinions on life and behaviour around her.

The biographer of the lives of the supporting staff backing up the military presence in Korea is fortunate in having items still surviving that give a clear idea of what the WVS actually did at their bases. Monthly reports were written, and some survive. When settled into routine at Seaforth Camp, Beryl wrote some of the reports. The camp was at Pusan. One soldier recalled that at Seaforth 'We had as much food as we wanted and proper beds.'

Beryl's official report is packed with important details of what was happening at Seaforth as 1953 began. The number of troops in transit was c.5,000, and there was a mix of British, Canadian, New Zealand and Australian forces. Beryl supplies the basic information:

The Club... was kept going by three WVS members and in these circumstances was open mornings (10-2) and evenings 6 a.m. to 10 p.m.)... we took 35 people on a picnic trip to one of the many good beaches... During August the big events in transit camp routine were the arrival of the Essex Regiment in HMS Asturias *from U.K. and the departure of the Royal Fusilers to Egypt in* Empire Halladale. *The WVS were at the station the next day when the Essex Regiment left for the Forward Areas.*

The troops going north were given 316 bundles of magazines and 48 packs of playing cards.

Beryl made several comments in the report that asked for help and improvements, including a desire for more snooker tables. Efforts from home had resulted in bundles of magazines from centres ranging from New Malden to Scarborough. The film service had had 66 orders, and a scheme called Say it with Flowers attracted sixteen orders. Games were a popular attraction; there was a universal clamour for table tennis, and once '... a Corporal Fusilier who had worked in connection with Regimental Welfare produced 131 balls and donated them to the club.' There was also card-playing, covering crib and whist.

At the very heart of Beryl's contribution was entertainment. The photographic evidence she left attests to the concerts she organised, and on top of games matches and a library that loaned out 70 books in one month, there was music:

> *As the weather was very hot for almost the whole month, it was often a case of fan or gramophone as we had only two wall plugs and one was in use for the radio. All skilled electricians were busy with the fittings for some new billets nearby. We used the pick-up mostly during the evening when it was cooler. We sent about a dozen of our latest records to Britannia Camp for the use of released prisoners-of-war. A new gramophone catalogue was compiled during the month. Radio was listened to quite a lot, particularly for the Jack Benny Show and Mail from Home.*

For further general details of the WVS of which Beryl was a part, there is also the WVS News Sheet. Each sheet included a summary of the year's events, and for 1953, in a background of terrible floods back home in eastern England, WVS centres across the world had sent clothes. In fact, Beryl had still been at home on leave when the floods hit, and she wrote to Chris:

I did lots of flood relief work during my leave in Lincolnshire, it was a dreadful business. Louth and Alford took most of the refugees. We sorted mountains of clothes and furniture etc. for them in a hangar at Waltham. 45 members of the W.I., the vicar's wife and me. The parents don't like the idea of my flying to Korea. Didn't have a very good leave – too cold and too busy.

Pat Whitall wrote a report on her involvement in an early foothold by the WVS in Korea at Inchon, which gives us an interesting picture of how the establishment began when they started a divisional rest centre: 'Here for three days men from the line had a brief respite from war, and convalescents became fit.' She then adds an informative summary of what was done:

This tented camp on the sea's edge had many luxuries to offer men from the Line, a change of food, unlimited beer, morning tea in bed, and endless hot water. Here we had a large lounge and a tea room. We found the men slept a great deal, and Read – magazines more than books. Eventually we came to handle most of the woollen comforts that were sent out to the men, and each man was given a parcel as he got on the truck to go back...

From these reports we gain a vivid account of each WVS centre. At Kure in Japan, for instance, in mid 1953, the place was 'for all Commonwealth forces at a busy period. It is most amusing to hear the accents of the Digger, Canuck, Kiwi and Tommy, mingled together in one happy family'. Much of the time served by the WVS organisers was in running tours, and in important chores such as shopping for and visiting the men in hospital.

The writer who summed up the time of the report settled on a crucial point about WVS work: 'These touches seldom go unnoticed, and it is the WVS who puts so much of herself into her work in the way of sympathy and understanding of the troops, and thought and care for her rooms, who is so repaid, and who realises that work Overseas is one of the most satisfying jobs there is to be done.'

Beryl was now in the midst of a frustrating, perilous and very modern war in its large scale and political influences, but paradoxically a familiar war, as in its core events it was a war of attrition, largely with troops dug in, fixed in trenches in a sadly stereotyped form of battle, imprinted in the British mind as being like the one most Brits had lost family members in. But the war in Korea was to clock up a horrendous total of around 5 million men killed, in an axis where east and west met in an unwanted theatre of war, which was composed of trials and tests for the manpower and fire-power of the great nations. The statistics are disturbing for a conflict known as 'the forgotten war': Britain lost just over 1,100 troops; sixteen countries were involved, and Commonwealth countries were drawn in, finding only confusion and barely adequate provisions at times.

After Britain pledged troops, as the war passed its first phase and the Chinese entered the fray, it became a war in which National Service youths took part, and a total of 40,000 British served there. The push north in October 1950 was perceived as a threat by China and, as so often happens, matters escalated soon afterwards. Chinese forces went into North Korea and things were set to get out of hand. There had also been personal and individual confrontations, notably in the sacking of General MacArthur by Harry Truman, the American president. In the country itself, Syngman Rhee, the South Korean leader, was not widely popular.

On the ground, the fighting conditions were dire. Stephen Kelly's book, which gathers lots of first-hand memories by combatants, makes it clear that there was 'Manchurian Fever' caused by the ubiquitous rats; there was a shortage of food; there were no facilities for washing and keeping clean; the low temperatures were far too severe for the military clothes to cope with, and too often, individual heroism and sacrifice won the day instead of tactics.

The most disappointing results were that, after peace talks failed in March 1953 (the month Stalin died) there was an impasse until the armistice of July, and a result that has maintained division ever since, in the creation of the two and a half mile Demilitarized Zone. Some of the main aspects of the war filtered into popular culture, notably in fictional works and films – *The Manchurian Candidate* and *MASH* being the most well-known.

Beryl's life in late 1952 and early 1953, found her in the thick of a war that existed on the edge of consciousness as far as Britain was concerned. However, she was so aware of international politics and of the situation around her in her various posts, that her surviving letters give testimony to her political awareness and the acuteness of her questioning mind. When the culture of the Far East struck her first, in a short time at Singapore before Korea, she was keen to learn some languages, but she was aware of universal issues and debates. In this respect, one thing she had in abundance was the press. In Korea and Japan she had not only the local cheaply printed *Korean Base Gazette*, but she also read *The Pacific Stars and Stripes*, printed by the USA, and *The Straits Times*. If we add to this any English papers and magazines sent out to the base, then she was well equipped to keep informed.

In the first few months at Pusan, where she was first posted, the preserved materials show vividly what kinds of chores she needed to do. For instance, a member of the Canadian Legion based at Inchon sent cash to pay for the cleaning of his flannel suit, and at the same time he requested some artists' materials such as poster paint and brushes. The writer sent some cash but had to add that he didn't know whether the cash sent would cover it all. In other words, Beryl was doing the shopping at times, and she would have to somehow pay for any short-fall and reclaim the cash later. It seems a very cumbersome way to operate.

As one might expect, there was plenty to do in terms of administration and procedure, including, after returning from the leave in Hong Kong, of making sure she had the right documentation for movement, and then having the required inoculation; from the Commonwealth Transit Camp she had to have certification of movement as when she went from Pusan to Kure, and there would have to be written documentation regarding her medical fitness and freedom from infection. Matter such as this, along with all the sights and sounds of journeys, figure prominently in the letters in her archive.

Again, thank-you letters and other social communications open up a wider social history around the bases, such as an airmail from Inchon to Pusan in which we have a glance at another problem:

> *Thanks for the little handkerchief... fortunately this last week the weather has been lovely, but have been to Seoul on a couple of occasions, meeting the WVS there. They have a very nice house but what a ghastly spot Seoul is! The NAAFI there had a robbery last week, and they stole £7000 worth of watches. Then our own NAAFI at the camp had a similar robbery amounting to £70.*

Also in this first phase of work in Korea there was a definite spirit of welcome and friendly association. It is an indication of the good impression Beryl made on soldiers that they wrote to her after being moved on, even if the messages were short, as in this: 'I have been back to the leave centre and was surprised to find that you had been posted to Pusan. I hope you are getting on alright there as I am now back with the battalion and we had quite a do on the night of 28/29. We had quite a few casualties.'

If there were Germans around, she found them, and some correspondence is with a man called Fritz who was in the 1st Battalion Duke of Wellington's. Again, his note gives some insight into life at the time:

I have only understood the text of the Deutsch on the back, but enough to know what you put. Quite a lot has happened since I left Inchon, and the best thing was Tokyo leave. I must say that it was the best leave I have ever had. I returned just in time to go into the front line, and we came out yesterday. We had one chap killed and 2 wounded, so we didn't do so bad. We have just had a memorial service for them. How about coming up and sorting out some magazines for the welfare of the troops?

Central to Beryl's work was the task of organising performance events and also encouraging and supporting all kinds of social occasions across the base. The photographic record of her life in the WVS gives ample evidence of her presence as a 'party girl' but images may lie. Often the provision of celebrations and sing-songs was part of a day's work and firmly entrenched in her job description, but of course, she enjoyed being popular, and the stack of letters written by men to her long after party occasions gives testimony to her success as hostess. One of her favourite hobbies for these occasions was reading palms, and a photograph exists showing her in costume, trying to be mystical and exciting. There were regular invitations to drinks parties and other celebrations, and one of these was even expressed in verse, at the end of the year, when an invitation came from the HQ of the British Commonwealth Forces in Korea:

This invitation comes to you
With hopes that you are free
To come along one afternoon

To have a cup of tea.
The day the party will take place
We hope you will remember –
Is on a Tuesday of the week,
The twenty-ninth December.
The time is sixteen hundred hours
And for our rendezvous
The Chief of Staff has lent his house,
In other words, House Two.

There were also much grander affairs, such as a programme offered at the Inchon Service Club soon after her arrival:

Cutting of ribbon: Colonel Carl H. Elges
       Commanding Officer, 21st T Medium Fort
Welcome Address: Lt. Col. U. M. Manning
       Executive Officer, 21st T Medium Fort
Dedication: Captain H. W. Ogden
       Chaplain, 21st T Medium Fort
Presentation of Club: Colonel C. H. Elges
Introduction of Service Club Personnel:
       Miss Vera Vincent, Staff Advisor
       Miss Julia Cook, Club Director
       Miss Ursula Coventry. Program Director

Music was by '110th Replacement Bn Combo.'

In addition to internal shows and celebrations, there was the matter of healthy and worthy relations with the Korean people, and an example of the kind of event Beryl loved organising was a presentation of Korean Classic Folk Dances fronted by Kim Tong Moon and Dr Lee Hoon Koo.

By March, Beryl was familiar with the routine and with the range of duties expected of her. From the central office of the WVS came a welcome letter. This noted that she had been sick on the journey out, but that she was now 'settled... and thoroughly enjoying it'. The letter included a job to be done, though: 'I have had a letter requesting various flashes to be sent, so I am sending the whole lot direct to her, including the ones you asked for. I am sure if there is some sewing to be done, you must be bitterly regretting that you did not take your old friend, the sewing machine!'

Naturally, in a war situation in which massive numbers of men who were in and out of battle, there would be some problems. Beryl obviously had a problem, but it remains a mystery. All that is known is that Lady Reading had to be in contact with a number of senior officers regarding some difficulty with troops in the rest centres. It may well have been something related to unwanted sexual advances or even a degree of unacceptable behaviour, but whatever it was, Lady Reading communicated the topic to Beryl and expressed herself very vaguely. She wrote, 'I do not honestly think it can be very easily handled but I am quite happy knowing that you will watch carefully and that the best possible results will come from our little talk the other day.'

Reading between the lines, and taking statements from some letters, the heart of the problem at Pusan (which led to a transfer north to Inchon) appears to be behind this: 'I was well tired of the 1000 men and two girls business that was the situation... The trouble was that my partner was too new to the WVS for the particular design of the opposite sex and she showed it in circumstances where the slightest extra smile or favour could set the camp by the ears.'

Lady Reading took immediate measures, and Beryl explained these: '... she suggested a scheme for economy in personnel out here... that is to do nine months in Korea and nine more in Hong Kong or Malaya. The second idea underlying this is to give the WVS from tropical climates a turn in a temperate one and vice versa...' This might, on the surface, indeed be related to 'economy' but surely it was also to give some relief to the outnumbered women. Beryl was absolutely content to have escorts – both for visits and as protection at events. That is, in a world of flirting, unwanted advances and no doubt some drunken actions not intended and later regretted, there had to be a 'buffer zone' for the women. Hence she always explains about the men who took her to dances or drove her to visits on leave time.

She had plenty to say about Inchon in 1953, and her report is excellent documentary evidence on the situation:

> *Near our own camp is a large hospital entirely run by Swedes.... An American transportation officer took us out by boat to the* Jutlandia, *a wonderful Danish Hospital ship. They, with the Swedes and Norwegians, are doing wonderful work for the sick and starving Koreans, apart from war casualty work. There are 40 nurses plus two women doctors on board...*

Beryl was getting to know the troops of the 1st Commonwealth Division, and the mix of nationalities might have been part of some unmanageable task. The Division was multinational, comprising British, Canadian, Australian and New Zealand men, along with Indians in a medical attachment. It was also united with the US 1 Corps, and these kept together until mid 1954, when Beryl was still there, helping with demobbing. It is not difficult to imagine the hundreds of potential problems that would be integral to the social and leisure activities of so many fighting men.

For several months in 1952 there had been a hiatus. As Lieutenant Colonel P.J. Soden told everyone in his farewell circular, 'Due to the comparative static state of the battle front since April, we have taken the opportunity... to effect substantial improvements in the standard of NAAFI service' and he added, that his period there may well prove to be 'historic days in the history of the Korean War'. For Beryl it was a situation she found would soon change. As well as helping with sewing jobs and shopping for the bed-ridden, she was supervising and supporting in all capacities, as a note testifies: sent to the 1st Commonwealth Division Rest Centre it asks for help: 'I would be glad if you would keep an eye out for 22579448 L/C James C.A. Royal Fusiliers. He is, I think, a rather difficult case and as his mother works for us in London, it would be nice if we could take an interest in him and help him as much as possible.' When many notes to her were for things such as buying pen nibs, this kind of caring (possibly psychiatrical) makes it clear exactly how ad hoc so many measures in health care were.

Beryl was coping with a mountain of paperwork, mostly dealing with correspondence. She wrote that on her birthday in May: 'I've had as many as 60 letters per month to write to people who send us magazines.' Still, soon there was fighting again, and she spent a long stretch in Pusan. Again, she reported on the place with documentary precision:

> On the harbour of Pusan one can see the infamous island prison of Koje. Pusan had one million inhabitants before the great exodus from the North; now it has five million. The extra four live in incredibly poor lean-to shacks, made out of tins, boxes and bottles discarded by NAAFI and American messes and canteens. The standard of cleanliness is, I regret to say (and the behaviour) of these refugees, is much higher than that of our slums and poorer areas!

She settled in thoroughly by May, and it had taken a long time to reach that point of confidence and near-certainty about things. It was not difficult to fill the day in between working sessions at the centre; she had her Box Brownie, and took hundreds of snaps with that. She had family and friends not only to write letters, but to send essential provisions such as her need for Beecham's Powders (she had a large stock of these by the middle of the year). Then in late May she announced: 'We are having a Coronation Ball in this camp so I really would like a new evening dress, but I can't get to Japan before the 2nd to get one. One can't get things in Korea, or buy them suitably cheaply.'

Back home, of course, the Coronation of Queen Elizabeth II was the talk of the press and the town, and the magazines and papers were stuffed with features on the topic. For Beryl this meant planning, listening to a range of possibilities and suggestions, and naturally, taking advice from the WVS organisers. Whenever there was a special occasion to be marked at the bases, there was an event. *Any excuse for a dinner party or drinks* might have been a suitable motto. After all, there was time to kill and fill in between the confrontations. The WVS and NAAFI staff welcomed these occasions, of course, because it broke a demanding routine, and although it meant plenty of work for them, it was all aimed at having fun, with the bonus of getting to know some of the staff across the wider establishment. At Beryl's first base at Pusan, there was always a feeling of the people being on the move; sometimes men were there simply for two days before going to the front or catching a train to someone, for a variety of reasons.

The celebrations for the Coronation were, therefore, special and universal. A typical invitation for Beryl was from the warrant officers and sergeants of Seaforth Camp, who requested the pleasure of the company of Miss B. Baxter 'at a ball to be held in their Mess on June 2nd 1953 at 7 p.m. in honour of the Coronation of Her Majesty Queen Elizabeth II.'

At home, it had been a tough, demanding time ever since the horrendous smog of December the year before. Then the East Coast floods had been a major disaster, just a few months later. Robert MacFarlane, in his book, *The Wild Places*, asked people about the floods, and answers such as this were given: 'The sea wall was breached in dozens of places. On Canvey Island alone, about 200 people were drowned. If you had been out at St Cedd's which remained

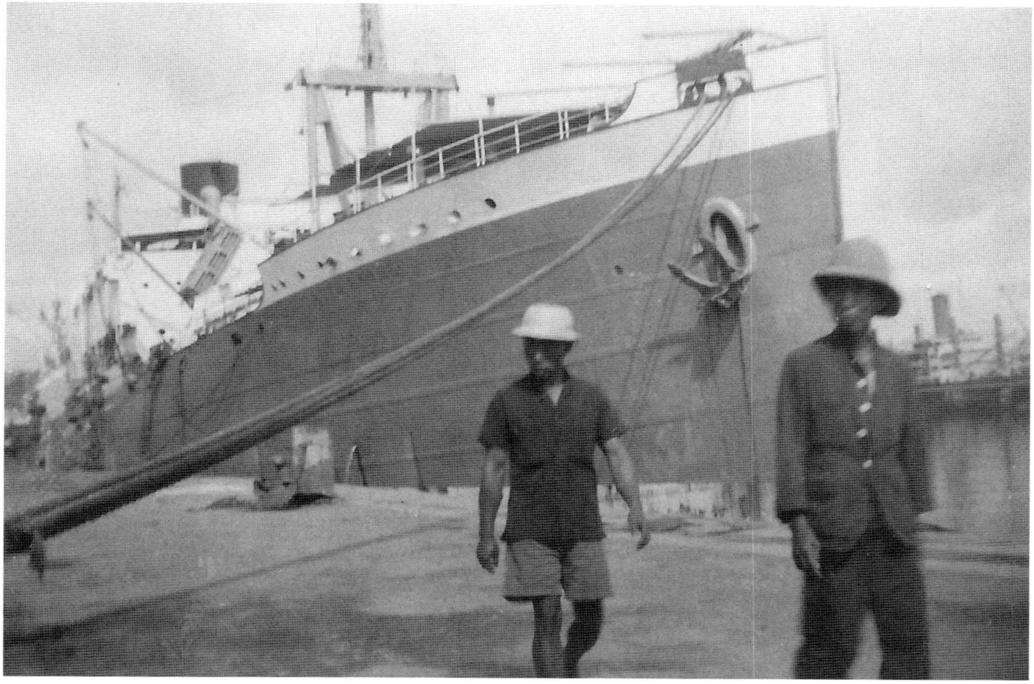

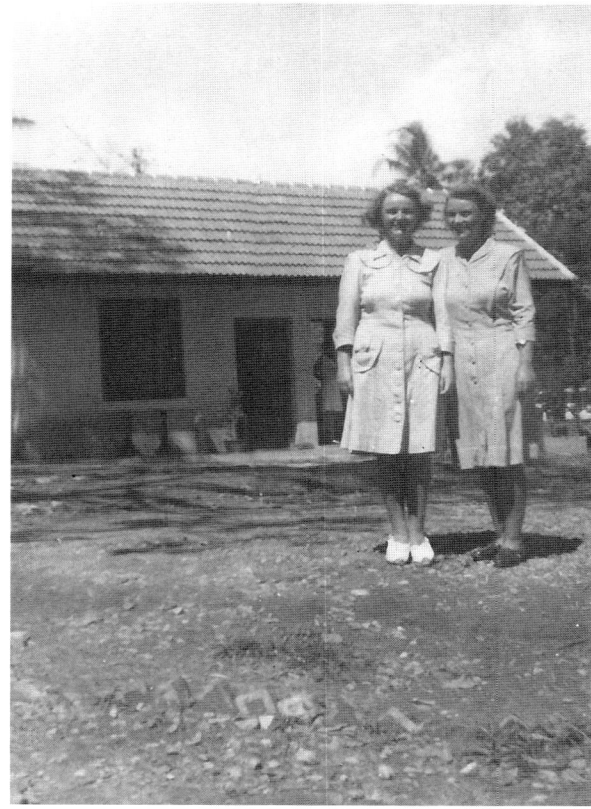

Above: A former Dutch troopship, the SS *Kota Baroe*, which was taken over by the US in 1942 and used by Beryl.

Right: Beryl was based here after the last Korean posting. Here she is with her sister Chris.

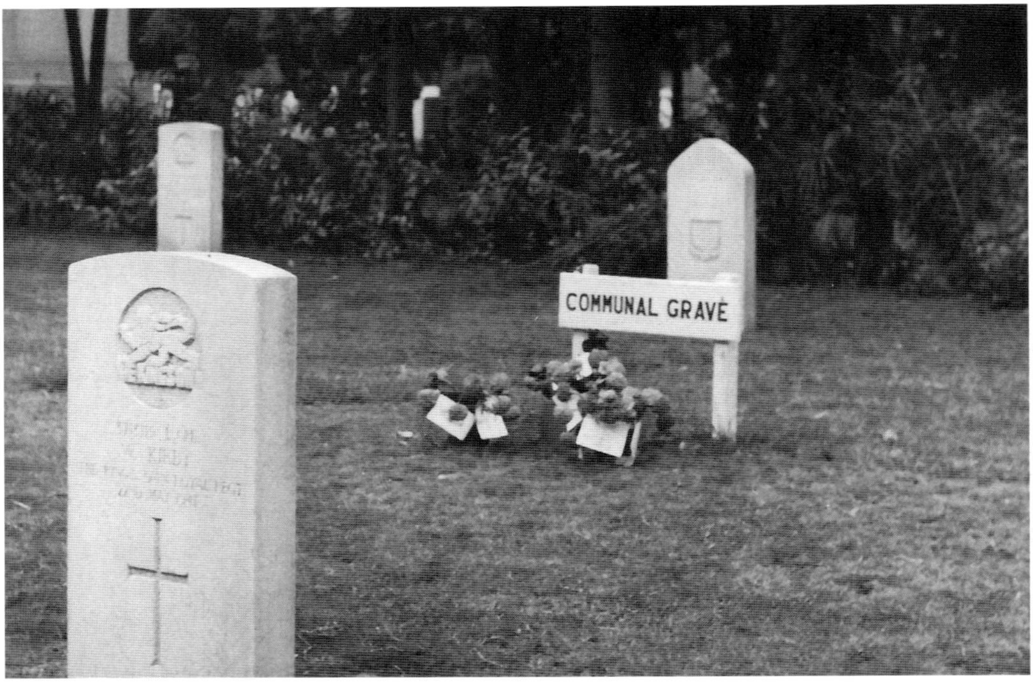

Beryl dealt with the aftermath of this crash in Jordan.

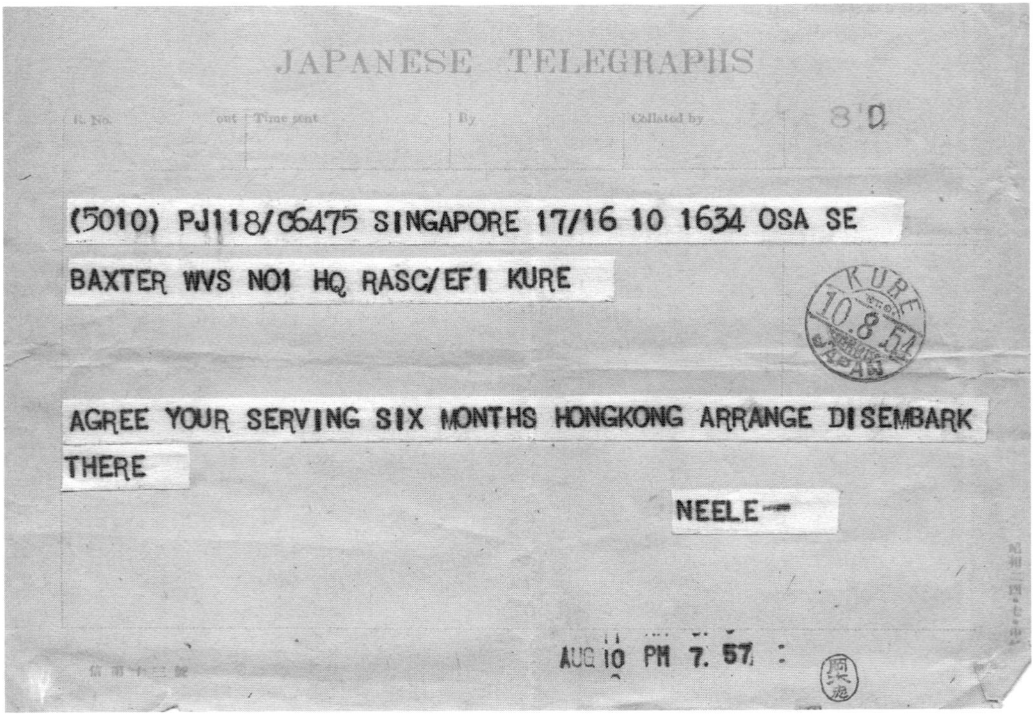

JAPANESE TELEGRAPHS

| B. No. | out | Time sent | By | Collated by | 8'D |

(5010) PJI18/06475 SINGAPORE 17/16 10 1634 OSA SE

BAXTER WVS NO1 HQ RASC/EF1 KURE

AGREE YOUR SERVING SIX MONTHS HONGKONG ARRANGE DISEMBARK
THERE

NEELE—

AUG 10 PM 7. 57

This message from Japan is one of many Beryl preserved.

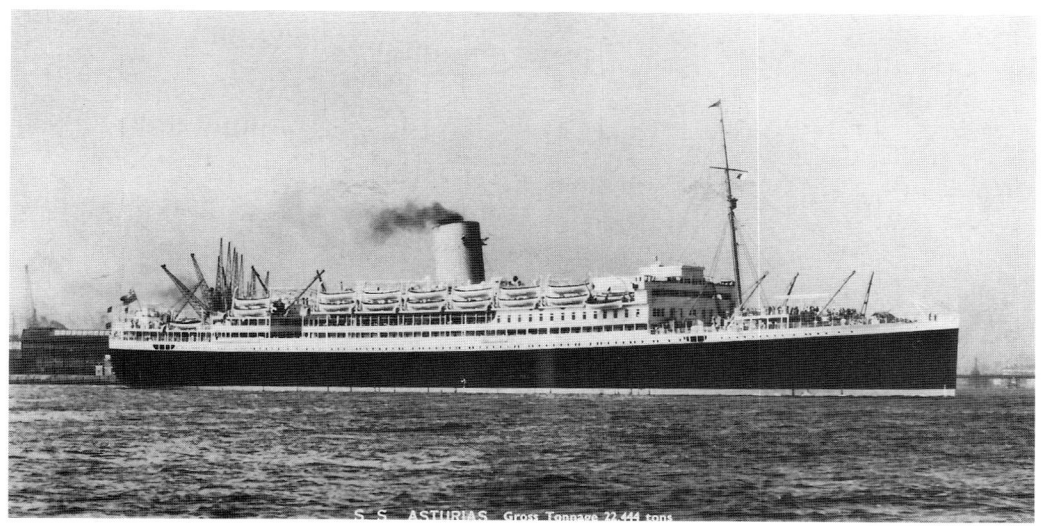

Above: Many of the troops in Korea were transported on this vessel, the SS _Asturias_.

Right: Beryl kept this flyer addressed to members of the Allied Expeditionary Force when in her WAAF days in Stanmore.

SUPREME HEADQUARTERS
ALLIED EXPEDITIONARY FORCE

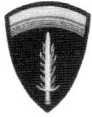

Soldiers, Sailors and Airmen of the Allied Expeditionary Force!

You are about to embark upon the Great Crusade, toward which we have striven these many months. The eyes of the world are upon you. The hopes and prayers of liberty-loving people everywhere march with you. In company with our brave Allies and brothers-in-arms on other Fronts, you will bring about the destruction of the German war machine, the elimination of Nazi tyranny over the oppressed peoples of Europe, and security for ourselves in a free world.

Your task will not be an easy one. Your enemy is well trained, well equipped and battle-hardened. He will fight savagely.

But this is the year 1944! Much has happened since the Nazi triumphs of 1940-41. The United Nations have inflicted upon the Germans great defeats, in open battle, man-to-man. Our air offensive has seriously reduced their strength in the air and their capacity to wage war on the ground. Our Home Fronts have given us an overwhelming superiority in weapons and munitions of war, and placed at our disposal great, reserves of trained fighting men. The tide has turned! The free men of the world are marching together to Victory!

I have full confidence in your courage, devotion to duty and skill in battle. We will accept nothing less than full Victory!

Good Luck! And let us all beseech the blessing of Almighty God upon this great and noble undertaking.

Dwight Eisenhower

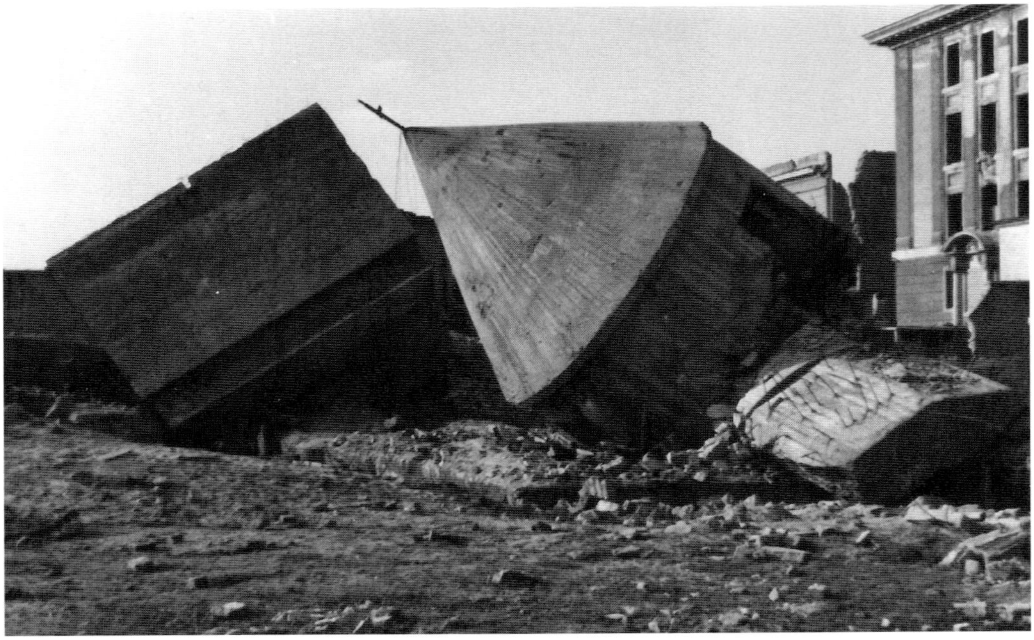

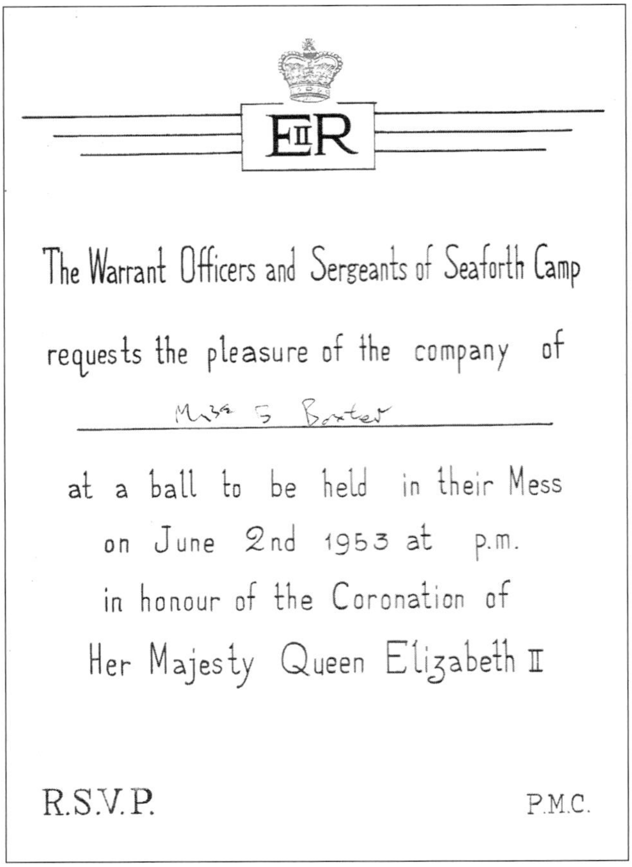

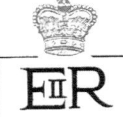

The Warrant Officers and Sergeants of Seaforth Camp

requests the pleasure of the company of

Miss S Baxter

at a ball to be held in their Mess
on June 2nd 1953 at   p.m.
in honour of the Coronation of
Her Majesty Queen Elizabeth II

R.S.V.P.   P.M.C.

Above: It appears that Beryl took this snap of Hitler's bunker while serving in Berlin.

Left: One of dozens of invitation cards preserved in the archive, this one being an invite to a Coronation Ball in honour of HM Queen Elizabeth II.

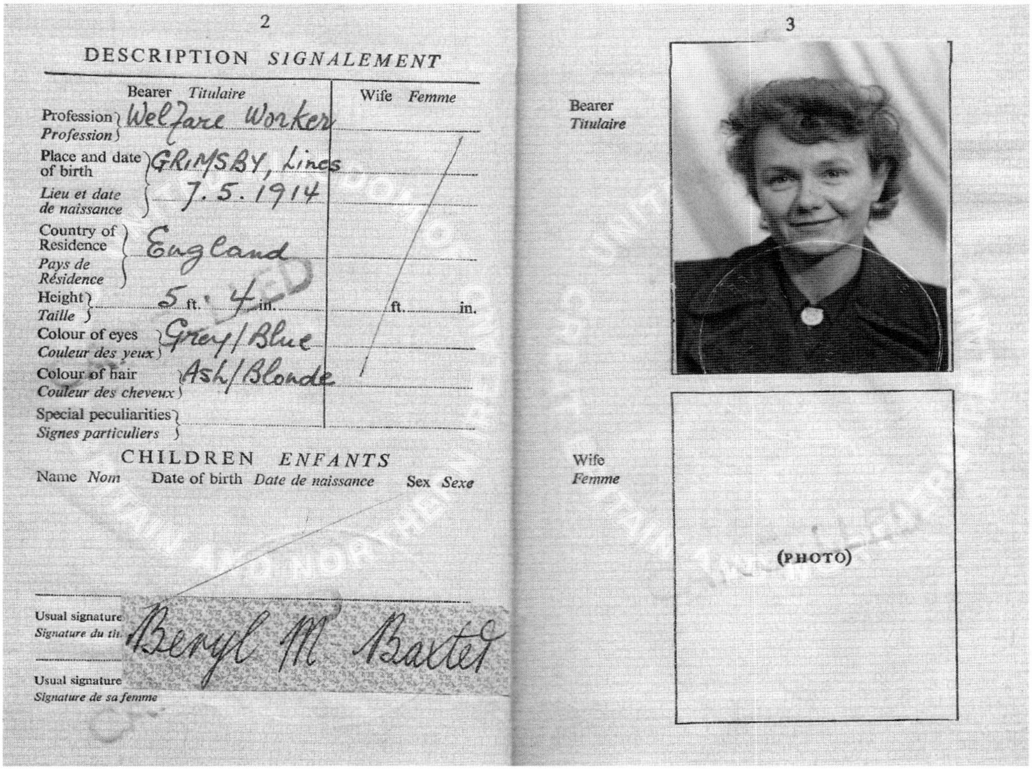

DESCRIPTION *SIGNALEMENT*

	Bearer *Titulaire*	Wife *Femme*
Profession *Profession*	Welfare Worker	
Place and date of birth *Lieu et date* *de naissance*	GRIMSBY, Lincs 7.5.1914	
Country of Residence *Pays de* *Résidence*	England	
Height *Taille*	5 ft. 4 in.	ft. in.
Colour of eyes *Couleur des yeux*	Grey/Blue	
Colour of hair *Couleur des cheveux*	Ash/Blonde	
Special peculiarities *Signes particuliers*		

CHILDREN *ENFANTS*

Name *Nom*	Date of birth *Date de naissance*	Sex *Sexe*

Usual signature
Signature du tit...   Beryl M Baxter

Usual signature
Signature de sa femme

Bearer
Titulaire

Wife
Femme

(PHOTO)

This is the first of many passports, logging Beryl's global journeys.

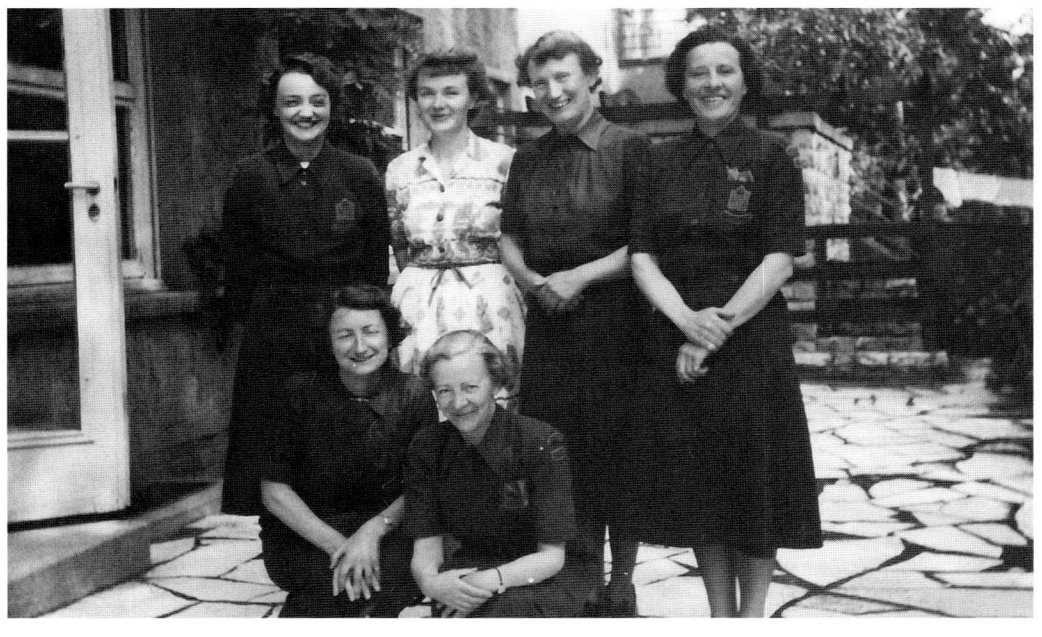

A moment captured in the Berlin years.

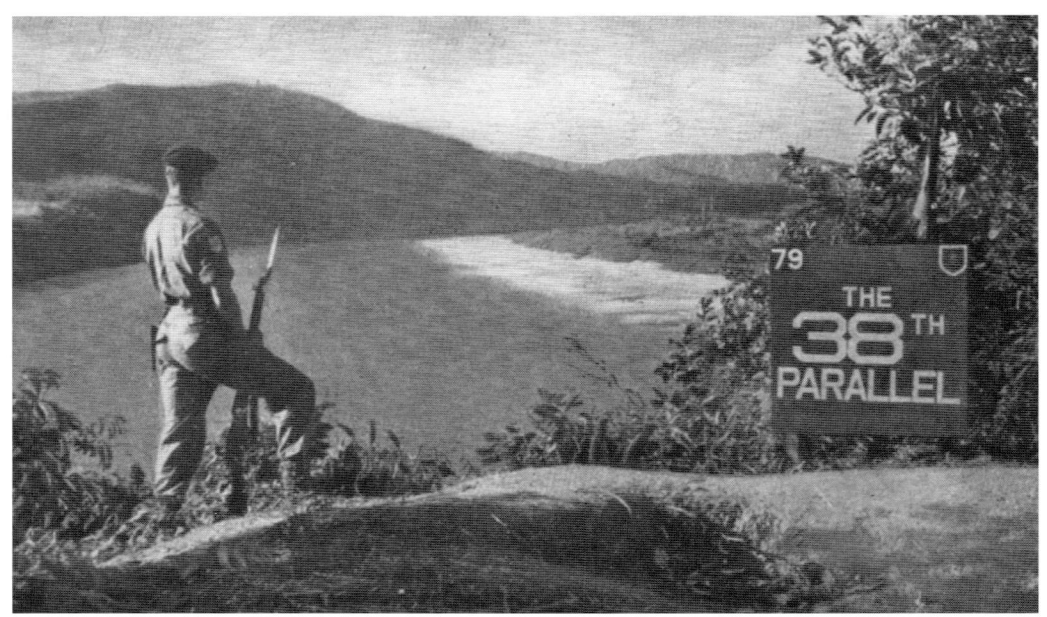

An image of the crucial geographical division in the Korean War.

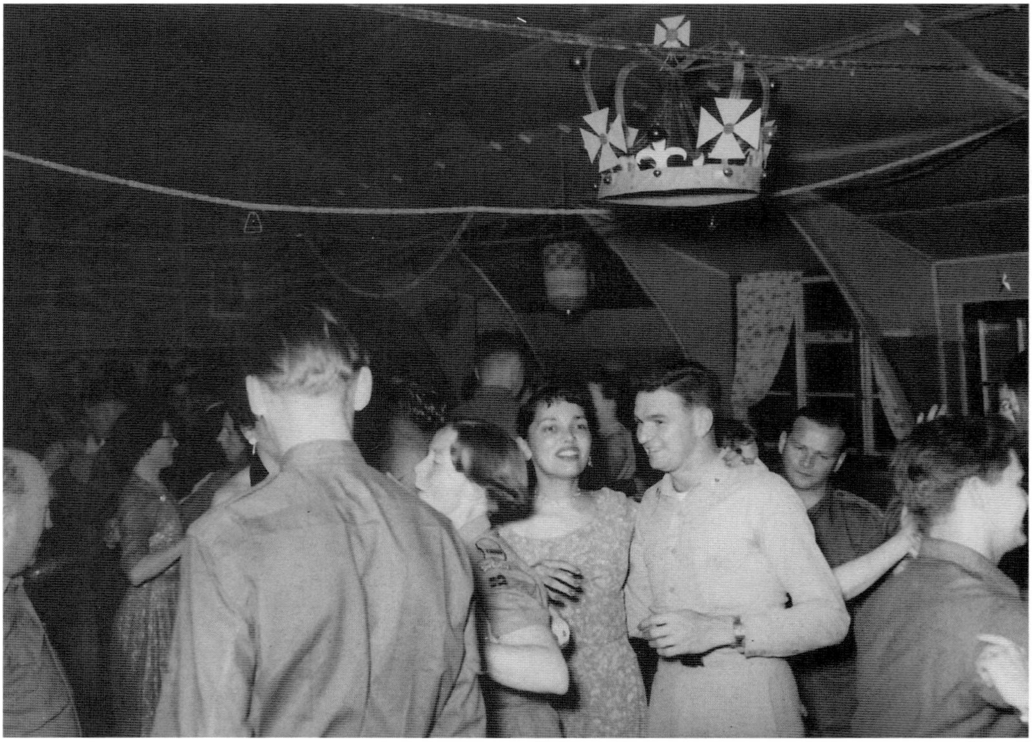

One of many pictures of dances at the WVS/NAAFI centre in Seaforth Camp.

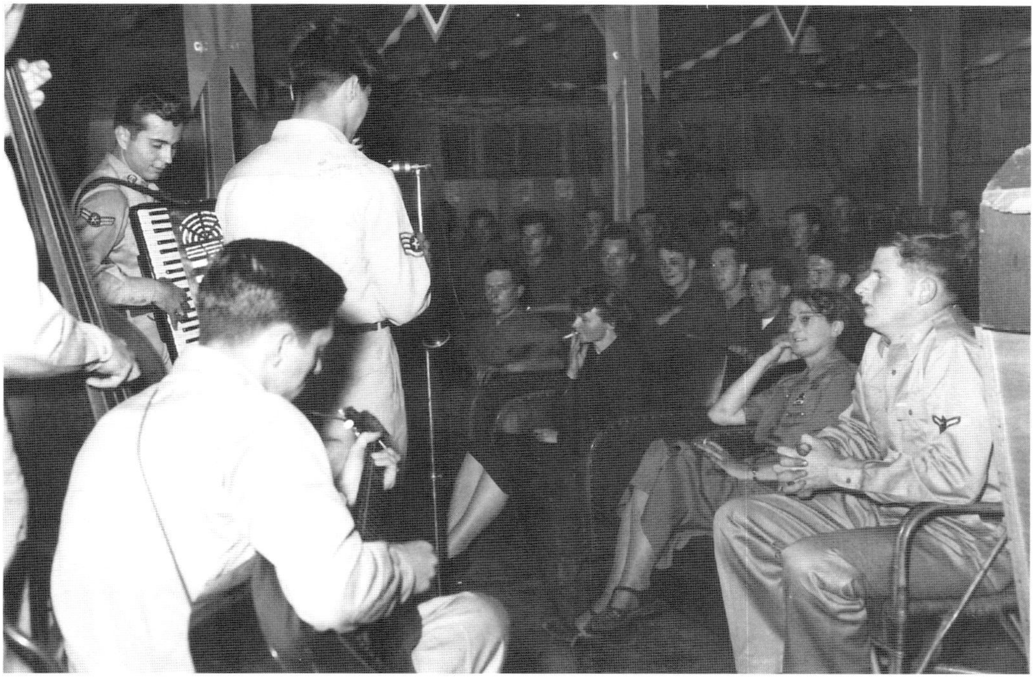

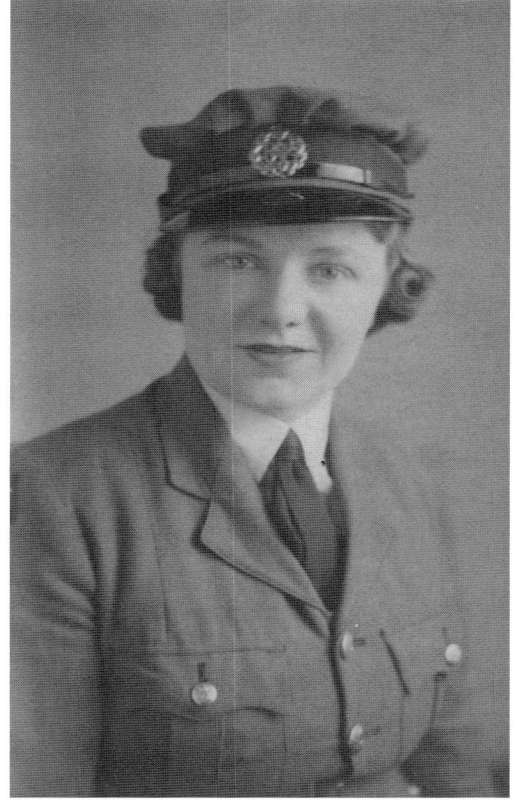

Above: A typical scene from a camp concert with an American band playing.

Right: A picture from Beryl's early years in the plotting centre.

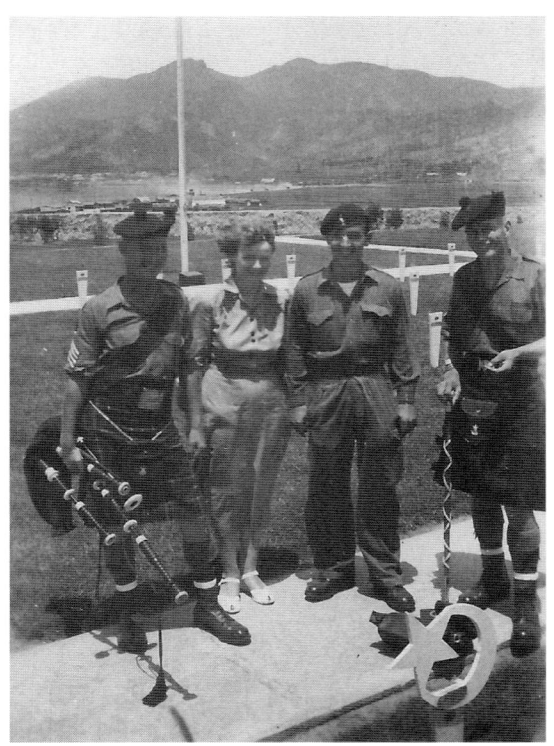

This photo of Beryl and soldiers shows the sheer delight of togetherness in war.

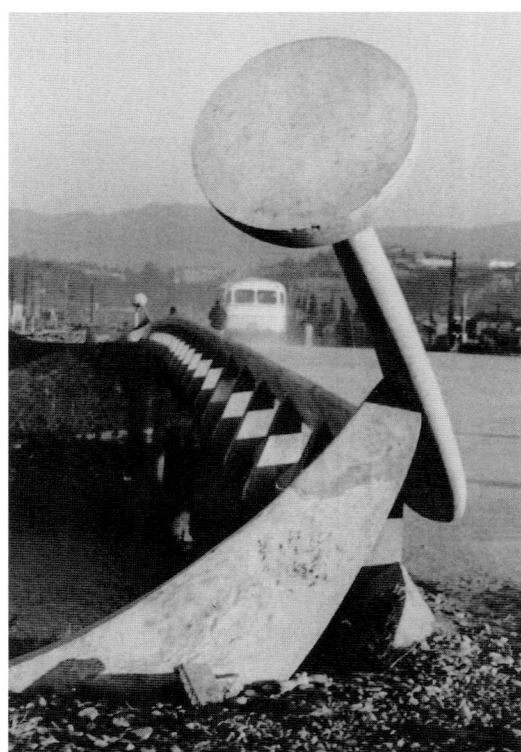

Completed in 1952, the Hiroshima Peace Bridge was part of a plan to reconstruct the town after the bombing.

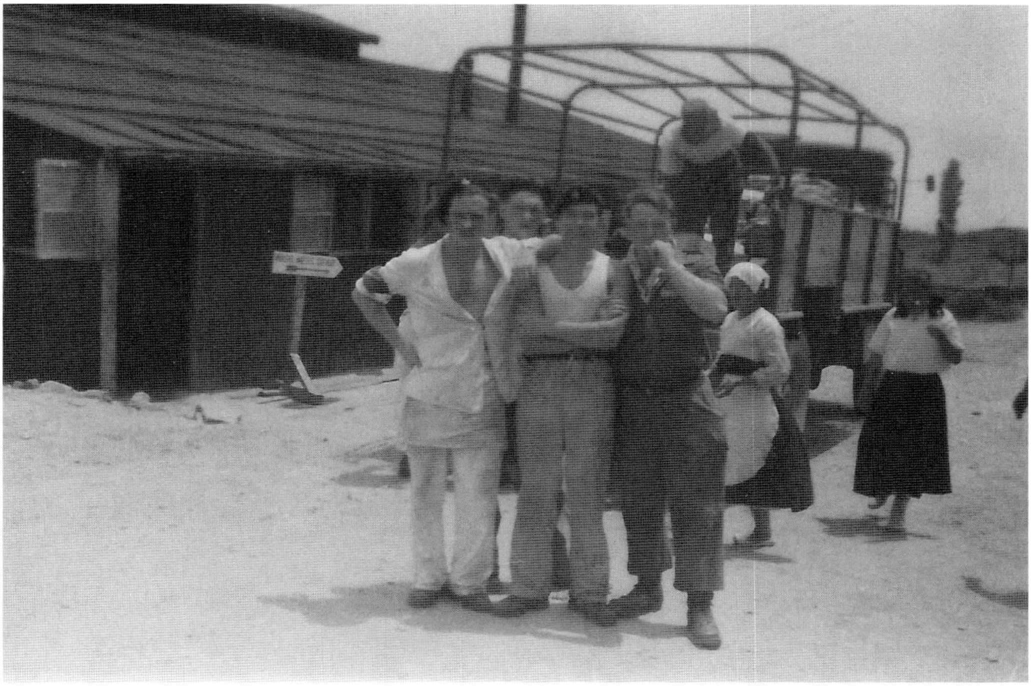

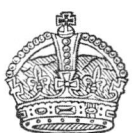

One of many photos of Beryl with troops, taken by the mess in 1953 when at rest from the front.

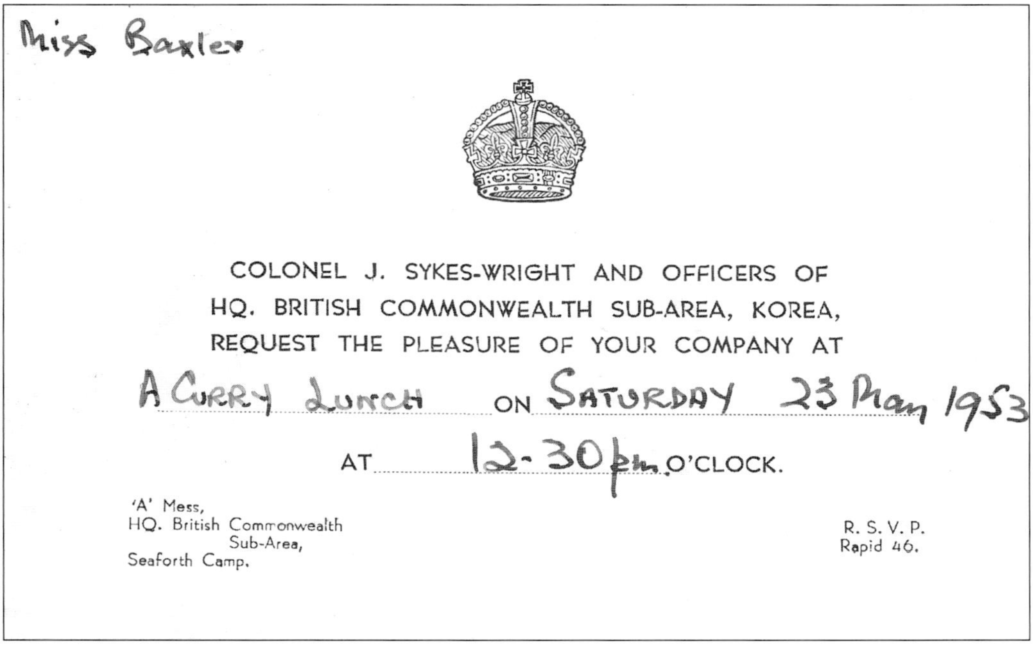

Miss Baxter

COLONEL J. SYKES-WRIGHT AND OFFICERS OF
HQ. BRITISH COMMONWEALTH SUB-AREA, KOREA,
REQUEST THE PLEASURE OF YOUR COMPANY AT

A Curry Lunch ON SATURDAY 23 May 1953

AT 12-30 pm O'CLOCK.

'A' Mess,
HQ. British Commonwealth
          Sub-Area,
Seaforth Camp.

R. S. V. P.
Rapid 46.

From May 1953, an invitation to lunch at the mess in Seaforth Camp from Colonel J. Sykes-Wright.

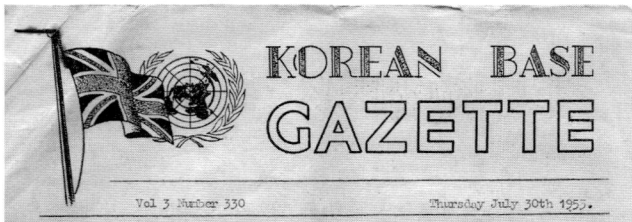

KOREAN BASE GAZETTE

Vol 3 Number 330   Thursday July 30th 1953.

DULLES TO MEET PRESIDENT RHEE

Korea : Wednesday - The American Secretary of State, Mr Dulles, accompanied by four Senators, leaves for Korea on Sunday. He is to have talks with President Syngman Rhee to endeavour to formulate a common policy for the forthcoming political conference. Also discussed will be the problem of Korean unification, the withdrawal of all foreign troops, the Korean and American mutual security pact, and the rehabilitation of South Korea. Mr Dulles said yesterday that he would oppose the admission of Communist China into the United Nations as the price of Korean unity, and that he thought America had enough influence in the United Nations to outvote any such move. He also stated that he was against the granting of any further concessions to China, and that although America reserved the right to leave the political conference after 90 days if she thought the Communists were not acting in good faith, she was not automatically committed to resume hostilities.

In a statement to the Korean people President Rhee said today, explaining South Korea's collaboration in the Armistice, that he had received assurances from the 16 UN countries engaged in Korea that they would come to his aid in the event of any further Communist attack.

On the front, both sides are still continuing their withdrawal. Work is going on to remove barbed wire and unexploded ammunition, and to look for unburied dead of both sides.

The United Nations chief delegate today offered to begin the exchange of POWs on Monday, but the Communists said they could not complete their arrangements in time; the first group of Communist POWs are due to arrive at Inchon today.

75 Swedish and 7 Swiss members of the Neutral Commission arrived by air today, and are expected to meet the Polish and Czech delegates at Panmunjom tomorrow.

+   +   +   +   +   +

GERMANY : Wednesday - The Federal German Supreme court has ordered the release of 2 leading ex-Nazis arrested by the British authorities early this year on charges of plotting against the regime. A British spokesman stated that it was difficult to understand the reason for their release, as no question of their guilt or innocence was raised. The West German Chancellor, Dr Adenauer said that he was firmly convinced of the 2 men's guilt.

+   +   +   +   +   +

NEW DELHI : Wednesday - Mr Nehru returned yesterday from his talks with the Pakistani Prime Mini-

TRUCE VIOLATIONS ALLEGED

Korea : Wednesday - When the Military Armistice Commission met again today the chief Communist delegate alleged that UN troops have violated the terms of the truce on 8 separate occasions. He said that UN artillery and a machine gun had opened fire after the cease fire, and that 3 UN aircraft had flown over the demilitarized zone. The chief UN delegate said that he would investigate, and asked for further details.

Before leaving Tokyo for Washington by air today, General Mark Clark said that as far as he knew there had been no violation on the part of the United Nations.

+   +   +   +   +   +

INDO-CHINA : Wednesday - 10,000 French Union troops yesterday attacked a Viet Minh force estimated at 2,000. Paratroops and armoured vehicles were used to encircle the rebels, while naval vessels patrolled off the coast to cut off escape that way. The French HQ in Hanoi states that the rebels have been unable to break out, and that already 100 have been killed and 400 captured.

+   +   +   +   +   +

CAMBODIA : Wednesday - The Cambodian Prime Minister said yesterday that he had asked France for a joint Commission to be set up to study the possibility of an immediate transfer of certain

Left: Beryl preserved a few ephemeral publications such as this copy of the *Korean Gazette*.

Below: A snap of a common experience – on board ship again, leaving port.

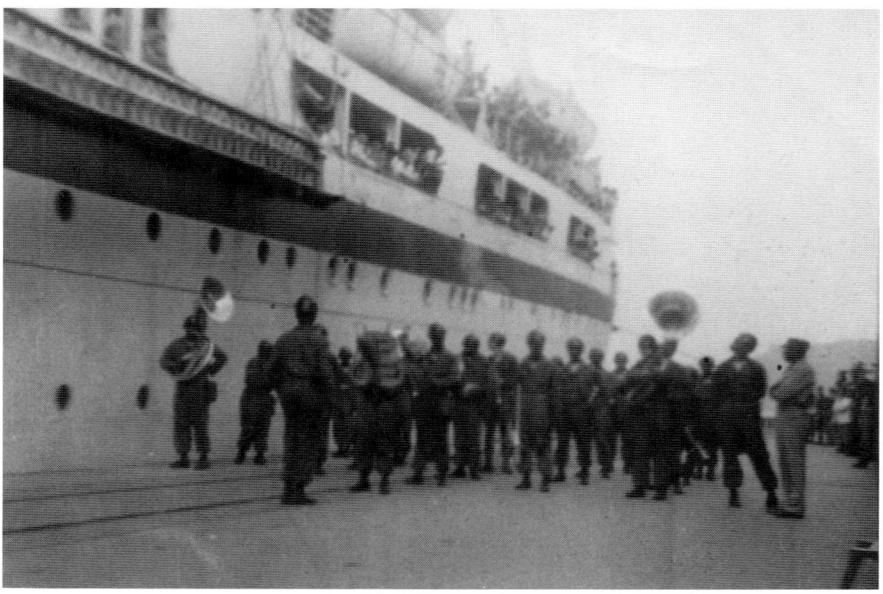

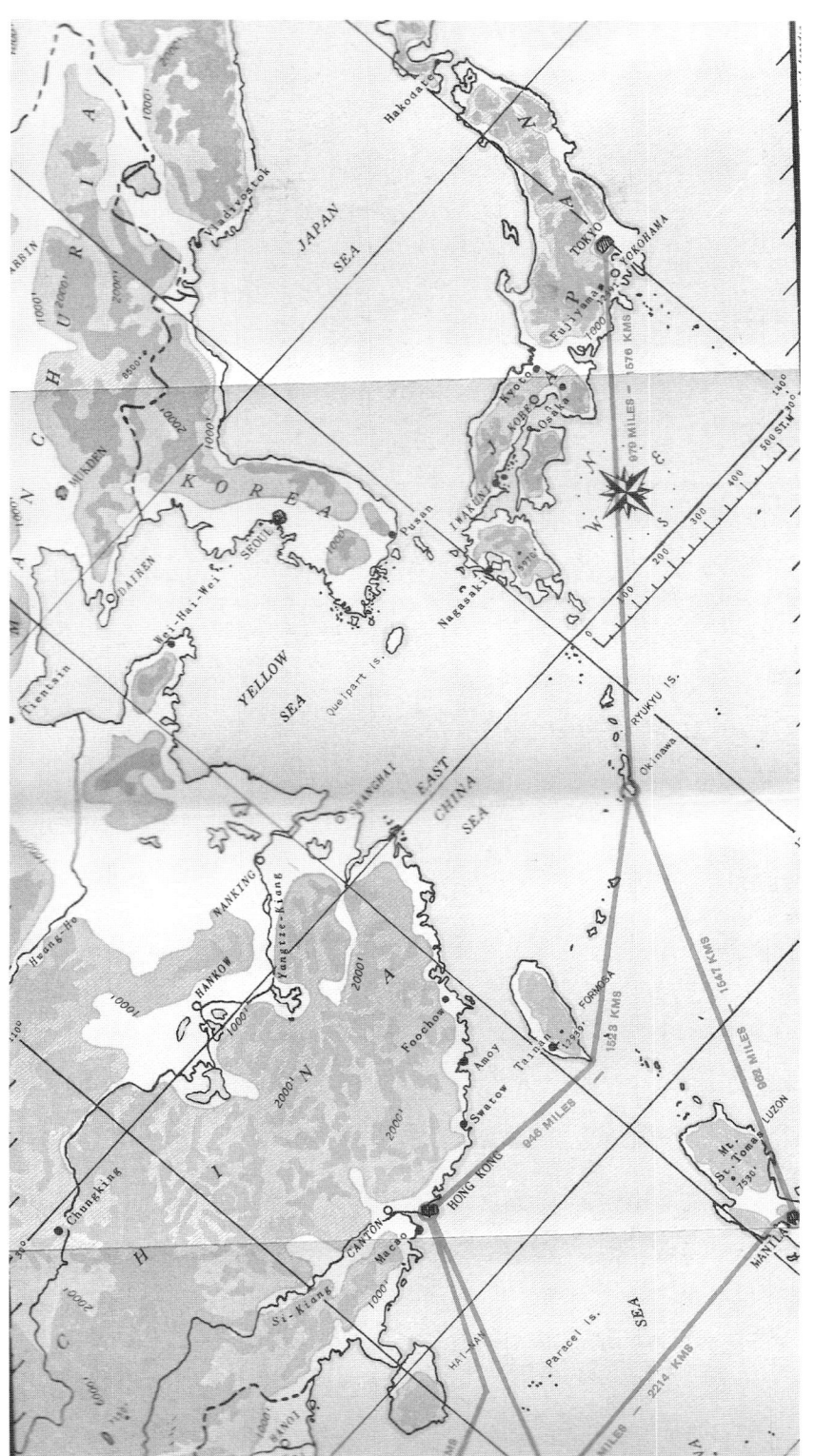

The BOAC air routes give a clear idea of the routes Beryl flew.

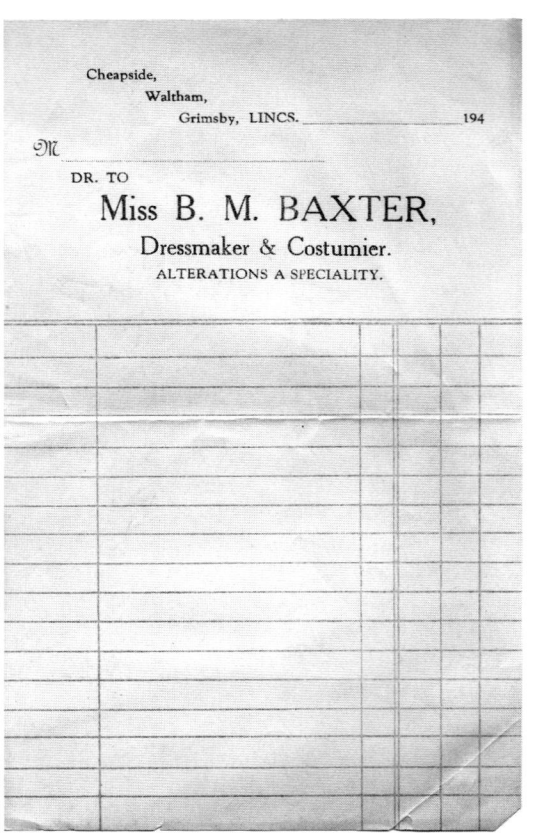

Cheapside,
Waltham,
Grimsby, LINCS. _____ 194

ℳ _____

DR. TO

Miss B. M. BAXTER,

Dressmaker & Costumier.

ALTERATIONS A SPECIALITY.

Left: Beryl, as she was meant to be, if war never came.

Below: Regimental bands such as this one played a vital part in all celebrations.

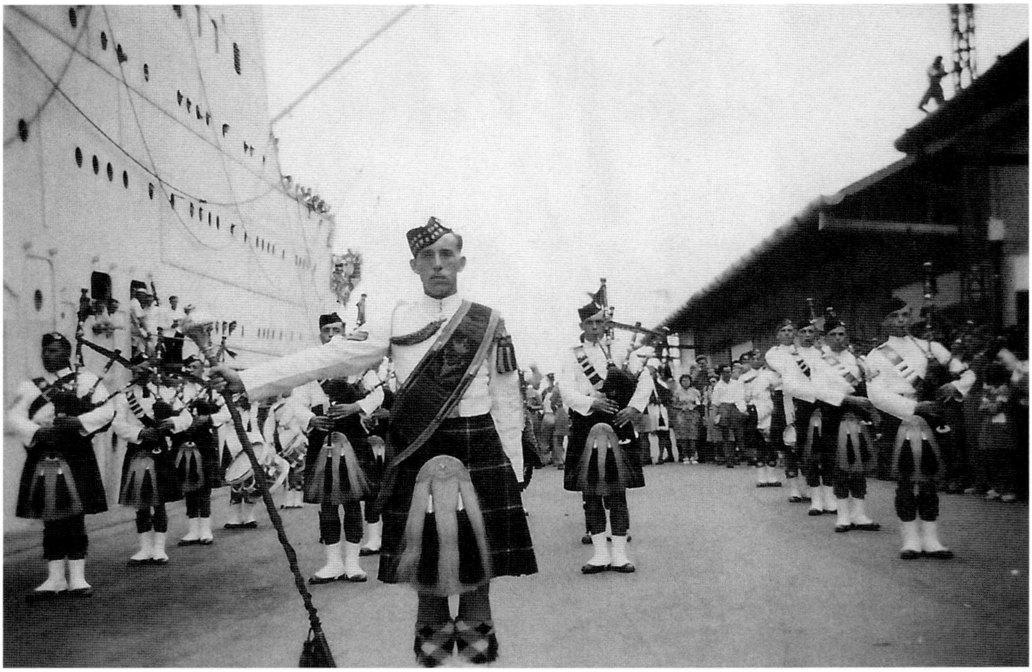

R.A.F. FORM 1394.

ROYAL AIR FORCE.
BRIEF STATEMENT OF SERVICE AND CERTIFICATE
OF DISCHARGE OF

The corner of this certificate to be cut off if the airman/airwoman is discharged with a "bad" character, or with disgrace or if specially directed by the Air Council.

SURNAME........BAXTER.................OFFICIAL No....2053718......

CHRISTIAN NAMES......BERYL MAY......

Date of enlistment 19.6.41 / enrolment 7.5.47 .... Terms of enlistment / enrolment ... D.P.E. 2 years under AMO A.926/46.

(a) Date reported for regular service.....7.5.47.....

(b) Branch of Air Force in which enlisted....W.A.A.F.....R.A.F. trade on discharge......CLK.S.D....

Date of discharge........3.6.49...... Rank on discharge.......ACW1.....

(c) Cause of discharge.........Termination of engagement. K.R. and A.C.I. para.652 clause 1.

(Para. 652 Clause 1 King's Regulations and Air Council Instructions.)

(d) General character (i) during service.......V.G.........(ii) on discharge.........V.G.....

(e) Degree of trade proficiency :—A......SAT......B.........—.....

Special qualifications........NONE.....

(f) Medals, Clasps, Decorations, Mentions in Despatches, Special Commendations, etc. { DEFENCE AND WAR MEDALS.

DESCRIPTION OF ABOVE-NAMED AIRMAN/AIRWOMAN ON DISCHARGE.

Date of birth ......7th JULY 1914.......... Marks or scars ....NONE......

Height......5....ft......2....ins.

Complexion......FRESH.

Colour of eyes......GREY BLUE.........Colour of hair......ASH BLOND.

Airman's or airwoman's signature ...*Beryl May Baxter.*

(g) Brief statement of any special aptitudes or qualities or any special types of employment for which recommended :—

During the period of three months she has been at this Unit, she has proved herself to be a hard working capable girl, always cheerful and co-operative. She is very keen on social welfare work and should be successful in civil life especially if engaged in work of this nature.

ADJUTANT

6 MAY 1949

FQ (Unit) 19 GROUP

R.A.F. Mount Batten

Unit Date Stamp

(Signed) ....

Commanding H.Q. (U) no.19 Group.
Royal Air Force.

Attention is directed to Notes (a) to (g) on reverse.

Beryl's discharge sheet from 1949.

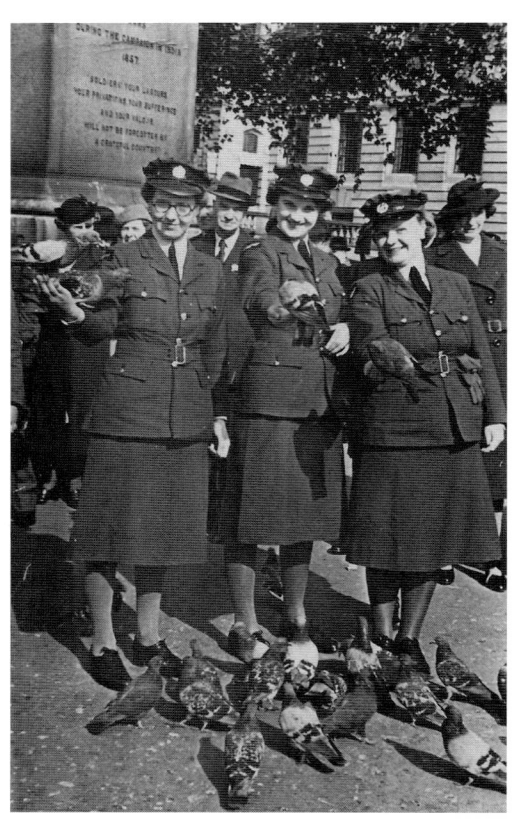

Left: Another group picture of Beryl with various friends and workmates.

Below: A rare image of the interior of a club in Japan.

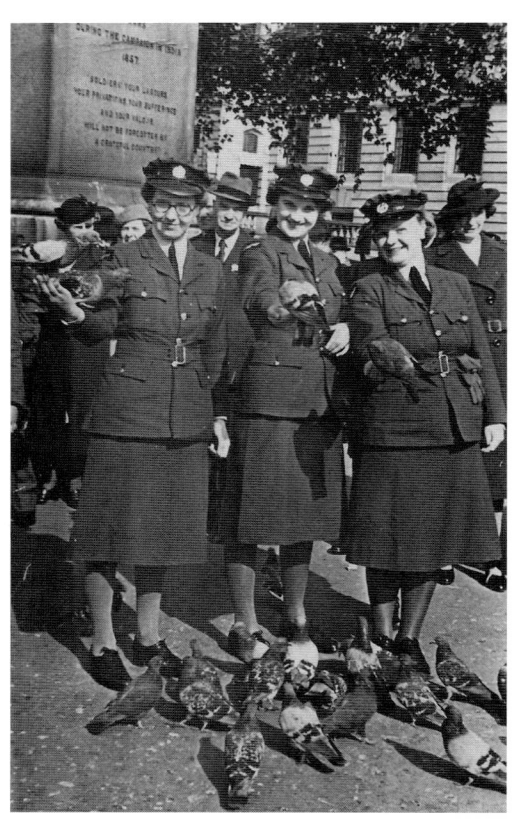

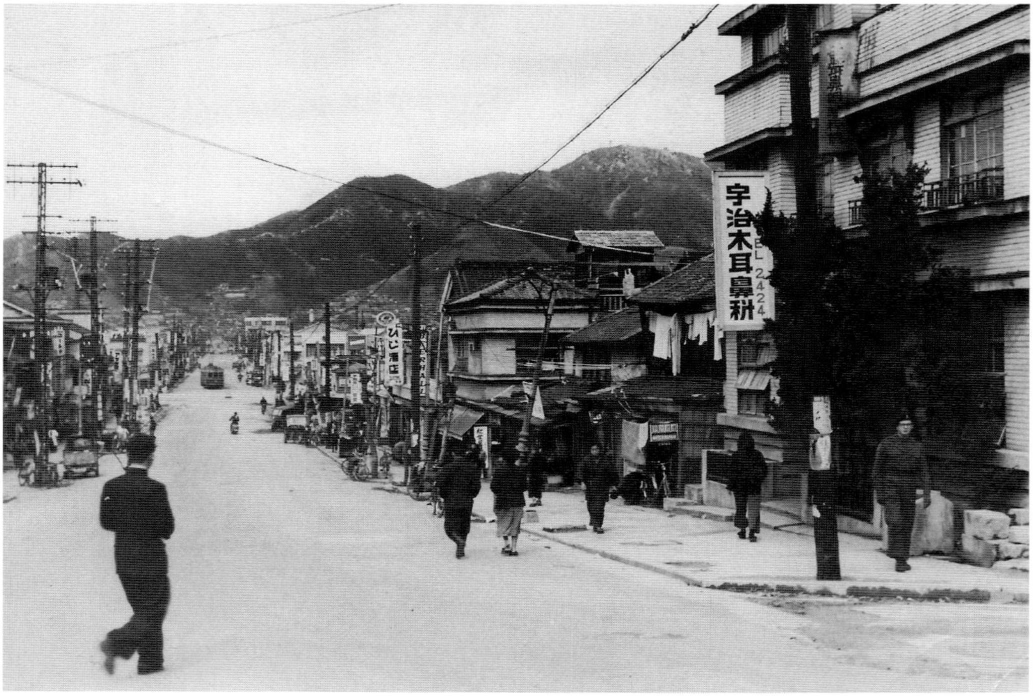

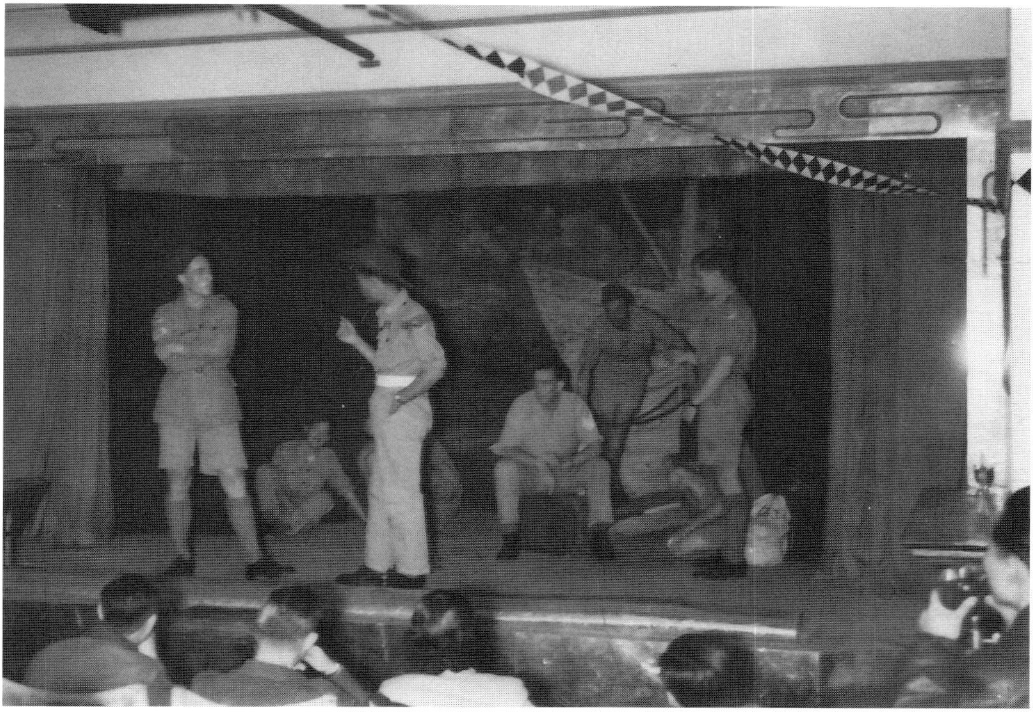

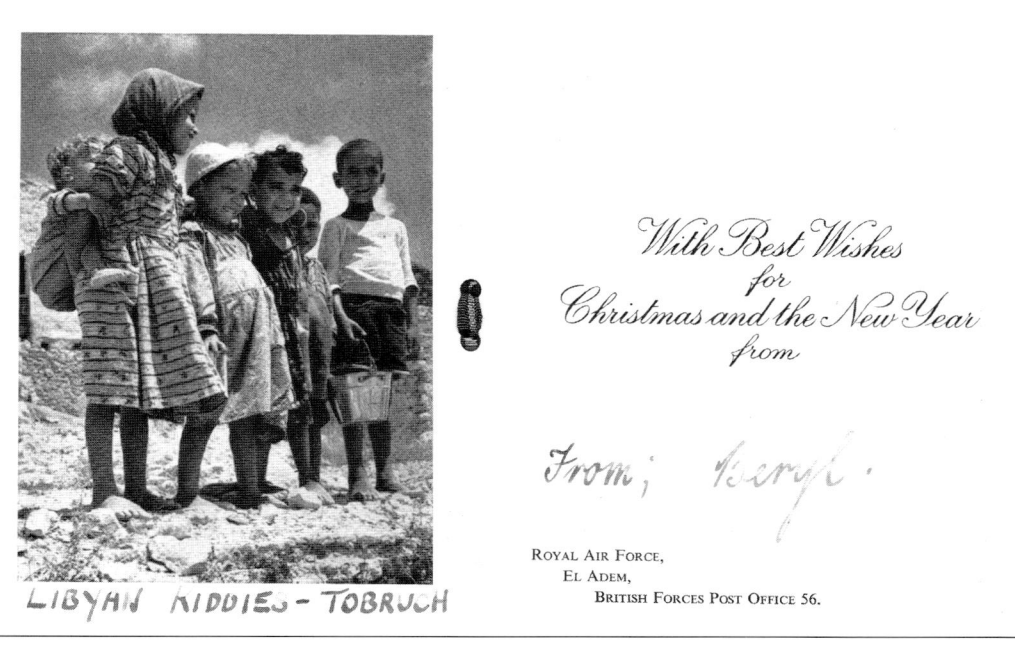

Beryl loved organising events such as this. Theatre was her passion, after dressmaking.

LIBYAN KIDDIES - TOBRUCH

With Best Wishes
for
Christmas and the New Year
from

From; Beryl.

ROYAL AIR FORCE,
EL ADEM,
BRITISH FORCES POST OFFICE 56.

One of Beryl's many Christmas cards from places she visited.

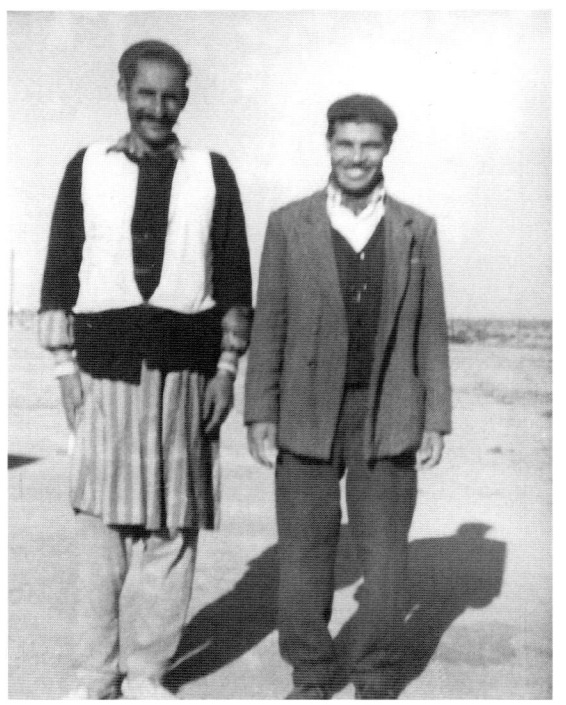

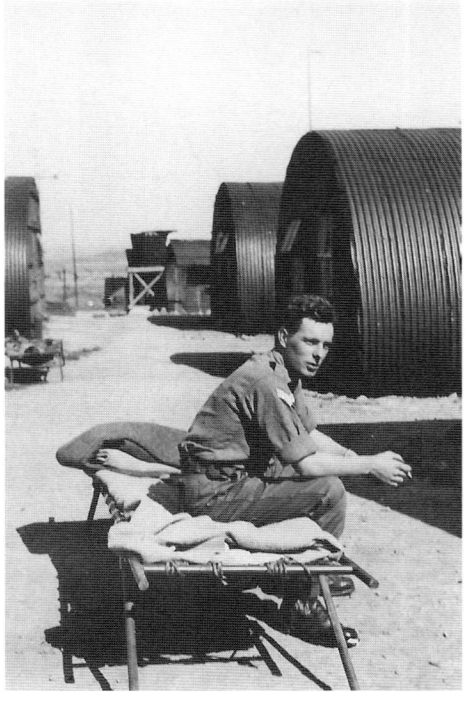

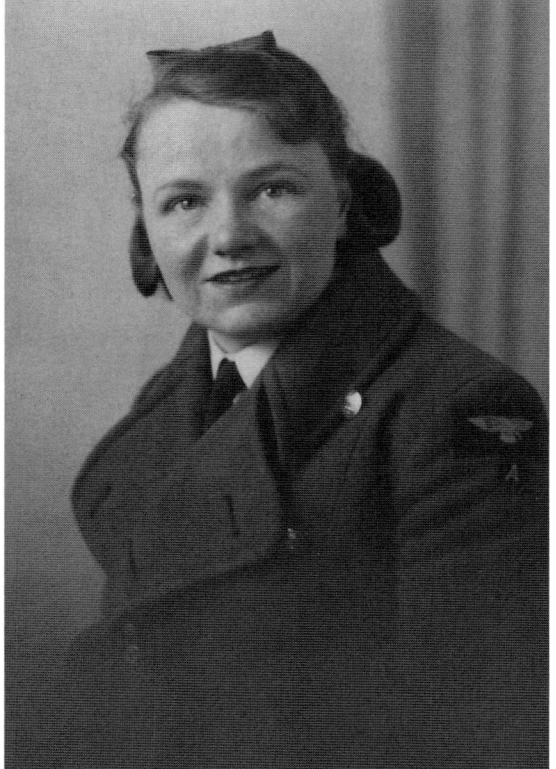

Above left: Two of the locals at Habbaniya.

Above right: A soldier taking five minutes at Seaforth Camp, Korea.

Left: Beryl in her RAF greatcoat at Silloth during her initial training.

dry, said Peter, and you looked back inland across the peninsula, you would have seen only the upper storeys of buildings.'

The smog of December there had been four days of thick yellow smog. People were breathing in a poisonous gas, and the official figure was that 4,000 people had died, over four days beginning 4 December. I have a memory of being caught in such a fog, in Leeds in 1959. I was on a bus going to the city centre when the smog invaded the road outside and then the bus. The situation forced a stasis on everyone and everything, and breathing was difficult. Finally, most passengers stepped out of the bus and walked, feeling with their hands along walls, to find their way.

Rationing was finally ended in the same year as the Coronation, and after the sadness of the death of King George VI there was a general sense of wanting and needing to celebrate life and the dawn of perhaps a new age, with a new sovereign at the helm. At camp in Korea (and no doubt in similar camps across the Empire) there was a profound enthusiasm to celebrate. In the milieu described above, there is no surprise in the fact that liaisons and friendships were often short and swift, with multiple attractions and a huge proliferation of male over female. The women were accustomed to new faces, fresh attractions and transient emotional involvement. Beryl often mentions men adrift, lost and in need of company other than their own mates in the ranks of the squaddies. There was a constant awareness, among the care and support staff, of the aching loneliness, fear and anxiety in the military ranks, and conscripts in particular, young and innocent, would be desperate for their learning experience to be fast-tracked. Every small demand or problem, from inspection to the next good meal, brought some stress. All this is to say nothing about the possibility of death whenever they were sent up the line, of course.

With all this in mind, it is easy to understand the popularity of the Coronation celebrations. At that point, with the events at planning stage, there was also talk of a possible truce. If the United Nations signed a truce, then North Korea might fight alone; Beryl's opinion that it would be a 'big blunder if the U.N. signed a truce, and the North Koreans fight on alone...' She had a sound grasp of what was then being called a 'Police Action' policy. Her criticism of this was written with a high degree of emotion:

> *This so-called Police Action in Korea wiped out 100 of the Princess Pat's Canadian Light Infantry last week, and also the previous month, three-quarters of the 1st Battalion Black Watch regiment. An ambush by 60 Chinamen on about 20 of the King's Regiment recently left only 30 survivors. This is just to give you an idea of how bloody this war is. The Americans lose even more than the U.N. troops all put together. Recently they defended "Old Boldy" – a much fought for hill – at the cost of 300 men, in less than three days! Please keep these facts to yourself...*

Beryl changed again in May, from Inchon back to Pusan, travelling by train, on a journey that took almost twelve hours, enjoying the 'lovely hill country and a little Lakeland'. Again she referred, when writing to her sister, of the 'Police Action' and added that 'I do not think the outside world has really much knowledge of it or much interest in it... but I can assure you that this is a terrible war...'

But, as Lady Reading noticed when she visited, the living conditions for the WVS were quite reasonable. Her quarters were better than ever on arrival, and with the Coronation imminent, she explained with a certain angle of pleasure that she had 'another bad case of young man love older woman on my hands again.' This time, the man in question was rather cultured and sensitive, and Beryl delighted in explaining that the man '... is quite humble with me and he doesn't care who knows about his adoration.' He spoke three languages, and that would impress Beryl. Nonetheless, there was a fundamental problem for Beryl and her peers in this work, and she explained this very clearly: 'It is not fair to single him out... I dare not show him even sisterly affection. I can't single him out from the many good types there are here who look to me for even a mild understanding, and affection, in a situation like this one where there is such a lot of emotional starvation.'

The Coronation shindigs went ahead, and there was a film distributed from London, and she noted that there was a news reel but that she missed it, as she was on duty. Again, in the celebration period, there was another difficulty with sexual relations and social intercourse. She started taking a Korean language class, run in the evening and organised by the Americans; the teacher was a graduate of the University of Seoul. She was the only Britisher in the class, and she noted that this fact seemed to fascinate the teacher. Then the inevitable happened – he asked for a date. Her response that their relationship had to be confined to the class interaction of teacher and student. Again, really explaining to herself as well as to her sister in Singapore, she explained very lucidly what the moral issue was: '... we are only four WVS and European women in the British community. We must never favour one more than another, or it creates an "atmosphere". After the happy-go-lucky attitudes of the Americans at Inchon, it is very stifling here...'

Then the Coronation celebrations began, and there was a general atmosphere of relaxation for a while. She had three weeks of hard work first, doing the preparation, and then she sat for hours in the sun 'making red, white and blue rosettes and small silver paper crowns, with ribbon streamers, all to be worn as Coronation button-holes. 'We sent 200 up to the boys we knew at the front,' she wrote home. Then came all the events:

We organised competitions for very good prizes, picnics (indoor and outdoor) and every evening we had a visiting American or Korean concert party or band. What a week. Phew! In a match where R.O.K. army officers played *our other ranks from the area and B.M.A. the former won 3-1. The R.O.K.'s* were a joy to watch, so agile and determined, and of course much fitter than our chaps. Our club looked wonderful decorated with lots of lovely flags and gilt crowns etc. were sent to us from Japan for it. The day began with a big parade of Commonwealth troops which was reviewed by our Colonel and the British Minister in Pusan. All the people (there are many of all nations and of both sexes) who work for the many welfare and civil assistance organisations were present. We were there too, to watch it, in full force too...*

* Republic of Korea

Lady Reading, who sent regular letters to WVS staff, had something special to communicate, as she was involved as one of the group of peeresses. The account of the day is very detailed, and she ends the piece with an interesting footnote:

In the evening I stood outside the Palace with several thousands of other people and I swear once or twice I heard my ribs crack as I squeezed harder and harder, but I also heard something I shall never forget. The Queen had just finished her broadcast – very moving – and the National Anthem was played. Nobody sang and when it ended the woman next to me said, "I couldn't have sung that for a thousand pounds. It was a prayer, to be spoken in one's heart, not a song to be sung with one's lips.

At the celebrations in Korea, Beryl was there to see Syngman Rhee (called by some servicemen Signalman Rhee) and also Helen Kim, women's leader in a Patriotic League. The latter gave a return party at 'an exclusive Korean women's club' followed by a dance and a cocktail party. But Beryl references a guerrilla war situation in the background, after an escape of some prisoners. She explained that 'The Yanks have been going about armed to the teeth but no other nation is doing this.'

The staff at different bases did sometimes visit each other. Beryl explained to her sister: 'It is only an hour and a quarter from Inchon to Seoul, and Mavis and I used to go in there to spend the day and stay the night at the officers' mess. They loved having us socially of course. The trouble was always to get away again...' There was always the steady stream of farewells and gifts also, such as this happy occasion:

Before I left Inchon, four of the naval officers of the port came to say farewell (I'd known them from the first there). They brought a bottle of Canadian whisky, two boxes of strawberries, two large tins of fresh milk, two fresh lettuces, two tins of crabs and some oysters. They never did come empty-handed. The Americans are great organisers but in the fighting they have to be rescued from complete massacre.

The more Beryl was steeped in routine and experience, the stronger her views became, and opinions such as the above are common in her letters. She was managing to save some money, consciously staying away from shopping in Japan and being tempted to stay at Japanese hotels.

By late summer things were moving on the professional front. Yes, there was a truce, but there was an immense amount of work to be done by the WVS. She explained to Chris: 'HQ are asking me to extend my contract to eighteen months. They seem keen on sending me to Malaya for part of it, but I'm more in favour of a period in Japan or Hong Kong... please tell me what you think would be best.'

Through Autumn, we know how busy Beryl was because her reports have survived. Her account of September was very heartening:

September was a very busy month. The highlight of life at the Transit Camp was the arrival of the Warwickshire Regiment in HMT Empire Orwell and the departure for Egypt of the Durham Light Infantry... In the club itself, the large spare room to the rear of the billiard room was repaired and painted out in an attractive green and white... we moved the contents of the lounge into a spare room, and found the move a very pleasant change. It was very nice to be in such a light and airy room. Everyone's morale, especially that of the WVS, was boosted.

The club was open for 19 days that month, and Beryl commented that more than usual Australians, Canadians and Americans came through the club and joined in with events. Her photos give evidence of some enjoyable music nights. As to games, all the usual were still popular: table tennis, snooker and board games were also in demand, and there were whist drives, crib and hospital visits. The film *The Queen is Crowned* was shown every day for the 26 days when the PoWs passed through. She notes that the film was shown before evening drinking parties – a statement with obvious inferences. A hundred of the 1,005 men who passed through the base that month were officers and sergeants, and these were given their own dinners and drinks sessions. The report gives a glimpse of these: 'We held a little dinner party for five Gloster sergeants, the only PoWs that day, in the Mess Hall at which five welfare workers, three Red Cross and two WVS were happy hostesses. After drinking a toast to the Queen, we escorted the sergeants to their mess and we went on to the canteen as usual.'

There was also the usual provision of books and magazines, and in August, the 56th US Army Band made an appearance. It was one of the best months for entertainments, with music from Korean groups as well as from some New Zealanders, and Beryl noted: 'The Durham Light Infantry produced a very good comedian, and he quickly found a stooge. They were in combination a very funny act. Two others founded a hillbilly and yodelling act. A third act was a pianist and a ballad singer combined.'

She received something special among her mass of correspondence, just after the Coronation events. She had been noticed from home locations; in the batch of mail in mid June came a letter of thanks from the office of the Lord Mayor of Sheffield: 'I am also asked to thank you for letting the Lord Mayor know about the Sheffield men who are on their way home on the troop-ship *Empire Pride*...'

In September there were health worries and something should be noted here about this in Beryl's life. She owned and clearly often consulted two card-backed booklets on women's medicinal matters. One was the best-selling *Ailments Peculiar to Women* from the Lydia E. Pinkham Medicine Co. (the source of the song by The Scaffold, *Lily the Pink*) and other was in two volumes, with the title *Woman: Her Generative Functions and Diseases for Maidenhood and Married Life*. Together, these gave the same body of basic anatomical and organic information as had been provided for centuries in handbooks for men about to marry, with material derived from Aristotle. Lydia Pinkham's booklet was sold as a 'private text-book' and dealt with menstruation, pregnancy, diseases of the womb, hysteria and nervous disease and digestive disorders. Beryl's vague references to a chronic illness – written to her mother – suggest some kind of illness related to a gynaecological malaise, probably dysmenorrhea or metritis.

Living the kind of life she had chosen, health would be a constant worry, hence her insistence on having supplies of Beecham's pills and having time and quiet for recovery after high levels of excitement or activity. That September, with the hard work of the Coronation behind her, there was a new fear. This time it was encephalitis. She wrote to her mother:

Actually in Korea just now there is an epidemic of encephalitis; it is common to this part of the world at this time of the year. That is another name for brain fever cum sleeping sickness. A WVS administrator in this theatre was invalided home from here, through contracting it in Tokyo. That happened in 1951. Symptoms of this disease are the same as for a severe chill and a 'can't keep awake feeling.

She pinned her faith on Beecham's Powders, and on trying to sleep for long periods when work allowed. December and Christmas must have helped her and lifted her mood. Her contract had been extended and she was to stay longer in Pusan and then go to Singapore, where Chris was still living (and married). She and her mates worked out a WVS Christmas programme that included piano lessons, a snooker tournament, a dance in a ballroom, a table tennis tournament, Scots country dancing, carol singing and Christmas carols. The highlights were:

Christmas Day: Christmas Games and Carol Singing
26th. Christmas Fayre and Party
  Competitions, side-shows and games

27th. Launch trip to Miyajima: bring your own lunch
  Modern ballroom dancing classes
  All Games Tournament Night

Beryl, as the star dressmaker, was always in demand, and in the middle of Christmas work, she had a request from fellow WVS worker elsewhere, asking for 'a piece of velvet, enough to make a sort of sash or alternatively some sort of fancy belt?'

At the end of the year, Lady Reading sent a circular around the WVS bases. In this she recalled the year of the Coronation, but also the immense flood:

> *We, in WVS, have had a second experience this year – the experience of a national emergency which made great demands on us, and strained us, as a service, to the full. This emergency not only taught us how much our members could undertake and fulfil, but also how great was the confidence in our Service, and it made us realise, once more, our great responsibility... History as it is read seems so different to how it is lived, even as the perspective of a building drawn from a distance is different to the photograph of the interior of one of the rooms within that building, and that is why I think the richest and most worthwhile gift I can send to you this year is the wish for you to have the will to think deeply, to examine carefully and to realise the example that is yours to live...*

Beryl had plenty of everyday issues and tasks to handle at the end of the year. Many of the tasks were essential but irksome, such as dealing with insurance. She had to read a considerable document of small print, and then list the goods insured. These tell us a great deal about her life at the time. Effects range from a tweed suit to four blouses, four poplin dresses, and of course, the ubiquitous greatcoat. Clothes were always a major concern for everyone. Notes from the troops to the WVS girls often relate to clothes, and to health and comfort, such as this from a man in the Commonwealth forces: 'Dear Girls, our hearts were full of gratitude when, last night in the mess, we all washed our feet, powdered them, and tried on our new stockings. How grand it was to wear, once more, stockings with feet attached to them. The "dear boys" are full of praise and might now be the best dressed men in Seoul.'

A request from Inchon was a regular occurrence too. In one note, Evelyn required two pairs of nylons, size 9, and the writer notes that the gift shop in Seoul had nothing smaller than a size 10. But sometimes the cries for help were more onerous, such as this: 'Dear Beryl, I hope you won't think me too much of a nuisance but I am wondering if you could do something for me... I have a case of kit in Miss Gibson's wardrobe... could you send it by internal mail?'

Beryl herself received clothes from home regularly. On one occasion she requested an item called a 'Scandale belt' and also she liked to have a strapless bra. But she sold her 'Scandale belt' as she couldn't get into it. She did enjoy some local items: 'Japanese shoes are in the main stylish and good. European stylish court, dancing and formal style shoes are however usually £3-10s to £5 per pair.'

Correspondence must have taken many hours in an average week. Family members wrote from home; workmates wrote from other bases, and troops wrote from anywhere in the world. But when Beryl wrote home she treated the occasion like that of a foreign correspondent, and anyone collecting her letters would have gathered a sizeable amount of geographical information. She could have written copy for armchair travelogues with great fluency, as in this report from a leave visit to Japan:

> *eighteen days were spent in and around Tokyo... then three days spent in Myalima, off the coast of Honshu. This island is a sacred one, and is the most incredibly lovely spot full of hills, small rivers and waterfalls and multicoloured shrines. It is also the island where the famous Jap suicide pilots used to spend their last hours. Whilst I was there, hosts of schoolchildren were sitting around the hills, painting pictures of the shrines. The best ones would have the honour of having their picture hung in the main temple.*

She means 'Myajima' – meaning *shrine island*. The suicide pilots in the Second World War took a last drink from a sacred spring; clearly part of the network of shrines that they would have in their scope for the sacrificial deaths of those pilots. More pleasant was a visit to a theatre in Tokyo, and here Beryl was in her element:

> *Theatre goers in Japan make a day of it, and take their meals with them, all neatly packed in metal containers, complete with chopsticks. For those who don't like to sit on the ordinary seats there are cushions in box-like enclosures on the floor in the box. Most Japanese women sit with their feet tucked underneath them. They even do that in buses and trains, which means they sit facing the windows, with their backs to the passengers.*

Beryl's sister, Rene, did not write often, but in mid year she wrote to report that Chris was in Kuala Lumpur but had bronchitis, and that one of Beryl's workmates had been interviewed on television. Rene shared Beryl's love of theatre and song, and asked whether there were 'any Italian singers out there?' The poor woman must have been ill at the time, reporting that she was sick of television as it 'promoted idleness'. A workmate also wrote at this time from another base and expressed a popular opinion: 'Our mutual fried S. Rhee is very unpopular with the man in the street here... everyone praying to be sent down to Seoul to run down rioters with a tank. The general opinion seems to be that the country and the people have never been so well off in their lives despite the war... but if the Yanks were to go, there would be many empty pockets and stomachs.'

Beryl's very first responses to Korea, given in a letter in late 1952, show that she was always attentive and responsive to new sights and cultures, and that early report, from Kure, set the tone for her attitudes – mainly that of mixing sharp insights with social and economic footnotes: 'We live in a delightful little Japanese house... with rice paper and plywood construction. We have two Korean maids and we get along okay.' Alongside this we have the response to Koreans: 'Seoul is a very attractive city, despite the ravages of war. Of course it has a large and flourishing black market. However a new "hwan" has been issued recently at 168 to a £1... An American P.X. Is the predominating feature of both Seoul and Inchon, with very loudspeakers making ordinary speech impossible.' The person who made those remarks was not really prominent in the letters at the close of 1953.

At the very heart of the confrontation of European and Far Eastern peoples was prejudice and the inheritance of the hegemony of Europe over the century before the war with Japan and the following Korean conflict. The clearest way to see this is in reading literature produced by Chinese writers, such as in the memoir *Falling Leaves*, by Adeline Yen Mah. She explains, 'In the 1950s racial prejudice was much in evidence in England. Chinese students were few and far between my English classmates and myself. Most of them had never been in such close proximity to a Chinese...' Taking this viewpoint also opens up fresh knowledge on the Korean War from the opposition side, as the same writer explains as she gives a man's response to the war's effect on his life: '"Import-export!" Gregory snorted, incredulous at my ignorance. "Haven't you heard of the Korean War? Didn't you know that the Allies put an economic blockade on China?"'

There was a deeper, more rooted inheritance regarding China's place in this war, too, and such understanding gradually emerged after the ceasefire. Adeline Yen Mah explains this succinctly: 'For roughly one hundred years (between 1842 and 1941) westerners were perceived throughout China as superior beings whose wishes transcended even those of their own mandarins. The white conquerors were treated with reverence...'

Beryl, always open to new learning and expanding her intellectual horizons, became aware of such things the more she enquired and observed. The PoW process was to force on her, and on all involved, a need to understand and to react to, the worst elements in this dirty, trench-embedded war, on the edge of the known world as far as ordinary Britishers at home knew.

Later, she became more critical of the situation, perhaps as she tired. At one point, maybe after a long, hard day, she scribbled a note: 'One or two of the WVS have been here as long as four years in tours of 18 months at a time. Two of them too long...' However, she had regular missives from soldiers in the thick of the war, and such notes as this, from an NCO, must have been pleasing, as the man unloads some compliments: 'I must thank you once again for the "settling in" attention I received at Inchon and congratulate you and Mavis on the success you are having in running the camp, not only from my experience but from some of my underlings.'

Beryl now faced the new year, 1954, and she knew that ahead of her lay a mix of places, new experiences, and the challenge of helping with the return home of the men who had suffered as prisoners. She had planned to end her time in the east at Hong Kong and Singapore, and that lay not too far ahead. It was a time when a turning-point loomed and there were the usual uncertainties of working on short-term contracts, at the mercy of world events out of one's control or influence.

As the process of 'clearing' went on, the farewells and tributes came, and Beryl preserved many of these, such as a letter from the WVS administrator in Japan and Korea, Lieutenant Colonel Janvrin, who wrote to Lady Reading:

> *Only one word will describe the selfless devotion, the kindness and influence for good of the ladies of the WVS, namely, the word vocation, in its highest meaning. They seek no material rewards, for their happiness is forever in giving rather than to receive. We love to have them with us, for they mean so much to a soldier's life out here; not only his spiritual life which so often requires their direction, but also his life of friendships in which they share so unselfishly and with so much good for him...*

There was the usual everyday chore on Beryl's list of things to do, as 1953 came to a close and she made plans for her next move, which was supposed to be to Singapore. A typical letter in this context was one from a fellow worker who was based with the Canadian Legion. The letter conveys the spirit of the time, the mood of dispersal and clearing up: 'Captain Hillman goes in a fortnight and we don't know the new man yet. We'll never get another Hillman unfortunately,' and also, 'Maris is going north for a month from Friday next to help Betty while Margaret goes to Hong Kong. The three of us will then run the two clubs...' Clearly, there was still plenty to do, peace agreement or not. This did not work out as planned, as will be shown, but whatever the destination, the fact of a phase of life coming to an end was impossible to ignore. Korea was still very much in her thoughts and letters carried on coming to her from friends back in that troubled land, but part of her tried to look towards the future, and part kept looking back to what she had come through. All her life in theatres of war up to the point of arriving in Pusan had been secondary, present in the aftermath of something. Now, she had seen the effects of a terrible war at first hand, and not until late 1953 had she had time to stop and consider just what had happened around her. Routine, as usual, had often distracted her mind, and only in letters home and to Chris had there been chances to unload emotional responses. The near future was to offer a space, a gentle hiatus, and time to reflect on the reality she had bravely faced.

The year 1953 had begun with many aspects of the Korean conflict being at a very low ebb, and gradually there had been progress towards peace, but the modern reader has to reflect on what the effect might have been on Beryl and everyone around her when they read reports such as this from January that year: 'The United Nations prisoner of war command reported from Pusan that three North Korean Communist prisoners of war at a compound on Koje Island beat an American soldier to death on Wednesday when he went into a building alone...'

Chapter 7

Clearing

PoWs Return Home

War always created problems when it ends. The appropriate image here is perhaps that of a monster shaking its tail, so that skin, dirt and everything else teems off its back. A war is like that, and the monster of Korea was such a thing: various small pockets of fighters and service staff were shaken across the sea and air, and many began their journey back into life by stepping into the nearest outpost of civilization. The NAAFI and WVS would be their nearest such haven in Korea. Yet, of course, travel was always difficult and the exhaustion of combat was complemented by the sheer nervous collapse experienced in a long journey without any element of domestic support. When the club came along, and the welcoming faces of civilians, it must have been like walking into a dream of heaven.

What Stephen Kelly's correspondents make clear, in his book of memoirs from Korea, is that coming home was a bland affair, and in a wider sense, there were many opinions expressed about the army's attitude in general, such as this, from Kelly's book: 'Not even the army seemed very grateful. Again, there were no thanks, no parades or letters of appreciation. When, and if, they did receive medals they came by post in a small cardboard container.' One is reminded of the close of a celebrated work on the experience of the First World War by Wilfred Owen. In his poem, 'The Send-Off' he wrote about the return home:

Shall they return to beatings of great bells
In wild train-loads?

A few, a few, too few for drums and yells,
May creep back, silent, to still village wells
Up half-known roads.

As early as October 1953 the process of supervising and supporting the return from war of the troops – regular and national service – was under way, and in one of the WVS bulletins, we have an account of how the return was dealt with. The PoWs had only started to be taken from the front towards a journey home in October that year. This was a log of the work done by the WVS:

> *The gathering at Britannia Camp: The troops spent an afternoon and evening there, then went on to Japan.*
> *Boarding the plane: at 8 each morning some board a plane. Before that, the process has started the previous day with this schedule:*
>
> *11.30 Reception tent*
> *1-2 p.m. the next group arrive*
> *Mid afternoon: to the dining room 'for their first good meal in years'. Two women from the team pour free beer for all.*
> *Late afternoon/early evening: Betty Stern reports: 'When the first ones through have had their meal, Margaret Murie and I go to our NAAFI gift parcel table and distribute these.*

Betty Stern, a co-worker in Korea who wrote the report, noted that 'WVS are present non-stop from the time they arrive until 9.00 or 9.30 at night.' Money from an anonymous donor was sent also, and Betty noted that this was spent in Japan. Part of the welcome included food, dancing and gramophone records, and even birthday cakes had been made.

Betty Stern, who had written for the WVS newsletter about helping returning PoWs, wrote a full report on what was happening at Britannia Camp, for the record, and for the office back home. This all related to 'Operation Homeward Bound'. Her summarising paragraph gives us a rare insight into the experience:

> *Now that Operation Homeward Bound is completed, we can look back on one of the most wonderful experiences in WVS welfare work, and we feel deeply grateful for the opportunity to help our British find their feet, during the intense excitement and turmoil of feelings, on their first day of freedom, and help them to realise that they have not been forgotten by the British people, who are so glad to see them return to their homes once more . Many times we have had to control a lump in our throats, especially when the men gripped our hands, moves them almost unbearably. We realised this and just talked calmly and in the most homely fashion about their home towns, wives and mothers, and look at innumerable tattered and dog-eared photographs that have been tenderly kept through all kinds of difficulties and privations.*

The camp was around one hour's drive from the exchange point at Munsan-Ni, and the returnees would have arrived at that point in the heart of a medical centre, run by the Canadians.

Betty Stern's report of the welcome given the returning troops is very thorough and shot through with caring and responsibility. She, Beryl and two other staff members supervised a string of events, going from the first reception to saying farewell as the troops boarded ship for home. They were dealing with 1,005 soldiers between early August and early September. Many of her charges were from the 'Glorious Glosters' whose bravery in the battle at the Imjin River in 1951 had become the talk of the camp. But the men passing through also comprised fighters from Australia, Canada, South Africa and New Zealand. Betty noted, 'There had been PoWs for periods ranging from almost three years down to a South African Air Force officer who was shot down six days before the Cease Fire came into effect.' That armistice had happened on 23 July 1953.

The offerings from Operation Homeward Bound gave the men rest, good food, a medical check-up and time to adjust themselves to the complete change of existence, with in addition the mental readjustment to something called 'peace' but which was still uncertain in their minds.

The entrance to the Britannia Camp was splendid: an archway had been put in place, and this had been painted with red, white and blue bunting. This was also on trees and flagpoles, and of course, the Commonwealth flags were all fluttering. Beryl also noted more detail: 'One man arrived waving a home-made Union Jack from his vehicle; this had been concealed from the Chinese, like their Coronation rosettes, which several wore again on their day of freedom. One of these had been brought through in an empty toothpaste-tube.' Part of the welcome was music from the Royal Scots Pipe Band. Then the men were helped to send cables home, and then came something they all relished with gusto: a proper shower. Betty commented, 'The schedule was thrown out a little, because they could not be persuaded to leave all that luxuriant soapiness!'

Then followed a solid meal in the Mess Hall, and the report described the highlight: '... this was when the two WVS acting as bar-maids put down glasses of frothy ice-cold beer in front of them. Each man was given two bottles of beer to have with his lunch, courtesy of the NAAFI. Beryl was one of the bar-maids. After that there was a distribution of NAAFI gift parcels; these had either 100 cigarettes, a bag of sweets and matches, sweets, chocolates and nuts, or a pipe and tin of tobacco. The weather was hot and sticky, and Betty had umbrellas placed over the tables which held the presents. She remarked that 'We were thus in constant view to answer questions, and set as an information bureau.' The real hit of this day of rejoicing was a scheme called 'Say it with flowers'. Betty, Beryl and the others were kept busy sending flowers to mothers, wives and girlfriends. Betty quoted a letter from home, and she explained that these words summed up the value and impact of the scheme: 'Last Tuesday my mother received a bouquet of flowers, sent on Bert's behalf. It wasn't until then that we really believed he had been released. He has been abroad for four years, two years in the PoW camp.'

The press at home enjoyed reporting on the chaos, and on the plight of the returnees from the war, turning up in all kinds of places, such as twenty-two men who arrived in Malta in May:

In the same aircraft were eight British soldiers who had been wounded on the Korean front. The former prisoners were wounded and will continue their journey to Britain by air tomorrow morning... The men were welcomed by the GOC [General Officer Commanding] in Malta and civilian women who met them at the airport with gifts, which included a Malta-made leather wallet for every man, with a personal note from Lady Mountbatten.

Letters home were written on the occasion too, but the WVS had to select, as there was too much demand for the few staff members to cope with. But then, at the very heart of all this, was the NAAFI canteen. There was a constant flow of talk, singing and shouting for hours on end; the Scots pipers kept appearing, and Betty noted that this was where the WVS women really contributed: 'Almost every evening, we two WVS, with other Red Cross girls used to join in Scots dancing... leaving one piper to play, and this was a very popular sight, received with enthusiasm, especially the *Dashing White Sergeant* and the eightsome reels.'

The WVS back at home kept in touch, and things were changing after the truce and the beginning of the repatriation process. One letter confirmed that books and magazines were still being sent out east, and also that staff manoeuvres were in action: 'You have probably heard by now that Mrs Morden is on her way to Japan to bring home the British Prisoners of War as soon as they are released. You may perhaps meet her...' Mrs Morden was travelling on the *Asturias*, and Beryl was there to meet her on arrival. There was such a lot of coming and going, and such large scale movements of men, that the press out in Singapore and at the bases had a good time offering gentle humour. One cartoon of this hue shows a face-off at a baggage counter at Panmunjom, in which a British officer argues with a Korean. The interchange is this:

> *Korean: Ah, you agree to sending the prisoner to a neutral*
> *country provided it won't take him?*
> *Naval Officer: Yes, provided he won't go.*

Beryl, in more routine moments beyond the celebrations and welcomes, was dealing with postal orders for clothing requirements, from other bases and further away. In August she wrote to Chris in Singapore: 'I've just managed to get my first night off for a week. During that week we've had the Essex Regiment arrive and the Royal Fusiliers depart. The latter went on the *Empire Halladale*, en route to Egypt, poor beggars.' Some outfits were moving from one war zone to another. She reported that 'The truce news was received by the Koreans with ominous quiet... They are pouring ROK [Republic of Korea] army troops to the demarcation line and speeding up the call-up.' There was a widespread belief that the truce had been 'staged' so that it could be broken, and there were rumours reaching Beryl that some wanted a chance to use atomic weapons.

More down to earth, Beryl had encouraged men leaving for Singapore to drop in and visit Chris. Beryl at that point was working with Betty and Margaret Murie, and generally, they were short-staffed at the WVS. She was certainly busy: she hadn't seen the 'Coronation flick' by the 15 August; the 'mossies' were playing hell with her and it was extremely hot. Chris made it clear that she thought Beryl's salary 'awfully small' and that she should be making plans for the future. But Beryl had a constant flow of correspondence, many of the letters coming from the military. One note, from a Sapper in the 1st Commonwealth Division Battle School, is especially interesting: 'I'm sorry I haven't written before but I have been awfully busy getting settled in, finding a place to live etc. Hara-Mura is a rather peculiar place, it is a large establishment, built here to teach soldiers how to conduct themselves in battle. That is its primary purpose. Its secondary function seems to be to supply customers for the surprisingly large number of houses of ill fame dotted around the vicinity of the camp...'

A letter written in October from Beryl's manager and area organiser gives us a very clear notion of Beryl's life and duties at that point. First, he wants to know when she wants to take her leave; she was planning one of her leave visits to Tokyo, and he needed dates. Then there was the issue of sewing and clothes. Beryl had no machine and so: 'The dressmaker is still busy making the ACS [Army Community Service] girls' materials and we simply can't get her for anything. I suggest you get your things made in Tokyo... I believe you wanted buttons for your green linen dresses: could you let me know how many. I do hope your rat plague has ceased – nothing more unpleasant.'

A month after the Coronation, Beryl wrote a long letter home. She said good things about the new organiser, and never mentioned the rats; she goes through the regimental movements, and then evidently delights in having used her beloved German:

> a soldier who has a German wife but who has been away from her for a long time in Korea addressed me in German, and quite unintentionally, I answered him in it. From then on, for three whole days he haunted me with German conversation, just to ease his homesickness I suppose, but the gutturals played havoc with my throat... it really is refreshing to meet one British soldier who bothered to learn his wife's language...

She was still absolutely fired up for learning new languages, still attending classes in Japanese and Korean. Equally, she was still acutely observant of conditions and life around her: 'The large reconstruction programme was underway the day after the truce was signed. Lots of the squalid refugee shacks are being rapidly replaced by artistic looking Korean houses with the traditional curved tiled roofs. Tons of wood for building and food and clothing, is building up at the docks and being delivered swiftly...'

Whether Beryl realised it or not, in picking out the roof tile for special mention, she was calling up something truly iconic in Korean civilization. In Neil MacGregor's great survey of *A History of the World in 100 Objects,* the roof tile is selected from the artefacts of the eight century BCE. He writes, 'The ceramic roof tile in the British Museum comes from one of these new buildings [in the Tang Dynasty period of China] and it tells us a great deal...' Beryl's simple note evokes something deeply and significantly Korean.

In the midst of the Coronation shindigs, Beryl had her moment of fame: she appeared in a magazine feature. The County Borough Organiser back home in Grimsby wrote to her: 'We are all intrigued by the article in *Woman* about you and your work. One of our people brought it in rather late and we all enjoyed reading it.' The feature had played up the angle, as in the heading, that 'The Dressmaker Goes to War.' Obviously this made a rare and appealing story for the readers of *Woman*. In fact, one reader, who knew Beryl because of a parcel interchange, wrote to her: 'Reading one of the *Woman* magazines last week I read with interest an article on yourself entitled Dressmaker Goes to War. It also contained a photograph of you so we now have the advantage of knowing what you look like!'

Earlier in the year, when Beryl was having some difficulties with the sheer press of men wanting attention and time, and her move to Seaforth Camp at Pusan had been arranged, we have a good grasp of the care and attention she had from her back-up team, and they were there again later in the year. But she had so many communications from servicemen she had worked with earlier, in those difficult times later in the year, that she was surely feeling much better about things. One man from the 1st Royal Tank Regiment is typical of the real friendships she had garnered around her. He wrote: 'very glad to hear that your leg is nearly better and that you are "skipping about like a fairy" (quote B.M.B.)... Troops returned up the line two weeks ago. I don't seem to have eaten, slept or washed properly since then...'

A rarity in Beryl's life as intermediary, listener, shopper and cultural correspondent is a letter written concerning a serviceman. Such an instance of this is a letter that arrived at the Coronation week from a woman in Nottingham. She wrote to ask about a problem with mail home from the writer's husband. The wife wrote: '... we have got the matter in the hands of our M.P. and he has instructed the Post Master General in London on the matter as it seems so funny that he is receiving our mail and we not his...' In fact, Beryl had asked a friend to call on the writer and try to help. The letter ends with profound thanks to Beryl who had 'asked a personal friend to call'.

By mid 1954 Beryl's life was all about sorting out practicalities. In March she had to check Japanese visas; at the same time she was dealing with such things as taking memento photos and sending essentials to workmates elsewhere, as this shows, from another friend: 'Very many thanks for seeing to my photos so swiftly... I hope you won't mind but I'm immediately sending you extra photo prints as directed; six large boxes of gramophone needles; 24 boxes of photo corners and 12 lighter flints.'

Then, as she was supposedly heading for Singapore, she wrote home that there was a change of plan. She wrote to Chris from the WVS Mess at Kimberley Road, Kowloon: 'Well I suppose that you have gathered from my telegram that I have stopped off in Hong Kong to help out for six months. I can't help feeling that I am being a bit mean to you by so doing.'

Then, before what was to be a posting to Hong Kong, she was needed back in Kure to cover an emergency staffing situation. For several months, before a final eastern assignment, she was back in Japan, a place about which she had mixed feelings. She was back at the ship-building centre near Hiroshima, and when Beryl returned, it was the location for the headquarters of the British Commonwealth Occupation Force. As far as Korea was concerned, the long stalemate had begun. The record makes it clear that there were staff shortages across the whole structure of the various bases, from Japan across to Hong Kong. The staffing was always a fragile concept, with so few women working in a situation in which they had to react swiftly at any time to cover and often, to step into responsibilities for which they had little or no experience.

The correspondence for the first six months of 1954 reflects a challenging time in Japan; she wrote to Chris that she had been 'left holding the baby' and that she had been temporarily in charge of the club at Kure for a month. She did not want to continue, and had her thoughts on Singapore, where Chris had a comparatively comfortable life in the club land of senior officers and higher officials in the colony. But she still had to maintain the shopping that was asked of her for long periods, including ordering the specific type of bra that was in demand from all her female contacts. A receipt from the famous Whiteways store 'The store of progress in the East' shows that she bought '1 incudenform bra' for fourteen dollars and fifty cents. Whiteways Laidlaw and Co. had centres at Ceylon, Straits Settlements and the Malay states. Before that, in the Edwardian years, they had been one of the most prominent stores in London.

Military contacts were still flooding Beryl with letters, asking for help, often in obtaining photos of time spent on leave; one request shows that she even sorted out cleaning jobs: 'Could you get this duffel coat and my suit jacket cleaned and then sent direct to Inchon? Miss Gibson told me that I would be moving up in about a week and having these cleaned now will save packing space.' (This was from an officer in Korea.) But many communications were from men who had formed a friendship in a particular base and now wanted to keep up the acquaintance, such as a captain who was in the 2nd Battalion Band of the Royal Scots, and his letter is typical of many:

Dear Beryl,

Thanks so much for your wonderful letter which I received two days ago. It left me very pleased to find out that you are in the best of health... The hand has not been working very hard lately as we have been doing only two parades a day, and a church parade on Sunday mornings; it is mainly through the weather that we have done so little because the coldness freezes up all the instruments. The WVS is sure looking good now that it has been painted. Good to hear that you enjoyed your leave though I must say that you spent it entirely different to mine, for I was never sober all the time that I was in Tokyo.

Some of the letters to Beryl contain surprises and interesting insights into the status of the WVS. Another letter from a man serving with the Royal Scots has this: 'You know Beryl, I never knew that the WVS existed until after the last war. I first met them when I was RSM of a reinforcement camp at Kalyan (India) not long after I was released from a PoW cage. I got very friendly with a lady there and through her I realised what a sterling job you ladies do and I have always admired you since...'

Many of Beryl's contacts sent requests but also informed her on all kinds of events, many of them packed with interest for the modern reader wanting to know more about conditions out there at the time. A man writing from HMS *Ceylon* for instance, in February, gave this information: 'There has been a very long delay in the letter getting here as it – along with about four hundred more – were wet through when the aircraft carrying the mail crashed at Singapore. My address was washed off the front but it was traced to me by your address inside.'

From a fellow WVS worker, writing to Kure, we have a rare insight into the kind of everyday bustle and activity that was part of the WVS life, and she writes with the knowledge that Beryl is standing in for someone else and feeling swamped by work:

> *My Dear Beryl,*
> *What a week we are having... there are always troops in and we are working all day and every day... we have had the plumbers in fixing a new bath. For two days the rain has just poured down and about four Koreans treading in and out... a bit of spare time has been spent mopping the floor and keeping the place reasonably decent. We've had no hot water until last night. Now we've got the carpenters in because the bathroom door won't shut with the new bath in! Today, however, the weather is perfect.*

Beryl's first long report appeared in May 1954, and in this we learn for the first time that there were worries about the physical toll of the work she was doing. She worried about her weight and about her general health. Although she does say that 'friends here still comment on the fact that my face is hardly 30 years old, but my figure below the waist is 50 years old.' She told her sister that 'They constantly bully about diets, exercises etc. However I contend that as I work very hard and am always active I just cannot exhaust myself with diet, exercise etc. The weather is getting warm and sticky. Seven-eighths of the time it is raining hard... This heat will affect my weight...'

In spite of a basic dislike of Japan, she comments often on the beauty of the landscape and of the flora: 'The chrysanthemums have to be seen to be believed. In between showers today I had a lovely sleep on a bamboo settee and woke up with half a face suntanned, and one leg. Our mess is surrounded by hills wooded near the summit and the rest of them terraced neatly with rows of golden ripening barley.' She found one aspect of life heartening: clothes and craft. She reported that 'dressmaking is cheap and good here in Japan. I'm getting together a wardrobe for my much needed leave.' She also took pleasure in her usual activity learning about the culture she lived in. She reported that 'I'm still trying to learn Japanese, and help with English classes for Japanese schoolchildren.' She made her accustomed efforts to be sociable and to be seen beyond the confines of the mess and the army facilities, going to parties such as one given by the Anglo-Japanese group, and with them she watched a series of films: 'One was Queen Elizabeth's life from early days; another was the Festival of Britain [1951] and the third was from all aspects on all parts of British life.'

She made the point that the Japanese were very anxious to know about Britain, and admitted that she struggled to give them a comprehensive account of the British educational system. After an initial worry about her weight, she resumed the report with the fact that she had lost 'five pounds with the advent of the warmer weather'.

From Hong Kong, in March, came a full account of the administrative troubles from an organiser. These problems are put plainly: 'I've had an awful job getting the list of shopping done for the girls in Korea; we just press on, I'm half area organiser and half Club worker or anything that crops up, and though it's all right for a little while, I certainly hope it doesn't go on...' This had all been prefigured in an account of the situation by Beryl in a full letter to Chris in Singapore, and from this we glean that even pleasures became very tiring work. 'We always work most when the service play, although some of our work consists in being very overworked partners for dancing for four and a half hours with the troops on Christmas Eve.' Beryl in January 1954 had no clear idea of where the next posting would be.

There is no doubt that at that time, Beryl was opening her mind to other career possibilities. She confided to Chris that 'As far as women are concerned I had a rotten time in Korea' and that she decided to be informed on other possibilities. She went with a friend from the Canadian Red Cross to Hiroshima to visit members of the Church Missionary Society who were running a girls' school. She noted that 'ten per cent of Japan is now Christian'. The work attracted her: 'I have strong leanings towards this kind of work and by this means I could stay for 3 or 5 year tours in Korea or Japan. I saw an English representative, and she obviously didn't want any competition, if you get what I mean.'

Not only did Beryl visit: she was so involved with the American missionaries and their work that she spent a lot of time with the women and their charges: 'When I visited them they introduced me to some schoolgirls whom they teach who had all been injured by the atom bomb. One of them had hidden in water in a ditch for 48 hours which was the reason she only got slight burns on the head.' During her cultural liaison activities, although she started by enjoying tea ceremonies and flower arranging demonstrations, something else developed:

> *This was a Christmas party, with a service and carol singing. As the representative of the WVS I was called upon to make a speech, which I realized was to happen two minutes before it did – in the middle of eating sticky iced cake and drinking green tea. My friend nudged me and said 'Look out... they are about to call on you.'*
>
> *I made a very impromptu one and said that my friend, Vera, was going to Korea the very next day. They immediately answered that she must be remembered in everyone's prayers, especially as it was so cold in Korea.*

In May she wrote home and had a lot to say about her turning-point in her life of service, and she had found out about something else, related to the missionary work but very different in what was possible. When she wrote to her mother she spelled out matters very carefully, almost as a teacher would, and began her letter with the statement that life was very different and that she was 'holding the fort with a staff of one'. She confided that the staff situation was 'somewhat chronic'. Then came an account of her new thinking: 'Recently I saw a possibility of doing something which interests me, even more than this work does. We had a lady spending a leave in our mess last week who belongs to the Save the Children organisation in Korea. She is actually a tuberculosis nurse working in Korea... the same organisation have a crying need for welfare workers too, so I'm going to apply for a job in this capacity.'

The WVS work was, one may affirm, taking a toll on her strength and resources. She explained that the welfare workers did good work and reflected that the lady visitor had 'done very good work amongst the Poles and Arabs'. She was currently working with a doctor in Pusan, and Beryl discovered that the contracts were for one year, so she must have thought in terms of trial and respond: after all, if the work was not for her, then she would return home, as she was soon to do from Kure anyway.

In spite of the hard work, she was still cultivating her interest in Japanese life and culture, visiting Kyushu and other places. She went with a nurse friend to Takayama and took a train to Matsuyama. She reported for her mother on the sight of a medieval castle and cherry blossom trees, and then wrote about the *Koi Nobori* festival: 'The carp are really a symbol or the little boys, and dolls are put on display for little girls in the *okonoma* or alcove that is part of every Japanese house...' Her weight continued to worry her, and she explained to the family at home that oysters were provided all day long, along with tea and coffee and all kinds of treats.

Soon after her arrival back in Kure, Beryl gave one of her most detailed accounts of the Japan she was to love for the rest of her life. She made much of the relevant information regarding her own occupation: 'The Japanese are the most exquisite needlewomen really and dressmakers are on the whole cheap and good. I have the urge to do some home sewing now...' She certainly did; she had an efficient Singer model sewing machine 'which only needs cleaning' and she knew, by February, that she would be in Japan until August, so she settled down to designing and sewing in whatever time she could find for that. She delighted in giving Chris a full account of Kure:

I do work in Kure, which was once a very important naval and submarine building base for Japan. It is situated on the Inland Sea, one hour's ride by bus from Hiroshima. Facing the sea this city is to the right of Kure, and to the left on this coast are such large towns as Osaka, Kobe, Kyoto, Yokohama and Tokyo. Last Saturday a nurse friend and I went for a ramble over the hills near the many bays and inlets. We came on several "out of this world" villages where the folk rushed out to see us, and in some cases the older people came up and admired our colouring and skin...

She gave Chris a summing-up about her situation, which was at this point very much troubled. She was searching everywhere for possible alternative work, while at the same time explaining the predicament: 'I was like you, overworked when I was in Korea but here it has been much easier. I have very little responsibility, you see, but the organiser goes home in May so I look like being her successor.'

Beryl also never missed a chance for some theatre or performance, and she was increasingly interested in Japanese art. In late 1953 she attended a performance of Kabuki-Za, which offered such entertainments as *Kyokanoko Musume-Dojoji* (The Dancing Girl at the Dojoji Camp). The theatre is still there today, in the Ginza quarter, a major theatrical centre. It is not difficult to glean just how much Tokyo had been developed and commercialised in the few years since the atom bombs. The Kabuki-Za material Beryl saved has adverts for the Latin Quarter, which offered Latin American music and 'tasty American food' and also adverts for golf courses, Mikimoto Pearls and 'A bit of Paris in Tokyo' where there was a classy restaurant and free parking.

Within a month of that letter, she wrote again to her sister, and the account she gives of a particular female dilemma provides material for any historian of lingerie and clothing in wartime. She begins with a plea: 'My dear Chris, This letter is literally an S.O.S. about brassieres. I've put on two stones in weight since last Autumn, so the consequence is that everything I have to wear is on the small side.' The following explanation of the provision and availability of underwear is a revelation for the social historian. She sent £3 in postal orders for the task, and then listed the options available for such shopping, each one falling short of the desired objective. She notes that 'one can't buy anything here but the small 33 inches type or 30 inches type of bust.' She found a lot of the 'WRAC officer type of underwear, which always treats the bosom as if it were some obscene thing – or to apologize for it.' She also had friends in the Canadian Red Cross, but to obtain such underwear from their store required a ration card. All this reflects on a dilemma that perhaps is rarely found in the social history of war.

Clothes were always a primary concern for staff throughout the war. From Pusan, as Beryl worked in Kure, came a note from a former workmate, and the focus was on such things: 'We have a house girl called Lee and the other day she got me a pair of Korean shoes which I think are rather nice. I will bring you some back – they are made of rubber and will be very useful in the washing room. They are like little canoes.'

Through the six months at Kure the requests poured in for help, and these topics range from the sublime to the ridiculous. Here is a small selection:

> *Dorothy asks me to say she has the sherry for you but she has found nobody reliable to bring it along... The 8/6 change is enclosed...*
>
> *My aunt wanted a photograph of his grave if possible but perhaps there is insufficient time...*

Dear Beryl, Tony here again. I have a peculiar feeling that when I was asking you to trace my cousin's grave I gave you no details. Here they are: Sgt. James Tait, Royal Signals.

I wonder if you could kindly pick out for me three tea sets and let me know the price and postage back to England. On receipt of this information I could then forward you the amount of money needed...

Could you please send me 2 dozen batteries like the one enclosed. They don't seem to be obtainable here. You certainly look after us very well. I wouldn't like your job...

I enclose two negatives of yours truly which I would like enlarging... two copies of each and when you see the result you can laugh as much as you like. I'm enclosing 7/6 but if this is not enough please holler loud and long...

Are you by any chance able to pick up grade pearls at reasonable prices – or Japanese tea services? I have been wondering if it's possible...

[This refers to a Graduate Pearls Programme guaranteeing quality and authenticity.]

The archive is packed with envelopes and receipts relating to all the photograph ordering Beryl had to do. This service was run by the NAAFI who ran a facility with the EFI in Korea. Later, in Kowloon, she had private firms at her disposal, such as the Mayfair Studio in Nathan Road, Hong Kong.

On the other hand, when letters arrived that reflected the harsh reality of the war, they offer an insight into the situation of Beryl's clients and friends, such as this from a man in C Squadron 1st Royal Tank Regiment:

Dear Beryl and Mavis,
At last I am able to tear myself away from futile jobs.
First let me thank you for helping us in no small measure
to have an excellent leave. It was a terrible blow to come
away and a greater one to arrive here. Within Minutes
I was slapping a brush paint two inches around a tank. Up
to my knees in mud I was experiencing that sinking feeling
that always comes at the end of a holiday. The reason we
came back early was the C.O.'s Vehicle inspection – not
the 'war' as we had hoped...

What she did have, fairly, regularly, close to the end of the resettlement and help given to returning prisoners of war, were requests about lost contacts and friends. A typical such letter has this: 'Now of course I am dying to know if you have seen any of the PoWs. Isn't it wonderful to think that they are free again? Wonder if you have come across Bob? I heard from him about a month ago.'

There is so much implied from behind such a question. Most of all, it suggests that Bob was a mutual acquaintance and that there were shared friendly memories. But deeper than that is the thought that each individual service person thought that they were a special memory, a significant relationship, when in fact, the three WVS workers in Pusan, for instance, had been dealing with thousands of men placed not far behind the front line trenches. This closeness, often in a somewhat artificial capacity, was surely the source of much of the stress the WVS women workers felt, and by the latter end of 1953, underlying Beryl's turmoil in her job, and the difficulties with superiors, stems partly from that accumulated anxiety and the toll on nerves and well being.

Beryl never missed a chance to describe the wider picture, and in this lengthy report, she says something very interesting about an important topic: 'By the way, one of our WVS was in the *Empire Windrush* wreck. When I was on it in 1948 its boilers failed once in the Indian Ocean and once in the Med. It ought to have been scrapped years ago.'

The move from Kure was drawing nearer as the year went on, and Beryl must have taken some pleasure in the fact that other centres were struggling too. One letter has a very succinct account of the very heart of WVS work in Korea, and in some ways this sums up Beryl's situation too:

> *In the meantime we have been visiting units in Seoul and up as far as Tokchon, getting to know the men and lads, and having a very nice task – if you can call it that – of distributing hand-knitted comforts so much appreciated. It has been a good thing for us to see just where the units are situated and how the boys live, and this week we are starting welfare work, beginning with a visit to K.16 airfield tomorrow night to run a darts tournament. Doris has boiled all the Garrison Church altar cloths in a bucket of Rinso water, and yesterday we routed some of the mounds of dirt in church...*

The stack of letters from the front have much in common when it comes to describing the conditions. Long after the Korean War, memories of this experience still appeared, and one such piece, published in *The Star* newspaper, gives a quintessential summary:

> *Our winter clothing for the hard Korean winter was a duffel coat and towel around the neck to help prevent the cold giving one frostbite. Yes, we did stink a bit but it certainly helped to deter the cockroaches from nibbling our feet. In fact we came to a compromise with these creatures. We allowed them to clean the plates after a meal if they allowed us to put a candle on their backs at night and walk around the mess so that we could write our letters home... (This was from Mr Harry Unsworth.)*

112

Close to the end of her time in Kure, Beryl had a letter from a friend at home in England, working with the WVS in Salisbury, and one note conveys the fragility of the WVS on the home front, in contrast to the same outfit abroad. She wrote, 'Here we are a small WVS centre. After the war, those in control first shut up and practically told it to die, so we have had to start from below zero in the last two years...'

By summer the thanks and appreciations came, and Beryl must have had a sense of having come to the end of her Korean experience. From a 'mother in England' came a letter that could have been sent by any one of a thousand such people, and it reached the heart of the matter:

Just a line thanking you all for the wonderful kindness and mother's thought you are giving my boy and all of them in B.A.P.3 Korea. My boy arrived there on his 19th birthday and has repeated to me how kind you all are towards them... My boy spoke of the WVS when he was in Germany. They are always helping and making the boys happy he told me, so I feel I can only send this thankful letter and trust in God for a peaceful world...

There was, of course, the leader: Lady Reading, and also the WVS administrator for South East Asia and the Far East. Both communicated close to the crucial date, 2 August, on which Beryl's contract expired. Lady Reading's thanks were to come later, but first, in July, came the area leader, responding to Beryl's request to go to Singapore. She wrote: 'Though we are very short down here in Singapore and the Federation, our extreme need for the next few months is in the Hong Kong area and I suggest if your transfer is agreed you should serve there for three months...'

Her future was decided then. She was heading for Hong Kong. The Japanese Telegraphs service sent her a message: 'Agree your serving six months Hong Kong. Arrange disembark there.' This was followed, in August, with a Marconigram, after the debate about whether or not she would be heading for Singapore, with: 'Neal advises disembarking Hong Kong after all. Confirm.' It was a difficult time. There appears to have been a maelstrom of activity, with superiors in various places deciding her future; this was complicated by the fact that Beryl herself was not entirely committed to the WVS, as her reflections on other career possibilities plainly show. The year before Kure had been a very demanding one, and as is the case with stress and overwork, damage had been done, but 'carry on' was the wartime spirit.

Top of the list of responsibilities was always 'the boys' though. She and her peers really cared; they were working in an area of war in which they provided perhaps the only truly meaningful caring factor. An army might look after its own, but the 'look after' has to have its limits, and much depends on ancillary workers for individual support. Beryl and the WVS were fully aware of this, and what had increasingly happened was that there was no answer to the question of *who cares for the carers*?

On top of the caring, what we must recall is the extreme range of daily and weekly duties. Letters refer to cleaning work and to setting up concerts and games, but there was general maintenance too. One of the most informative footnotes to that work is a list of 'extra items for attention' sent in a memo from NAAFI administration to workers in one centre:

> *This letter gives an up-to-date list of work required: Coco door mats to all doors to canteens and clubs. Repairs and replacements to 3 ceiling lamp shades broken during work. Repairs to window-cords. Completion of furniture in WVS Club to enable NAAFI staff to withdraw furniture on unauthorised free loan. Fit dartboard light in WVS lounge. Refit one dartboard light in canteen.*

One of the last letters Beryl received before travelling to Hong Kong has in it something that perhaps sums up so much of what she had achieved. A soldier from REME wrote this: 'I know I have been away for five minutes but I felt I just had to write to you as from now on, if you don't mind, dear, I am going to write to you as my own mother. "Hello Mum." 'He added, 'The ride back nearly broke my heart.'

There was a general sense of exhaustion across the board in terms of all who had participated in the Korean War. There had been constant criticism and disagreement about all aspects of that conflict. As far back as 1950, the debate around the US leader, Douglas MacArthur, had generated dissent and reappraisal. At one point there was even the rash prediction, from MacArthur, that the war would only last six months; then in early 1951 there was a general feeling that it would last another three years. Beryl's charges read papers or heard about the latest issues in debate. The prediction nearest to the truth was put in a feature in mid 1951: '... it would have to be known that the fighting would develop into a static war where shell consumption was unusually high.'

Beryl must have felt that sense of the war dragging on and on, and announcements such as this from *The Times* a month before the war ended was typical of many reports: 'The discussions today, which went on for more than an hour, were secret. The chief United Nations delegate, Admiral Joy, told correspondents that he regretted he could make no comment. Another United Nations spokesman added, "I think it is obvious that no agreement was reached."'

Beryl had lived and worked through the long struggle of seemingly endless discussions and she had seen the stalemate arrive. She must have looked with deflation as the years advanced, on the maintenance of the demilitarized zone and the continuing gridlock. It was indeed to be the 'forgotten war' and one of the first expressions including that phrase came in 1971 with this brief report: 'Colonel Hickey, who went off to fight at the age of 21 as a second lieutenant in the Royal Army Service Corps, straight from Sandhurst, said, "It is the forgotten war. There was no instant television coverage, just *Pathe News* with sanitised black and white film of flickering figures in the background..."'

Chapter 8

Beryl Takes Stock
Kowloon

It is a striking thought that, as Beryl's story draws to a close at the end of 1954 when she moved into a new phase of her life, that the Communism she had experienced via the battlefield and its results was to bring into the news reports when she went home some alarming news that shook the foundations of everyone involved with, or had suffered at the hands of, the Eastern Bloc as it had then become. Mary Lovell, in the process of recounting the lives of the Mitford sisters, explains this powerfully: '... in March 1956, the transcript of Krushchev's secret speech to the 20th Congress of the Soviet Communist Party was published, detailing Stalin's horrendous crimes. Ten million people had been killed in the thirties because they opposed him...' In the last months of 1954 then, and through to early 1955, all areas of the Far East were sorting themselves out, as men were all home or going home, and there was instability in every quarter. A military presence and police work, were needed, and along with the action came the support. Beryl was still very much needed, and the echoes from the last gunfire in anger in Korea were still being heard.

Two years before she arrived in Kowloon, Beryl had been invited to meet Commander John C. Hunt, Commanding Officer of the United States Naval Reserve, in Inchon. She had met Lady Reading and also other people who had figured in the press and in war publications. In contrast, now she was well behind any trace of the Korean War and its terrain or supporting bases, but there were fresh concerns. If one

116

considers just how far she had come since being the WVS beginner in Germany, at the end of the War against fascism, her achievement is staggering. Through all the basic hard physical work and mental stress, she had maintained a deepening curiosity about other nations and cultures, and continued learning and acquiring new skills. Her circle of friends had expanded significantly. Experiences had ranged from the everyday medical needs and essentials, such as vaccines and medical checks, up to confrontations with men suffering from the shock of war – what we now know as PTSD.

Now here she was with a fresh challenge, but one situated far away from any 'front' except for the border problems and the proximity to the new China. Britain was clinging on to the vestiges of its pre-war Empire, and Hong Kong had been a peculiarly sensitive location in that respect. After all, Japan's two actions – Pearl Harbor and the fall of Singapore – had shown that traditional dominance and prestige were never going to be eternally dominant and powerful. Every mountain had its cracks and fissures, and now, after the defeat of the enemy, what was to be done with the 'old' bastions of the Empire in the Far East? In that scenario, Beryl and thousands of others were called in as tiny parts in a massive machine.

One aspect of her life that must have struck her like a thunderbolt was the emotional one: friendships, reliance on close association and intimate experience of feelings, desires, co-operation and so on had figured in her life as a member of the WAAF but that had been nothing when compared to the situation of work with the WVS. Affairs of the heart and important friendships had now been occurring close to the front in a major war. The sheer volume of thank you letters and official appreciation Beryl preserved gives evidence of success in the necessary tasks of showing empathy and understanding; giving a shoulder to lean on sometimes leads to closer liaisons. She had several proposals of marriage and all were turned down; she had many male friends who clearly shared their hopes and fears. Letters from officers always referred to 'the most excellent way your staff look after the welfare concerns of D Company personnel when on leave at Inchon (from an officer of the 1st King's.) But this kind of presence and attentive listening was always going to open up opportunities for very cordial relationships. Sometimes letters merely hint at relationships far closer than a simply professional one, such as this in a letter from a corporal in the 1st Commonwealth Division: 'You see, B, if I was to say anything to your face you would say I was a nice liar.' That 'B' speaks volumes about the carer and client.

At Kure she was obviously worried about 'friendships' in their various degrees of intimacy, and she was concerned that she was older than the norm: 'Talking of hair, I've got a wizard layer of curls and a curly fringe now. I'm afraid it is too youthful though for the implied dignity of my position in relation to the very young people with whom I mix in my work. I am already involved trickily with two nineteen-year-olds.' She was still worried about her weight, and although the particular bras she asked for had arrived by the end of March 1954, she was ashamed to convey her physical dimensions: 'Many grateful thanks for the "visible means of support" received today. What a relief it is to have them and you will be pleased to know that they fit perfectly. I wonder by the way if you can send some literature showing light but controlling type corsets... something to get my tummy and hips back where they ought to be. I am 42 inches from the waist now. Ain't it a shocker!'

Hong Kong was to offer something very different; the closeness to emotional turmoil, together with an immediacy of the needs and cries for help from serving soldiers near a determined and ruthless enemy was left behind. She had worked primarily with the more fragile and vulnerable elements in the military structure – in most cases, National Service people. Their needs had been clearly evident, and the geography of the war in Korea had been deceptively simple, with positions to be held and co-operation with allies always a delicate challenge. Now, there was a microcosm in turmoil, a place in which capitalist modernity was growing alongside teeming humanity, on the run, frightened and in need of a new life. All this was close to her in Kowloon, and she soon began to perceive that she was in a cocoon – unlike her previous postings in a more brutal, visible world of suffering.

As she sailed for Kowloon surely her mind was swimming with the rich and complex humanity experienced in her last years of work in Korea and Japan. From the mass of evidence we have, it is obvious that networks of friendship were formed constantly; some came and went very quickly, while others persisted. Among Beryl's letters is one in which the writer actually expatiates on the nature of friendship and offers a substantial quote from a classic author:

> *Ah Beryl, at times it's nice to drop the mask of levity and tell people what you really think. Laughter and gaiety can cover lots of things and serves a Good purpose. I can always remember Charles Kingsley's thoughts on friendship or 'the water of life' as he calls it. He says, 'A blessed thing it is for any man or Woman to have a friend – one human soul whom we can trust utterly, who knows the best and worst of us in spite of all our faults... who will speak the honest truth to us whilst the whole world flatters us to our face and laughs at us behind our back, and leaves us to fight our own battles as we can...'*

Many letters show very clearly the friendship circles around her, such as this from a man serving in the Black Watch:

> *Sunday morning my dear, and way down in Pusan what are my 'two girls' doing? Although both of you have now deserted me it is very nice to think of you all together again. Tich was looking forward to rejoining you and I must say she missed you every day when you left Inchon. Can there really be all this attractiveness in the WVS in Korea? But I cannot see myself in Inchon without you two being there...*

One may imagine Beryl going towards Hong Kong with all those thousands of temporary acquaintances lodged in her memory. Some called her mother and some thought of her as nurse. Most simply wanted a friend who would listen, and when it came to the clearing and progressing of the casualties and returning squaddies in her last detail of duty as the troop ships arrived and departed, she must have valued her cache of mementos with a flush of pleasure.

She was on board ship again, and one thing she relished above all else in her life, as is clear from what she kept and treasured, was travel by sea and air: long distance journeys where she could temporarily forget all duties and responsibilities and be cared for by staff, with herself at the other end of the transaction for a change. Her world was one of expanding sea travel. Just before the war, the famous White Star Line advertised twenty cruises each year between May and October, and the airlines were still expanding. Hong Kong itself was undergoing a revolution in social life, communications and building. She was heading for a huge sea port.

She had also seen and witnessed at close hand some of the significant landmarks of twentieth century history, from Hitler's fallen bunker to the D-Day build-up. Later, she was to return to Berlin, and she would see the results of the less than successful attempts by the Allies to resolve the issues and problems so evident in German life that she had known.

Now here she was in a new place, although she had partial knowledge from her sister, Chris, who knew Hong Kong and Singapore very well. Chris was now married and settled with her husband Denys, who had survived imprisonment by the Japanese, and although they lived a fairly comfortable life with a rich circle of friends, they were both recovering from massive trauma, and from being at the very heart of one of the crucially important theatres of war in the conflict with Japan.

Soon after arrival, Beryl had her copy of a circular letter from Lady Reading, still in command of the WVS, and she had more than basic thanks to say; she offered, in fact, something of a sermon, and

120

this was based on her need to give a gift as well as thanks, and it ended with a compliment to Beryl and all her staff, although it was given in universal terms:

In her doing of everyday tasks, woman has the ability to collect much information – which she puts into the granary of her mind, and during one of her many routine jobs, she works almost unthinkingly on the sifting and final placing of this stock.

She has the power to assess, and a vast store-house in which to place – and the things which she amasses will often come into use because they are stacked ready to call upon in a number of directions. She has the zest to seek, and this is of infinite value in following the threads and tying up loose ends, and she has the urge to discover, to continue and to persevere.

Far below such rhetorical and grand thoughts, in Beryl's case, was the need to recover from the turmoil of her situation a few months before Lady Reading's circular. Then, she scribbled a note to Chris explaining her dilemma: 'I shall sail for Singapore in August. I wrote to the administrator of your area and asked if I could serve in Singapore or Hong Kong for 6 months... and London sent a telegram to confirm...' This was cancelled, and Beryl had to find help elsewhere. She even spoke to the colonel in charge of movements and he made a booking for her aboard the HMS *Asturias*. All this was a waste of time, and it was in the complexity of vocational politics that all was changed to Hong Kong.

By September she was in Kowloon. After the hell of the war, Hong Kong was still a British sovereignty; the Japanese had gone, and still the threat from Communist China was there. There surely could not have been a more marked contrast between her last posting and the new one. The Civil War in China meant that, as always happens, there were refugees. The overall population of Hong Kong by the time Beryl arrived was slightly over two million. Although on the surface this seems to be a recipe for all kinds of problems, one trend created the foundations of what was later to become the 'economic miracle' in modern Hong Kong history. Basically, capitalism shifted its base, and firms arrived in Hong Kong to set up stall. Adeline Yen Mah, quoted before in this story, explains in her memoir what the atmosphere was: 'Those were uncertain times. Every other family with property, Kuomintang [the Chinese nationalist party] ties or even western professional training agonized over what to do next: to stay or to go.'

Beryl's arrival was one little element in a large-scale reinforcement of the island in general, as Britain worked hard to preserve the place within the ever-increasing area of new Communist political influence. Crucially, when the Chinese expansion led to the People's Liberation Army there approached a potentially aggressive position regarding Hong Kong, and advances stopped. To maintain Hong Kong as a trade centre and fully working port, the commercial base had to be kept and strengthened, and indeed that happened. The years immediately after the end of the war allowed free movement across the China-Hong Kong border, as there was no control in place, but as far as Beryl's arrival was concerned, as she set up in her new posting, there was a massive problem of homelessness, which was partly due to a great fire at Shek Mei, just before she arrived. Quick housing had to be done, by whatever means. High rise was the only way, and the result was that Beryl, dressmaker from Grimsby, came at a momentous time for the colony – a time when there were notable extremes before her. On one side there was desperate social crisis and overpopulation, and at the other end was the rich, appealing cultural life of this vibrant place. Just before Beryl arrived, there had been price controls as well, and this meant a monopoly on staples.

Kowloon itself today is made up of the peninsula and New Kowloon. In 1954, however, its features were the Kowloon-Canton Railway and the Wharf; it was packed with people and housing when

Beryl arrived. By 1939 there had been 750,000 refugees arriving there. But whatever the situation outside, the WVS and other back-up outfits for the services took an active part in the cultural life. After only a few months there, the invitations came for Beryl. A typical invitation to her came from all ranks of the Royal Engineers to a dance at the NAAFI Club in Chatham Road.

Beryl produced her accustomed long letter to Chris when she had just settled in. The good news is that she was happy, based at Kimberley Road where the WVS mess was situated. She wrote, 'Here I live in a very nice little flat which contains three of us and we all get on OK... When I arrived here a friend was waiting on the quayside and she said, "You're getting off here. Hurry up and pack!"... Dorothy rushed on board to help me unpack. It is a lovely place but very expensive...' She was very happy to disembark, judging by her comments on the ship: '*The Empire Orwell* was an awful ship... the stewards were mostly slatternly, needed haircuts and shaves... only when they found out I was leaving the ship suddenly they act like real stewards ought to...'

She had a holiday feel first day, going by cable car up the Peak, and then, 'We were able of course to see all the multicoloured lights come on, one by one, a wonderful panorama.' She was on the mainland, and had less onerous tasks than direct contact that the war had forced on her. One duty was to visit the King's Regiment Club. There was a WVS worker there every night, on a rota. She helped at the Kowloon Club as well, In between social duties she had time to check out prices, and she reported that clothes were half the price she had found in Kure. But it was not paradise. There were always problems to overcome. In this case it was the fact that water was only available for four hours a day. She told Chris that 'We have had two very rainy days since I arrived four days ago but up to now there has been no increase in the household supply.'

Washing had to be done at night, and she could only bathe at 5 p.m. She found that the service wives were 'a discontented lot' always moaning about maids. But regarding the heat, in Kowloon there were fans – as opposed to Korea, where there were none. She refused to complain, but enjoyed reporting on the various discontents. Summing up her attitude to hardship and the trials always before her, she told Chris, 'I'll always be poor whilst I lead the wandering life.'

From the balcony of her new flat she could see the centre of Kowloon; the view reminded her of a sea-front in Belgium with 'the same type of ornate white buildings with balconies and in some cases, window-boxes'. She refused to go deeply into the chaos around her, accentuating the positive as usual, and reporting on seeing a Jerry Lewis film, and had a ride in a rickshaw.

Her first report to Chris included the kind of information that sister has given to sister since the world began. It concerned a man. This account is not at all typical of her:

> did I tell you that whilst on leave at the American hotel... an absolute honey of a man from Texas, a marine officer. He was about 30 years old, more aware of horses, dogs, study and travel than he was of the fair sex. He was six feet three inches in his socks and liked all the things that I do. Unfortunately he arrived only two days before I left. He was having a last leave before leaving the service...

Her conclusion was the familiar Beryl stance: '... meeting anyone special was the last thing I had in mind. I needed a rest and a change too badly.'

One of the first things she did in between club duties was visit the war cemetery at Sai Wan. This is on Pottinger Peak, on Collinson Hill, and so she was living close by. The camera was soon in use, and she preserved plenty of snaps. Of course, the memorials signify much of the nature of the battle for Hong Kong as it gradually fell to the Japanese. The cemetery was constructed in 1946 and is looked after by the Commonwealth War Graves Commission. There are 1,528 casualties of the Second World War in the place.

She was considering alternative work and new horizons. There was still some interest in the Save the Children work, but as she worked in Sek Kong that was out of the picture. She told Chris, 'The Save the Children people wrote a very encouraging letter back and although they have no vacancy they said they would be delighted to keep me in mind for one.' In mid January, her mind was swimming with mixed emotions regarding both home and foreign potential in her notion of the course of her working life. She took pleasure in her usual people-watching reports, such as this, 'there has always been, out here, a blatant man-hunting faction (rich civilians and brigadeers are the usual type of quarry). Up to now results of the chase are two perfectly happily married husbands who are not averse to being amused till they get home to their wives.'

The Save the Children possibility had made a deep impact on Beryl, and she wrote more than once about the appeal: 'I'm sure I would like the work O.K. A doctor, a nurse and a welfare officer usually work together and form one ménage. I have a friend who is a nurse with it and she advised me to try to join. There are lots of good jobs offered in the Hong Kong newspapers, especially teacher or secretarial jobs...' The last remark is patently not what she wanted, but there was an underlying need in her reflections on staying away from home, living on the move, being useful and seeing all there was to see of foreign cultures.

The people-watching also gives a rare insight into the kind of relationship developments she had seen perhaps too often, and one story on this she relished telling her sister:

> most of the young men for whom I do a little welfare are as emotionally pent-up, or affection starved as it is possible to be. After a time out here they either get a girlfriend, drink too much or get a "thing" about older women. A young man with whom, strangely enough, I've had a little contact, has proposed to me by letter. Now,

*I vaguely remember he was quiet, seemed the sincere type,
and sometimes used to put on gramophone records whilst
I kept an eye on the whist drive. He once did say he was
going on a course to get a third stripe and that as a regular
she should get married soon. I'll have to refuse his proposal
on paper, having already said no on the telephone.*

The man was in Singapore and Chris and her husband would be seeing him, so Beryl, humorous as ever on such topics, wrote that she would 'leave this problem to the Peeks who could 'gently let him down'.

As for Beryl, she maybe took delight in showing that she was desirable and was something of a 'honey pot' among the men.

After Christmas, 1954, the end was in sight for Beryl and her Far East experience. As the new year began, her friend Dorothy wrote from Korea to remind her of what she was missing: '... we had a very busy time at the Club and it was packed out most days. We had a talent contest with great success and a Carol Service in the courtyard. On the 23rd we had a show in the ballroom and then a free tombola. I had Christmas Day off.'

Beryl learned about staff movements and the familiar reports of people coming and going. She was clearly the same restless soul now that the future was unclear. Dorothy refers to something Beryl had not mentioned in letters: 'When do you go to Malaya?' She never did. One of the very last letters she had before heading home was the usual mix of requests and accounts of changes, including the familiar shopping questions: 'Do you think the Hong Kong pearls are as good as the ones here? If so I'll ask you to get me a graduated string and I will send a postal order for them and any material...'

The life in Hong Kong turned out to be a complete contrast to anything experienced in Japan or Korea. It was mostly socialising and helping with activities in the clubs. Policing and supervision were a large part of military duties; one comment from a serviceman in Stephen Kelly's book of memoirs adds to this context: 'Whilst in

Hong Kong we had cultivated a friendly relationship with the local army garrison and as part of a liaison party of NCOs had been invited on board for a trip to Japan.'

Around Beryl in her last posting east of Suez was a sense that the colony was in the midst of a great upheaval. The Chinese revolution had shaken a vast area, which covered the globe from Hong Kong to Korea, and Beryl had seen most of this expanse.

In March 1955 she was home in Grimsby. Just before she returned, there had been the great freeze of February, and on 1 April, the Greek nationalist terrorist group, EOKA, initiated a campaign of violence in Cyprus; four days later Winston Churchill resigned.

The WVS sent a letter; this was from the regional staff office in Cleethorpes, and the note simply said, 'I do hope you had a good journey from Hong Kong and that you will have a very happy leave. You must have had a very interesting time. Do call at the County WVS Office when you can.' When she finally settled at home, she sent an account to Chris, as usual. It is clear from this that she had enjoyed her last long journey back home. She gave details, and it is obvious that coming home was an anti-climax, and she was not at all settled and adapted back into civilian life as she talks about her very exciting journey with all the stops along the way:

> *You will see by the above address that I made the journey safely. We spent the first night at Colombo, actually arrived at 2 p.m. and stayed at Mount Lavinia. I travelled with a nurse and we did the city and suburbs by taxi as there was a bus strike on and trams were few on Sunday. We called at Bombay, Karachi, Bahrain, Cairo, Rome and Frankfurt – mostly about one-hour stops in each place. We arrived London 7.30 p.m. on Tuesday 22.*
>
> *One of my 'fragiles' got left behind at Colombo so B.O.A.C. are bringing it on a later flight. I spent two days in town before coming home, and was given a very*

good welcome by WVS headquarters. I was asked to go
overseas again as soon as I can manage it...

This was guaranteed to bring on the recurrent restlessness, and it did, but there she was, back in Grimsby, and the letter she wrote was packed with discontent at having to do all kinds of domestic work, even down to putting paraffin on the suite and sweeping up layers of dirt everywhere. In a letter, a month after this, we have some candid introspection, given in a lengthy response to her sister's wedding:

My dear you have married a treasure and I admire your
courage in having risked marrying him at all in our
circumstances. I know I will never have the courage! It is
less hardship to be a spinster and luckily nature adapted
me to the role. I wonder if you will believe it if I tell you
that should those circumstances change for the better
from now on, I can't change. This I am sure. I've lost too
much, too often, emotionally, to care deeply any more. All
I care about is staying well enough not to be a financial
burden to anyone, any time...

In a mood of serious reflection, after merely a short time away from WVS duties, Beryl had been soul-searching, and this is deeply personal self confession. One had the sense that such statements had been a long time brewing. Now here she was at a real crossroads. Scarcely had she been back home, when there was a new offer. The WVS wanted to keep her in service, and they wasted no time in making an offer. They knew her wanderlust and they knew her reliability. She had proved herself in the heart of that 'forgotten war' and there had been no complaints directly to them, in spite of criticisms and complaints made in confidence to family and friends. Incidentally, the reference to 'in our circumstances' almost certainly refers to a gynaecological condition, as previously mentioned, when her medical books were discussed. Through all her time abroad and in the Battle of Britain, she had worried about her physical frailty, the repeated reference to her taking Beecham's Powders and having weight problems relates to the advice given on her malaise.

The important factor in her reflections is the reference to her independence. This naturally depended on income as well as on independent life and resources. The massive cache of correspondence quoted in the foregoing narrative did include plenty of reference to finances, but I have not put this together. Basically, she saved, and clearly saved from expenses. She also may have had a small amount from the shopping tasks and postal services, in addition to all the ordering of photographs. Her archive contains around 300 photographs, from group pictures of servicemen to war graves and ships. As a WVS worker (similar to being in the armed forces) there was bed and board and a uniform. Very little would be spent on food and nothing on accommodation unless this was on a leave period. In the leave time she obviously treated herself to such things as clothes and some luxury overnight in hotels. But there was small pay and saving was essential.

There was an irony awaiting her in this respect in terms of her independence and any plans she may have had for the future, and this is evident in the 1955 conditions of service material from the WVS. The crucial statement is this: Pay: For the considerations aforesaid the Member agrees to serve the Corporation without pay. The point here is that the contract by that time was with the NAAFI. The contract was headed 'NAAFI/WVS' and now this was really voluntary work.

It is easy to understand the appeal here though. After all the world travel, she had the wanderlust in her, and what the WVS offered was essentially a free holiday that lasted for eighteen months. There would be no worry about clothes, a roof over her head, or about food. No bills would drop through her letter-box. It was a kind of refuge from what her home was like. After all, she had gone home to mother and found that she was little more than what the Irish call a 'slavey'. Her letter to Chris about being at home reads like a report from some penal colony. With the WVS she even had, in some postings, servants and cooks. What was there to dislike?

We have to ask questions about home life back in Blighty. Her letters make the place seem worse than any shanty town she might have encountered abroad. It could be that she used some hyperbole, but Cinderella she was not. The reader feels a deep sense of unfairness that Beryl should go home only to graft like the lowest servant in some Victorian place.

Nevertheless, she had been first a WAAF and then a WVS worker from 1939 to early 1955. This life of service had become all she knew, and it was a life of choice, relished in spite of those temptations from such work as with Save the Children or with eastern missionaries. She had the contacts and she had knowledge of the system underlying the WVS. It was a time for decision, and she had very little time.

After Kowloon, at the very end of her Far Eastern service, she was for a short time in Sek Kong, in the New Territories. The main establishment at Sek Kong was the RAF station. It had been built from 1939 and work had been completed by 1950. A brief memory from Bill Griffiths describes the place then: 'In those days Sek Kong was just a big open area at the foot of a mountain range separating the border between Kowloon and mainland China. There were no stone or brick buildings, just tents.' The New Territories Beryl saw must have looked like a vast waste land, but she would have enjoyed the vista.

She was thinking about home, of course, but enjoying the last short stretch: 'This last week I have acquired a very nice WVS room-mate, just as I am due to leave here. I have just unpacked after another house move and now must start packing again.' The fullest account preserved of the time in Sek Kong is a report sent to Chris in Singapore.

Preparations were stressful then, at the verge of such a change of life. She wrote that 'I must admit that at the time of writing I feel a bit depressed about the whole prospect – 66 pounds of luggage only is allowed you see...' Officially, her posting ended at the end of February, but such facts always seem to be moveable in Beryl's life. There she was, her situation perhaps best described as marginal, in the stretch of flat land called the New Territories, and she was well away from the press of the crowd that had been her lot in Korea. Neither was there the strong cultural attraction she found in Kure. She must have realised that all had ended in a hiatus, a kind of limbo; it was a pause, and one that gave her the space to reflect and to think about alternatives, but all the documentary evidence from early 1955 suggests that she was ready for a change, and that 'home' meant something arduous, demanding and very dull in comparison with the life she had come to know and value. It is hard to dismiss the response, reading her words from the last phase of Far Eastern work as she looked over the vast airport and beyond, to the mountains, that what she had dreamed of way back in 1949 when the German period ended had been even more exciting and challenging that she had expected. She had been tested to the limit, but along with that experience had come lasting friendships, trials and tests, which had shown her what profound qualities of strength and resolve she had in her, and above all, she had proved to herself that she was a person very far removed from being the seamstress daughter in a Grimsby family.

Her life of service had stretched beyond anything she imagined. What would she do next? That would have to wait until she had gone home and spent time with her mother. Returning home from a war has been a theme for many writers. They have addressed the issues around how a person adapts, how the trauma stays inside, and how a new stage of life, caught in an anticlimax, has to be understood or the results may be painfully extreme. A determination to stay with the WVS is hardly apparent. The line of her thoughts generally links to something new, but something that would use her skills and experience of course.

One take on Beryl's thoughts as she travelled home is in an anecdote from an unknown source, and quoted in Nigel Rees's collection of tales from social history: 'A somewhat effete Englishman was asked what it had been like to be in the midst of battle. He replied: "Oh my dear fellow, the noise... and the people!"'

Chapter 9

With the WVS at RAF Habbaniya

In his book *African Genesis*, Robert Ardrey was looking at mankind at a time when since the end of the Second World War and the advance of the Cold War, there had still been endless conflicts in the world, from strife among the smaller nations to hot-spots in which the issues related to the greater themes of global war were apparent. In other words, there had been no 'war to end wars' and the twentieth century's most intelligent and sensitive leaders had certainly not brought peace, or even the pre-conditions of peace. His conclusion was a powerful and resonant statement on the world around Beryl Baxter in the Middle East in 1956, and he ends with optimism:

> *But we were born of risen apes, not fallen angels, and the apes were armed killers besides. And so what shall we wonder at? Our murders and massacres and missiles and our irreconcilable regiments? Or our treaties whatever they be worth... The miracle of man is not how far he has sunk but how magnificently he has risen.*

Beryl had witnessed some of the results and effects of war at close hand. Each experience did not deter her from further participation in similar work. We had come a very long way in the fifty years previous to her time in the WVS.

Now she was going to Iraq – a place when known as Mesopotamia had suggested a desert war and a conflict between modern armies and tribal outfits. But there was much more to it, as she was to find out.

After her time at home to make important decisions, Beryl finally decided on another stint abroad with the WVS and this time it was a posting in the Middle East, at the RAF base, and now here she was, flitting around various locations, all of which had an element of political ferment and potential violence in their cultures. After some brief stops to cover workers in Cyrenaica and Cyprus, she arrived in Habbaniya, Iraq. This was a base around fifty miles from Baghdad and it had been viable since 1936. It survived until 1959 when political ferment led to revolution. It was alongside the great Euphrates River, and fighting had been long and determined during the war. It covered a very extensive area and was chiefly the RAF command centre for Iraq.

The WVS in the Middle East in 1955 was active in fifteen centres, ranging from NAAFI facilities to officers' messes. In the Canal Zone they had staff at the Moascar Staium Club, the Moascar 1st Battalion Irish Guards, the Fayid Old Victorian Lido at Fanara, the RAMC (Royal Army Medical Corps) at Fayid, Tel-el Kebir Camp (where Beryl was listed along with Mrs Paul and Mrs van Unen), 1st Battalion Royal Warwickshire Regiment at Fanara, the RASC Column at Keren, Abu Sueir RAF, Geneifa, 1st Royal Tank Regiment, Port Said, 2nd Battalion Grenadier Guards, Port Said, Sea View Leave Camp, Famagusta Golden Sands Leave Camp, Troodos Pine Tree Holiday Camp, Habbaniya SHG RAF Club, and Khartoum South barracks. All this reads like a very strong presence, but this establishment covers a vast area.

From surviving records, we can see that the total staff for these places was thirty-four. Beryl was ensconced by then, but there had been a longer period of hesitation and alternative planning. The Save the Children Fund had replied to her application with 'Although we might in the future require additional personnel in Korea, at the moment there is no vacancy which we can offer you.' She had a farewell and a renewal of contract, confirmed in a letter from

133

Lady Reading, in which there was plenty for Beryl to be pleased about:

> *Dear Miss Baxter,*
> *I am glad to be able to inform you that the WVS*
> *Appointments Committee has approved your appointment*
> *as a member of Services Welfare Staff (overseas). I know*
> *what a splendid job you have already done for WVS and*
> *I feel confident that you will continue to do everything*
> *possible to maintain the high standard of WVS overseas.*
> *As agreed in your contract, WVS must reserve the right*
> *to recall you if circumstances necessitate such action in*
> *which case you will have the right to place your views*
> *before a committee of Reference if you wish to do so...*

Beryl was moving to a location with numerous facilities; compared with her previous postings, this was positively metropolitan, and in fact the place was known as 'Second London'. There was even a power station in the centre, and after the war, as many families of the services were there, a school was opened. Beryl was to become very fond of the place, as her letters and photographs show. There had been extensive construction around Habbaniya, and around the base there was virtually another town – the agglomeration of buildings for the construction workers. It was also on a mainstream air travel route; one celebrity connection is that the writer Roald Dahl was there for a time.

Numerous units and related outfits were stationed there throughout the 1940s, such as signals units, seven RAF squadrons, an armoured car company and plenty of Iraq levies for the RAF. Even more to Beryl's delight, as it fostered her love of flying, was the placing of a stop at Habbaniya for the famous Imperial Airways. BOAC, with whom Beryl often travelled, ran a passenger service between the base, Africa and other places across the Middle East.

The broader picture, and the background to what led to the base at Habbaniya, is to be found in the year 1941 when Iraqi rebel forces confronted British troops; Britain occupied Falluja, where there was a bridge, and the road to Baghdad was kept open; there was then a bombardment by the RAF of Falluja military targets. It has to be recalled that there were German planes at Palmyra, and these too were attacked. There was only one casualty on Britain's side – a naval aircraft. The report on this action was issued: 'Although a large area between Habbaniya and Falluja had been flooded by the retiring rebel forces, a successful detour was made by our troops.' The revolt was being led by Rashid Ali, and he led an attack on the damaged aircraft.

After the 1941 revolt, there was a steady infiltration and settlement by British forces. Eventually, only a few years before Beryl arrived there, several projects had begun, aiming at help and progress for the Iraqi people. A press report explained, as British aid was planned:

> *The first problem which any government here has to face is that of water. Great stretches of potentially fertile land are desert, either because they have no water or because, being subjected every year to severe flooding, they are salted up... The simple solution in theory is to divert the flood waters to the lands in need of irrigation. Certain schemes have already been put in hand, notably the Euphrates scheme to use Lake Habbaniya as a control point...*

Then, in May 1955, just before Beryl arrived from Cyprus, the Habbaniya base was transferred to Iraqi command. *The Times* explained: 'Habbaniya, together with other British establishments at Shaiba and Basra, is being handed over to Iraqis as the result of a temperate and adult exchange of ideas and proposals between the British and Iraqi governments – arising directly from Britain's adherence to the Iraq-Turkey defence treaty.' The Habbaniya Beryl went to comprised three forces working together: the RAF, the Iraq levies and the Iraqi army itself. The important point was that gradually the levies would be disbanded, and some absorbed into the national army, while as far as Britain was concerned, the RAF would withdraw in planned stages.

It can be seen from this background that Beryl's new home was part of the result of an innovative scheme of co-operation, and that, after a rebellion and violent suppression many years previously, was arguably a bold experiment in which political and military matters took a secondary position. All this was, of course, based on a long-standing British presence, which followed the actions in Iraq (then Mesopotamia) during the First World War. This phase of that war is perhaps best known to British people through the film *Lawrence of Arabia,* as the Turkish army figure in that film.

Beryl had a shock in store. The regime she was to work in was very different from the one she had known; the conditions of service she was under shows a complex bureaucratic administration, and she was actually now under martial regulations. A brief statement from the WVS headquarters in Famagusta to all WVS workers made the situation clear: 'WVS headquarters in London have asked me to make it quite clear to all members of staff that WVS members serving overseas, sponsored by NAAFI, become liable to the provisions of the Army Act, 1955 and consequently to trial by Court Martial in the event of prosecution.' That must have been a startling communication.

Some of the stipulations of the conditions of service seem draconian, and details of subsistence and pay were very meticulously stated and listed. For leave, after nine months of service, a woman could take 21 days; for service over 18 months, 10 days at the end of the tour could be taken locally. There were very precise definitions and descriptions relating to sick leave, class of travel, national insurance and local transport.

The other aspect of her new life was concerned with post. A circular specified that 'Private mail when censored is to be forwarded by officer i/c [in command] Sections to Wing or Unit headquarters for safe custody pending collection by the Royal Air Force Post Office staff.' More severely, the conditions listed offences against the Air Force Act:

Use of any stationery embossed or printed giving the location of the writer or Unit other than the correct postal address.

The concealment of such matter beneath postage stamps.

To mail any correspondence in civil mail boxes.

To convey or have conveyed by transient crews or passengers uncensored mail.

To transmit to unauthorized personnel any document, private diary, photographs or films.

To communicate with the Press except through authorized censorship channels.

Two months after leaving Sek Kong, there she was, at Habbaniya and already travelling around the Middle East, covering a number of countries. In early summer, 1955 she wrote home to describe her new life. After commenting that one of five other girls was told that it was a distinct honour to be sent to Egypt at such a historic time. She noted that it had been a subject for speculation exactly when she would arrive. Then she described her impact, and it was a boost to her vanity:

People who haven't known me before keep saying on introduction "Not the famous.Beryl Baxter? We had been led to think that you never would arrive!" At Tek with me is an old friend from Japan and two newer WVS – a happy set-up really. We live in a lovely airy mess, in its own gardens, with all modern conveniences, surrounded by desert as far as the eye can see. Mark you, there is a car at our disposal, two boys and a cook. They are both excellent and very cheerful.

Her home was at last a settled place. In the first months of her work in 1955 she had been moved around frequently. At one point she was in the Canal Zone on the side of the Bitter Lakes; while there, she went to Tel-el-Kebir, by the Sweetwater Canal, where she spent two months before going to Iraq. She was near the Pyramids and Luxor, and this pleasure was after something she always relished – an interesting flight from London. She travelled with BOAC, stopping at Cyprus, and then at a base at one end of the Suez Canal. She made a point of describing the plane, which was 'a Viscount, not a Viking' and on board, as she notes, they 'tried to kill me with kindness'. In August, at last she managed to meet up with Chris and her husband Denys, and they met at Tel-el-Kebir, with the temperature at 95 degrees Fahrenheit. Her sister was en route for Europe, but they managed to snatch a few days together. They went to the Pyramids with a Dutch party, She wrote home that 'We all had lunch at the Luna Park hotel... We left Cairo at 11 and I took the ferry to Port Said, to stay at the army leave centre.'

She sent a vivid account of the scene at Tel-el-Kebir:

> This is a very healthy climate. From Tanara we can see the Bitter lakes, and they are very near for bathing. At Tel, the garrison is surrounded by desert but in this camp there is much greenery, particularly rose bushes and flowering trees. Our servants are all male, mostly Sudanese or East African. One very seldom sees an Egyptian, Sudanese or any native type of women. Those who do venture outside their homes are dressed from head to toe in black... One sees a variety of work animals in the fertile areas near the canal: mules, asses, buffalos, horses and cows... I have not started in my job, and no-one seems to be in a hurry to make use of me.

This could almost be a section from a memoir of a Memsahib back in colonial days. But she was soon busy, and before routine kicked in she did something that was always at the top of her list: she set about finding a sewing machine. After a while, she made a discovery and set herself a challenge. She borrowed a machine from a local teacher. She needed clothes, and she comments that the sun out there soon fades any clothes people have.

The daily work went on, interrupted by a number of things, in particular a dock strike, which deprived the WVS of a large supply of books and magazines for a while. All the usual tasks that filled the days at a NAAFI/WVS centre began to keep her busy. There were the usual treats such as invitations to dances and tea. The RAOB (Royal Antediluvian Order of Buffaloes) were there, with an Old Boys' Association, and they invited Beryl to an 'informal dance' and they called themselves the Bedouin Lodge, getting into the spirit of the place. Otherwise, it was a round of providing entertainments and being cheerful in all the socialising events.

Then came the switch to Habbaniya. There, she could do such things as take a trip into Baghdad to buy records for the club. She saw the golden mosque at Khadimain, where she was not allowed to enter; but she was well. She told Chris that she was 'Getting plenty of fresh air, sleep and a carefully balanced diet. She notes that she did not want a repeat of the 'gippy tummy' she had experienced in Egypt. In addition, as she explained, 'The blessing of the heat here is that there is always a breeze from the river and lake and that is of course, cooling.' She spent some of her free time in an idyllic spot – sitting under a tall tree, 'with droopy leaves like a willow' and she noted that there were plenty of places to swim around the base. She adds that 'If anyone gets an overdose of sun, they are whisked off to the air-conditioned hospital on camp. In the course of my work, I visit the sick airmen there.'

On another trip out she had a very memorable experience:

> We were taken to see the Royal Mausoleum. This is a beautiful building like a mosque. It was guarded by the Iraqi army, and just inside the first court two elderly imams were sitting and intoning verses from the Koran, helped by an electric table fan... I have been able to

visit Babylon and Ctesiphon, to see the ruins of buried
civilisations. We managed to get these trips in before the
heat became so intense...

What Beryl was experiencing in part was the consequence of the Operation Musketeer, which had taken place just before she arrived in Iraq. Nasser, leader of Egypt, had declared the Suez Canal to be purely his own, so Britain, after signing an agreement about the area, which Nasser had now broken, had to act, and there was a military invasion, to control Egypt and crush any armed resistance. Britain then had to withdraw, after American pressure. The result was that the British presence around the eastern extreme of the Mediterranean was in a very delicate situation.

In a wider sense, if one looks at the global trends behind so much that was creating imbalance in the Middle East, it is clear that various versions of nationalism in the Arab states was mixing with other influences. The historian Albert Hourani sums up this situation when he writes of socialism in the midst of these wider changes and influences:

the idea of the control of resources by government in the
interests of society, of state-ownership and direction of
production, and equitable distribution of income through
taxation... The increasing strength of this idea was partly
a reflection of what was happening elsewhere in the
world: the strength of socialist and communist parties in
Europe, the growing influence of the USSR and its allies,
the coming to power of the Communist Party in China...

With this context in mind, her life at Habbaniya was somewhat idyllic, and in some ways a rest period for her after the theatres of war she had known first-hand. If we add to this a wider panorama of the unrest throughout the world in the 1950s, the situation of Beryl and her workmates, in the vortex of so much political imbalance, becomes far more than the image of a favoured few, with house-boys and cars, hermetically sealed from social divisions,. On the contrary, she and her peers were protected, an integral part of a substantial British presence in Iraq.

In my own experience, and that of my family and friends who grew up in that decade, the atmosphere across the world, as reported to our sitting rooms on the television screen or broadcast on radio (the latter would apply to most people then) was one of a concatenation of warlike images, from troubled societies. A survey of the decade in this context reveals such topics as atomic testing on Bikini Island; social dissension in Algeria; Malayan political divisions; the ongoing stalemate in Korea; violent civil war in Cyprus and the always present resentment in the Suez area.

If we look at the whole picture of British occupation of Cyprus, Egypt and Palestine between the years 1948 and 1960, figures provided by Richard Vinen show that in those years, total deaths of service personnel came to 922. Compared with figures in other theatres of war Beryl had known (notably Korea) these figures are small, but that does not mean that she was in a totally safe area, cocooned from any trouble. Her main concerns, though, were partly linked to the rapid movements of WVS staff across all postings, and the need for the staff to meet radical changes. In one letter from a workmate in Sek Kong, we have this reflection on such subjects: 'Doreen doesn't know yet whether she is going to Japan or not... she is working herself up into a nervy state and is quite tearful. She has decided she hates it here...'

At the very beginning of 1956, from Habbaniya, Beryl wrote to her mother in Grimsby that she was in the thick of such manoeuvres as had been described by her friend in Sek Kong: 'Like several other of my colleagues, I was originally destined for Cyprus or Tripoli. However, I was lucky to be chosen for this one, which is a two WVS posting (two separate clubs and one person in each). Everyone is moving out of here... backing up our troops in Cyprus, where there are lots of men.' Two WVS workers with her had been chosen to transfer to Cyprus, and Beryl witnessed two clubs being closed; she did her usual social visits, including some time spent with the sergeants of the Royal Warwicks at their mess. She was obviously pleased to have avoided a long posting in Cyprus and had a lot to say about the situation there:

> *I suppose in Cyprus it will be difficult, as one won't know*
> *who one can trust. In the circumstances I can't see the end*
> *of it in Cyprus, we must compromise to retain the island*
> *as a base, but we've no right to be there at all really.*

But at least at the level of everyday work, Beryl had plenty of pleasant support and good facilities in her temporary home: 'the tonic effects of the 60 degree temperature – all our rooms have ceiling fans and double roofs to keep them cool and here mosquitoes, flies etc. are few, as the RAF have a good D.D.T. spraying system carried out regularly and thoroughly. Our windows are covered with very fine wire net which keeps out all but dust... the insects seem to come out fully at night...'

There had been odd and aborted supposed moves before, such as back in May 1953 when Beryl had written that 'H.O. are asking me to extend my contract... they seem keen on sending me to Malaya. I'm more in favour of Japan...'

With sheer triumph and delight, Beryl found a sewing machine, and that gave her a welcome boost. It was a tough task to obtain and work on it: '... here I found a disused, rusty sewing machine, Singer make, standing in a tent, attached to a mess... I asked if I could try and make it work and was told there was little hope of that as many people had tried and failed...' But this was a challenge, and she found some help. A boyfriend of a fellow WVS worker worked on the machine and cleaned it thoroughly; it was taken to her quarters when ready.

Beryl was acutely aware of criticisms of her location, from home, and from the tabloids in particular. She found a headline: 'Operation Luxury' in which the accusation was made that money was being wasted, handed out to the contractors on Suez, after they had taken over from the army. But as well as being aware of the politics, she still kept up her reading and self-education and added some humour to her first letter home of 1956: 'I've just finished reading *Murder in Mesopotamia* by Agatha Christie. Mystery solved as usual.'

What Beryl did not tell her mother, but confessed to Chris, was that in late 1955 she had been genuinely worried at the situation regarding Suez and the actions of Nasser, the Egyptian leader. She wrote, '... our future here hangs in the balance, on the whim of the fickle Arab nature. Every day we expect to wake up and find ourselves prisoners of war. We none of us give a fig for our chance of life, even if Nasser doesn't get satisfaction at the London conference, and we are not using our sense of drama either.' At that point, having just arrived, she looked around and what she saw increased her worries. She noted that 'We are a very small force here now.' She also gave Chris a version of her life there very different from reports to her mother: 'During the night life is one long scratch. I go hospital visiting a lot to sit in an air-conditioned ward for an hour. We are getting the hot 'date winds' and choking dust storms often now. I went in a dust storm to Baghdad last week, but came back safely...'

Throughout the year, there had been the usual round of events, and although most were general socialising, some were by specific groups, and in fact they were invitations to travel, as they covered the whole string of bases. Such an event happened in June, and was hosted by the NAAFI at Tel-el-Kebir by the Secretary of the Ball Committee. Such was the value placed on social assemblies. In this case, it was a real communal affair, with appeals for subscription:

It has been decided to hold an open air Officials' Invitation Ball at the Imperial Club, Mosscar, on Saturday the 16th

July, 1955, commencing at 9 p.m. and ending at 2 a.m. All RTE and GHQ officials and members of the WVS may act as hosts and if they decide to attend they would each be expected to subscribe PT.50 to cover the cost of the band, buffet supper and other incidental expenses. It is hoped that each official will invite one guest preferably of the opposite sex.

As 1955 closed, Beryl had good things happen on the financial front. Money was always a worry to some degree doing voluntary work, naturally, but at least she noted that her cost of living allowance had doubled between April and September that year; She also had a £25 payment for a year's completed service and on top of that, there was a small gratuity. She always did her best to try to save, as life after WVS work was always going to be uncertain.

With time to write now, more than previously, Beryl took on the role of adviser more often, and some letters show that she was skilled in being 'agony aunt' during her life in Iraq. One typical instance of this is this mix of philosophical reflection and practical opinion:

Only sex makes men tick. I see it proved a lot in my job. Wind has changed to lashing rain now... by the way, you are much more adult than me in many ways, but men are always children. Our garrulity only comes from nerves about what the other person may be thinking of us, acting as if we are always in the prisoner's dock. Cut it out dear, in your own sweet self and you'll still be better than your criticizers. Sufferers have conscience anyway.

The end of January, 1956, brought a sense of balance and routine to Beryl's life. Though she was now in a much more populous and well defended gaff. She wrote to Chris, to the sound of jets 'screaming overhead' about the new life, thoroughly settled in Iraq.

This was one of the most vivid letters she ever wrote, and she even revealed what her short time in Cyprus had been like – something she had kept from telling her mother:

I had kicked around for seven days in Cyprus... I did manage to visit Famagusta for a few days... apart from the weather restricting sightseeing opportunities, there was the terrorism. One day of sheer terror and confinement to hotel, was a Sunday, when Archbishop Makarios was preaching in the cathedral. You can imagine I was very glad to set off for here finally. I had a bumpy passage and arrived in the dusk, dropped down into a terrible, waterless rocky surfaced plain (desolate, sublime)...

Her first impressions of Habbaniya, as expressed to Chris, were of a place where everything 'moved at a snail's pace' and she concluded that 'It is very like what Russia is reputed to be and we are only 600 miles from the Russo-Iraqi border.' Of course, Beryl was interested in the languages heard and written around her. She told Chris that one person at the base spoke six languages; then she explained some of the tongues in use: 'Assyrian – an Arabic basically like the Egyptian one but with an overlay of Turkish nouns, and Kurdish.' She also adds that she had 'found a few people who understood my Egyptian.' As was her habit, Beryl was enjoying the sheer delight of speaking foreign languages, and had gathered a smattering of several in her global work. She also adds, for the sake of Chris and Denys who seemed to enjoy high culture and the good life, that there was oil. She briefly noted, 'The dining room was full of oil people. Most of them were French, English and America, plus one Chinese.'

One significant step forward that becomes evident in the letters relates to their mother, and the crucial insight is, 'I do feel her life is too narrow for her to be able to advise us on ours nowadays. I'm treading on delicate emotional ground when I say that you don't want your life to become a repetition of hers.' Again, she was increasingly in a mood of giving moral advice. It comes as no surprise, if we reflect that she was now a senior member of staff wherever she was posted. Experience had given her a sense of her wisdom and more than a touch of *gravitas*.

In May she wrote a long report to Chris, and the Beryl here is more comfortable and assured: 'The whole camp is a mass of perfumes, and their relatives the blooms that produce them. We have roundabouts, private gardens, full of roses. They seem to grow everywhere, even on the roadside hedges, big pink and red cabbage roses...' She had also made a friend, a 'very sweet and warm-hearted Irish girl in her early thirties.' They had met in the Canal Zone, and then they were together again in Iraq. The girl was a great asset, 'She is very fond of social life (she is a very pretty blonde) and she has lots of contacts as many pilots come here. However, she always wants to take me out and about and is always looking for a nice man for me. She has produced four "suitable" already.'

As had happened so many times before in her life, there was an entanglement. Still, as has become the norm with Beryl by now, the approach is to weigh and consider a man and to remain distant: 'I hated to have to rebuff this officer as we so obviously clicked. I know I hurt his feelings and I also sense that he thinks I think he is not good enough. The trouble is he is obviously a very good type who doesn't know his own value with women. He is very kind and considerate – a great asset in a man!' A more problematic liaison was to follow, and this casts a light on the kinds of relationship difficulties faced by people in such circumstances. The man in question was in the NAAFI and he had a wife. He had his wife with him, but made a play for Beryl, who describes the situation:

> I knew he had his roving eye on me... the day after his
> wife left for home, he came to see if he could take me
> to the lake... he is commodore at the Yacht Club... Today
> I went to see him about curtains for the mess and he said
> how about the cinema this evening?' He was repelled,
> and Beryl was skilled at doing that. But it was all too

much for her. She confessed to Chris, 'The more I live and
work in such a predominantly male atmosphere the less
I can suffer them.

Her work in 1956 as she adapted to the routine that took a long
time coming was primarily housekeeping and running the club. She
explained that she had one night a week off; she explained at one
time, 'We work in our respective clubs 10 a.m. to 12.30 noon and
then 6 p.m. to 9.30. She also had to deal with servants and wrote a
brief explanation of her policy with them: 'The servants here respect
my knowledge of methods, amounts etc. That keeps them more
economical. By the way, it is bad policy I feel to flatter servants by
letting them see that you care about their opinions. They are not there
to sit in censure on you, they are just there to do as they are told.' This
is truly a revelation. After years of written testimony about Beryl
Baxter, here she is showing a forthright martinet kind of attitude.
There has indeed been a change in her. There was some stress, as one
might expect, and one time she hints at how she copes: 'In any of
my affairs I know I didn't need to worry about physical adjustment,
mental worried me more because when that is okay I feel well...'

Above all her concerns with weather, club socialising and affairs of
the heart, one aspect of life in Iraq remained deep in her sensibility –
the flora and landscape. Her most expressive account in this respect
is surely this: 'we have gladioli, beds of stocks, and sweet Williams...
all but root vegetables have finished now. Of European style there
are marrows, tomatoes, apricots, peaches, apples and green peppers.
These are 'in' now... it could be a paradise, and will be when the
irrigation projects get properly going. The rain in late March brought
the usual river floods but the newly opened barrages at Ramadi and
Sammara diverted the waters to needy areas.'

The first phase of life in the Middle East had been one of a precarious
hold on her world and its demands; then, gradually there had been,
after settling in Habbaniya, a sense of stability, and the necessary
routine of her work had helped to root her in the small pleasures

in between satisfying work. If we put together the references to the nature and scope of her duties, we find a mix of routine socialising at the club, hospital visiting and keeping up contributions to the camaraderie around the base, between civilians and military. What strikes the modern reader from the hundreds of letters is that Beryl's personality had deepened; maturity and experience have moulded her into a senior member of every team she worked with, and if we factor in the evidence of her short spell at home being very much an anticlimax, and also most arduous, our conclusion has to be that her deep need of working in service where she was needed was by mid 1956 very much in evidence. At times in the letters from the early 1950s onwards, one finds it hard to locate the woman who first travelled from Germany out east to the call of a new world of excitement and a new test. For sure, after her many postings up to the mid 1950s, she had proved herself equal to any task presented to her.

Towards the end of 1956, Beryl was fully aware of a diplomatic situation and of a degree of unease around her. She wrote to Chris, 'Right now we are in a very unsettled state of mind as King Faisal [Faisal II of Iraq, who died in 1958] has gone to Syria for talks this weekend. When we invaded Egypt there was a Lebanese squadron here but they of course didn't stay long when Syria decided on a difference of opinion with us.' There was a strong mail censorship, and there were fears of invasion as Beryl wrote home in October. There was trouble close to hand: 'Feelings run amok very quickly here, and whilst the invasion was on, one of our corporals was stabbed by two Iraqi soldiers while he was just leaving his billet for the NAAFI. He was left for dead but he is slowly recovering.'

As Beryl was aware, there were 5,000 Iraqi troops by the side of the camp, and they were there ostensibly to guard and protect from communities not far away who were militantly anti-Christian. Beryl reflected that everyone was on their best behaviour, to avoid fomenting bad feeling.

To make matters perhaps more tense, it seems that the Commanding Officer at Habbaniya had made it plain (perhaps in a memo) that he was worried about drunkenness at Christmas. Beryl thought that there had been some reference by him to possibly violent incidents with the Iraqis. Not far away, In Baghdad, there were at that time some strikes, intended to make public a general feeling of 'Middle East for the Arabs' movement. As this was happening, Beryl still had six months to serve.

More intimately bound up with routine life in the mess and club was the Irish girl, who was now a problem in Beryl's eyes. She commented:

> *She is in her thirties but always seems to be in "man trouble" – the sort that she acts a sixteen-year-old about. All this would not worry me unduly however if she would wear her uniform when on duty, and at least stop wondering how she can fit her work around her private life! She even opposes me or refuses to support me in joint welfare such as running a dance. She is also the kind that seems to let a gang of boys in the club dictate to her. The RAF authorities here don't like her...*

Matters in Iraq really escalated that October and November. In the latter month there were serious riots in Baghdad, and 69 people died. Beryl commented on some startling news also: '...the BBC seems to know that we British have been given 24 hours to get out of Jordan...' Beryl referred to her life there, to Chris, as being in a 'false peace'. Even more alarming news filtered through to her when it became known that a WVS worker in Cyprus had been killed by terrorists.

To alleviate the stress, Beryl, in November, did what she always did: she learned a language. This time it was Russian, and she found a teacher in a signals officer. She told Chris that most of the airmen signallers already spoke the language. She needed something to help her mental state. Her account of asking for a switch of accommodation suggests a high level of anxiety, 'Recently I asked the administrator here for another, smaller mess. This one is transit type and large and unwieldy, especially in the heat. She luckily doesn't like it either and has asked the RAF for a cosy, small place.' She aptly signed off in

Russian, and no doubt turned her thoughts to Christmas. There was restlessness everywhere. In Singapore, Chris had witnessed riots. The world seemed to be in increasing anarchy to the two sisters as 1956 came to an end.

The beginning of 1957 must have seemed like the last furlong in an epic long-distance race. She had just six months left, although she was thinking of extending the time at Habbaniya, but in the first months of the year the family were all helping as usual. Chris wrote to say that she was feeling the sense of uncertainty: 'I understand Beryl was leaving Iraq in May and I wanted you to know about things in case she needed them sending home to London.' This was to their mother, and it looks as though, at that time, everyone in the circle of letter readers and writers was in the dark regarding Beryl's future.

Then letters are back in the archive, and Beryl wrote to Chris with an angry tone: 'A week ago I had a letter from WVS in Cyprus to say that I must take all arrears of leave due in this theatre before I leave. Such an ultimatum makes me seethe, that both my opposite number and I have both foregone our due leaves so long, on account of shortage of staff and Middle East crises etc.'

The political situation had hit the WVS and others very hard; she had hoped to travel to Jerusalem via RAF Mafrak, and also to Mosul, but the chance had gone. There was also the factor that around Mosul all reports said that there was local hostility. Her workmate was taking leave for a few weeks, so that left Beryl alone, holding the fort. Such a pattern of events was always happening in Beryl's line of work, of course. But she was still planning a fortnight in Singapore with Chris and Denys. She wrote that staying with them 'would do me an awful lot of psychological good and I feel perhaps that you might like to meet me once more before you move...'

Beryl could not give any dates for travel, but she knew most ships and their possible dates of departure, quoting the *Umaria*, which left Basrah and vessels of the Gray and the Mackenzie lines. Still, such complicated matters as booking journeys were alleviated by the humour of basic necessities and their availability. She reported to Chris that a towel had arrived, but there was a commotion and some anxiety involved: 'The towel arrived today, plus a note in a pick envelope from Iraq postal authorities. I died a thousand deaths whilst the Arabic in which it was written was decoded by the canteen manager for me, as everyone thought it was a telegram. However, it turned out to be a notice that I must pay import duty on the towel... I can't tell you how much I owe on it.'

The first months of possibly her last year of service brought no let-up in the business of wining and dining – and courting. This time, she started going out with 'a well-known glamour girl here... I bless her for her large-hearted nature and Merry Widow tactics (she is a widow) and is very fond of the opposite sex. I naturally feel an awful heel and can't bear it when the man (who has also liked me) keeps looking at me...'

By July, the situation regarding the leave and various payments was sorted out by the administrator in Famagusta. She wrote to Beryl and to her friend Betty about the problem, and she confirmed that they could both take the leave they had planned. She added a compliment: 'As I mentioned this to my superior he said that circumstances prevented it in your cases and it's not really anyone's fault. I think you have both done very well to stick it out so long and I thought your Clubs were charming and a credit to you both.' The superior administrator dished out the cash; they were awarded £18 travel allowance and she added, 'However, the daily subsistence allowance is £2 a day so this will mount up in both your cases quite a bit...' The topic and the way it was handled shows what stress and pressure everyone was working under, because of course, matters specified in contracts are hardly going to run smoothly in a wartime context. In one of her letters, Beryl had written, just before this, 'All H.O.'s are panicking about me not having had more than five days leave in two years. I am due six weeks in that time.'

Beryl's last letters home or to Chris were written when swapping and changing was still happening in the various clubs and centres. There were still around a thousand men based in Habbaniya when she wrote in May, and her letter explains the kind of situation on staffing that was still not running at all smoothly:

> *It has been decided that Habbaniya will only have one WVS when I leave. (It needs at least two.) However, the C.O. of the camp here is horrified at the idea. He thinks the camp numbers have not run down enough yet to manage with one, but by August this might be the case. The Iraqi army and air force already control most of it, but we still have over a thousand British here, including families. The final number is to be about eight hundred people. Anyway, my number two here closed down a large club here and opened another one as big as mine on April 8th. It was folly to open that one...*

It still irritated Beryl that her assistant still did not wear a uniform; a decision on whether Beryl was to go or stay was still up in the air. She was considering going to Aden, by May that year, and that interested her because she thought of Africa being so near. Her wanderlust was as strong as ever.

At this time, polio becomes a topic of communication. The disease was in all conversations at the time. I myself was in the generation that received the vaccination during the time of sheer panic. In the mid 1950s, my school friends, family and I were terrified by images of the 'iron lung' on the television drama, *Dr Kildare* (a little later, in 1961). Beryl mentions it first in May. She wrote:

> *There was a polio case here... a boy who left for the U.K. on a plane, with several Nurses and doctors and with all reasonable care taken, but he died in his sleep in Malta. I saw him before he left and he seemed well on the way to recovery. We now have a woman victim here in the hospital. She is never out of the lung. Six Nurses*

and three doctors attend her and I understand she is a
difficult patient (thirty years old). She had to be rescued
from a very badly run Baghdad Hospital. Polio is a
scourge in this part of the world and one should never
neglect a frequent head or limbs ache...

One of Beryl's most satisfying tasks undertaken when she was in Iraq concerned an air crash. She referred to this once: 'Lately an airman here took some photos with a new Contina model of a mass grave here at Habbaniya, of the 23 victims of an air crash in Jordan on April 17th. He took great care of them; I watched him, but they came out shadowy and with bright sun patches... I was asked at the very last minute to produce a wreath for the second funeral on Easter Sunday morning.'

This refers to a crash known as the Aqaba Valetta accident, which happened on 17 April that year when the Valetta plane, from 84 Squadron RAF crashed and was destroyed when taking off from Aqaba airport. The plane was carrying troops – mostly from the 10th Royal Hussars from Jordan to the UK all people on board perished. Beryl played a major role in the aftermath of that disaster. She wrote to Chris:

The wreaths for that one were very amateur affairs, but
through nothing less, I swear that the hand of Providence,
I had two ladies, wreath makers, in the club at the time of
the message regarding the crash... I went to the funeral
and believe me when I say the fewer of such occasions
that I attend in life, the better I shall like it. I am now up
to the eyes in keeping up supplies of wreaths, photos of
graves etc. for birthdays and wedding anniversaries, at the
request of the many next of kin. Five laddies used my club
whilst in transit waiting for another plane to U.K. having
been off loaded from the one that crashed. Their narrow

escape was their constant topic of conversation. Some of the victims had served three years in a back-of-beyond place like Aqaba... Several of them were married men...

Beryl, even in her last months of the posting, was still studying Arabic, run by the headmaster of a local Iraqi school; she was also finding time for parties, and there were many invitations. She went to one party, in Mafrok, at which she was very ill, and she reported that the crew of the plane she used were very worried about her. But typical of her, she wrote that she was 'ashamed to be such a nuisance'.

When it came to June, after all the busy times and some medical fears, things were more equable, and her letters betray less angst about the world around her. The air crash had filled many of her hours, as she had written to relatives of the victims and offered whatever help she could give. She took plenty of photographs to send home to them, and they would have been welcomed, even though they were small 'Box Brownie' types. A letter of thanks from a colonel in the Royal Hussars. He wrote that 'I and my officers were very impressed by all the sympathy shown and are very grateful to you.' He offered expenses to cover the cost of the wreaths. The episode has to be one of the most satisfying and fulfilling actions of her long career.

Beyond all that, basic work went on, with just the one club, and now there was the leave to come before the important decisions of the year had to be made. In June she sent Chris a full report on matters in Iraq. Beryl was keen to take her leave and go to see Chris, but staff matters were problematic, as usual. They could find no way to take a RAF plane to Singapore, and could have no billet there. One has the feeling that Beryl was thoroughly embedded in social liaison and schmoozing. She was becoming the best advert for WVS in the area, by sheer activity among officers and men, and also with the forces families. One could spin this another way and pinpoint a women who was overworked, in intense heat, and coping with under-staffing. She wrote, with the further stress of a man who was courting her most actively as well, 'The hot weather makes people think only of themselves here. The fat is in the fire and I am managing two clubs, now Betty is away. I'm camp heroine suddenly! This is after being a bit of a Cinderella. John keeps pressing me in his cups as well as in other circumstances... He is treating his other lady shamefully, and it's worse because I'm here until October now.'

She notes that the WVS in the Middle East was running on '50% staff now... and there is no relief in sight.' Her last letter to Singapore was written in September, when the end was in sight. She was at the time desperate to have some leave, and this situation is described in extreme terms:

> *The snag is that I cannot prove that I have had an inoculation since I came on this tour. I know I've had one, before I set out, but it is not recorded on my papers. (They last six years you see.) Anyhow I am due to have one at 10 a.m. tomorrow and then another snag is that the M.O. cannot sign the paper until ten days after it. I am very pally with the three M.O.s here. They live in my block, as we are near the hospital. One of them did suggest he forged the paper but then began to wonder if he would be struck off the register for it! However, all this nonsense aside, there is another plane for Changi due here soon and I will have a seat on it...*

There was a golden opportunity at last for Beryl to meet and express her concerns with the area administrator, who wrote to say that 'It seems such ages since I saw you both that I want to try to pop over to see you the week after next. It must be quick but at least we can have a chat about things. Do you think you could be a sweetie and cable me if this is quite enough for you, or impossible?'

By November, life was all about preparing to leave Iraq for good. Then came a letter confirming that she was urgently needed to see the place and its people into the new year. Lady Wenham wrote the request, and it was in her capacity as special assistant to Lady Reading:

> *I have just spent a most fascinating twelve days seeing all the WVS in Cyprus and I only wish it had been possible to visit all the WVS members in the Middle East. As you must understand with the present economy drive this would be far too expensive. I however want to send you a few personal lines to tell you how sorry I am that I have not been able to see you. Miss Wilson tells me that it has been arranged that you stay on in Habbaniya until after Christmas. She will be writing to you about this very soon and I thought you would like to hear the good news.*

Was it good news? Given all the pressure Beryl was under, maybe she was desperate to get out. The reference to the economy drive explains much that was clearly stressing Beryl. Her area administrator wrote to confirm the extension, but added a caring note: 'However, you must go home as soon after Christmas as we can get you a passage for I really am worried about your long stay in such a bad climate.'

It must have seemed as though the help and understanding had been somewhat delayed, but of course, the tough time she had undergone was something that impacted on everyone in that very stressful and violent period in modern history. She had been a tiny part in a huge enterprise, and this was something that had developed in the aftermath of a world war. Naturally, Beryl understood all this, but still, the reader has to reflect that she had spent a long time in a place in which there were dissenting native groups around, along with political unrest and most disturbing of all, attacks on British personnel at the very base that had become her home.

Maybe, she must have been thinking, that this Christmas 1957 marked the end of her saga with the WVS. On 13 December she received a note – a copy of a booking with Lufthansa:

Air Passage
Confirming our conversation on 12 December. Kindly
Book the following air passage in respect of
Miss B.M. Baxter:
Baghdad-London 17.1.1958.
The cost of the above air passage is chargeable to
Headquarters,
NAAFI, RAF Staging Post, Habbaniya

If one compares the situation in the WVS across the Middle East when Beryl left Iraq with the figures for 1955, the emphasis on Cyprus is very clear: that was where the epicentre of violence and confrontation was most fierce and prevalent. The lists of staff and centres, issued by London, showed that there were fifteen staff across Cyprus, and in Iraq, merely Beryl Baxter and Miss L. Mangan. Other bases covered Cyrenaica, Tripolitania, Aden and Kenya. There was one staff member awaiting posting and one returned home.

If one had to sum up her time in Iraq, perhaps the words beautiful but testing would cover most of the situation. On the plus side, she had attracted all kinds of relationships, from the needy to the greedy; on the negative side there had been violence around the corner. The thought of departure must have been largely one of relief.

The new year this time really was a departure for home and for a period of decision making; after so long working in service, it was in Beryl's blood and she clearly wanted to continue in some way. The course of her work across the world, from Korea to Iraq, and from Germany if we include the time before the Far Eastern adventure, had entailed a number of trials and challenges, each in its own way unique and packed with difficulties. She surely saw that she had proved herself to be a leader and a manager, as well as a reliable servant, and the young woman who initially switched from RAF status as part of Bomber Command, had now gone through seventeen years of life abroad, well away from her Grimsby home. The last years had been fraught with troubles and complex work situations, but the written record shows conclusively that she was respected and valued by all with whom she came into contact. Catching that Lufthansa flight, she surely reflected on what she had become and how she had triumphed. She had always longed to see the world, and more than that, she had wanted to take in all she could, from language and culture to foreign ideologies and governments. But she had done far more than that, in fact, she had adapted with style and method to a series of tough regimes, and demonstrated a rare ability to communicate with people at all levels, from the private soldiers to the higher command and even diplomats.

She also came home with a massive photograph collection. Her archive contains hundreds of snaps of places and people from Japan to Iraq; these images also present a visual biography of herself, in small frame pictures, always with others; sometimes she smiles, surrounded by troops and at other times she sits at a desk or smiles in the open air with workmates and civilians.

A deeper level of scrutiny is required here, as biography demands that the writer reflects on the elements and topics that stayed with her and were constantly repeated through the correspondence. I would suggest that these are: preoccupations with health; coping with possible affairs and close friendships; managing the various strategies required in staff relationships, and of course, the adaptation to a range of alien cultures. Of all these, my selection for special attention would be that element in Beryl that always kept her stable and involved – her empathy. On the surface she did such things as attend language classes (Russian, German, Korean and Arabic) but more profound was her involvement with the particular needs of her charges and friends in terms of surviving in a theatre of war.

One strategy she always maintained in this respect was to create a normality, a routine. She held to the view that everyday matters staved off anxiety; sometimes this could be joining in with the locals, while at other times it was a matter of getting jobs done and allowing physical labour to oust any hint of stress and strain.

As so often happens, it was the elements she absorbed in her first few years that remained and tended to comfort and feed her. This was a combination of a number of things: the German nation and culture; the need to retain a valuable place in a hierarchy; the sustenance provided by popular culture (ordering vast stocks of magazines and books for the common rooms) and arguably the most fundamental value she had – that of ensuring that basics were always under control. Working for the WVS meant that these basics were cash resources, clothes and travel. She hungered for these, and her efforts done towards the experiences of leave trips were the main factor in enriching her education and sense of knowledge for each place she came to know. It is impossible to overestimate the need she had to see other places. Her accounts of such trips read like informative travelogues, taking her mother and sister into those places of reality as well as of imagination. She tells her reader about the flora and fauna, the habits of the ordinary people, and the smell, feel and touch of foreign materiality.

Beryl Baxter was heading home then. What was waiting was well known to her and to her sisters: domestic chores and helping her mother cope with daily tasks. There was always catching-up to do. Working overseas meant that all the necessary paperwork of existence had been shelved, so the adventure was a hiatus, a time out adventure. Going home was to face such matters as banks and savings, insurance, medical matters and household burdens. She can't have relished that, heading homewards. Her last report from home, a year earlier, had been like a report from the front in the war against grime and filth. She surely felt that she was transferring herself from servant to skivvy. But nonetheless, the destination was Britain, and she had lots of friends there, all willing and eager to meet up with her again. The next stage of her life is crammed with correspondence and meetings with former workmates.

She could never have prophesied it, but she still had half a century of service ahead of her, in work beyond the WVS. She was to be a house-mother and she also returned to her beloved Germany. The wanderlust continued. There might not have been thoughts of roots, families and husbands in her mind, but the Beryl who boarded the plane (now turned 40) was perhaps sadder and wiser, although it has to be stressed that most of her voluminous correspondence is joyous. She was largely a radiator, not a drain when it came to friendship. There is a feeling, in the sources from her last months out in Iraq, that the struggle to be encouraged and rewarded was now engulfed by a fight to remain at all visible when the demands made in Cyprus were so strident and persistent.

One last, wonderful flight then, was coming. The excitement of a plane journey must have buoyed her up, in spite of perhaps a shadow of apprehension, thinking of the air crash she had just been busy with, faced with all the relatives of young men who had died. The real reward, though, for all the work and enterprise, lay in her spirit: her very soul had been nurtured by all that immersion in humanity. As I completed my reading of her correspondence I thought of Joseph Conrad's epigraph to his novel *Lord Jim*: 'In the destructive element immerse.' I always felt that he thought of that element as a beneficent one – that a destructive element presses one to compensate by escaping, coming out new and refreshed. One would like to think that such a thing was in Beryl as she went home.

Conclusions

In modern history, the subject of women in action or in support of action, in war, has a rich and intriguing history as far as Britain is concerned – it was a long time coming. We think of the Nightingale nurses in the Crimean War of the 1850s as the first landmark. But fifty years later, as reported in the *Harmsworth Magazine* reflecting on the Anglo-Boer War, the delicacy and oddness of the trend was expressed in the wording of this statement: 'Among those who may be styled amateur nurses, Mrs Richard Chamberlain, the youthful widowed sister-in-law of the Colonial Secretary, were among the first to actually start for South Africa, amply provided with those minor comforts which make so much difference to the wounded.' Then of course, along came the First World War and the general influx of nurses to the front in France and elsewhere.

I spent some considerable time reflecting on why I wrote this book, and among many minor reasons, there was one central one, and the clearest explanation of this I know (in print) comes from Simon Heffer, in an essay on 1950s films: 'I have long thought that one of the many reasons why we should watch these films is that we are still the sort of people we really were; we just occasionally need to be reminded of what that means.' Beryl Baxter's life is another such reminder.

When I was a schoolboy in the 1950s, the only history we learned was British imperial. The history lessons consisted of a map with all the imperial pink on it, and stories of the Black Hole of Calcutta, the Mughals and the Munity. Good and bad in past times were clearly demarcated, and there was no whiff of doubt about why and how our

161

military retained those pink lands. In the process of researching this book, I came to realise that the National Service recruits would have had a similar experience, and the country they found themselves in would hardly have figured in that education. They would know about India, Africa and the Levant, and maybe even Australia or Canada, but not that obscure land north of Japan.

However, what I found in telling Beryl's story was that I had a powerfully angled view on the sometimes horrendous experience of those British, United Nations and American soldiers: I saw it through the prism of a woman; in fact, through several women, because friends and relatives wrote to Beryl and gave their perspectives too.

It is well documented that in the Second World War, British women were skilled in finding ways to contribute. They filled roles and did duties in all corners of the war, in all theatres of conflict. A few became national figures, such as Stella 'Jaye' Edwards, the pilot who died during my time in writing this biography. The fact that Stella excelled herself in the Air Transport Auxiliary meant that she really stood out, being truly exceptional, and I feel that she was a role-model for many others. Beryl, in contrast, did what many did, but there is no denying that her achievement was exceptional. I limited my material to the events of c.1939–1953; but she continued in various areas of social service, being a house-mother in Germany and also in Lincolnshire, in later life.

I have been impressed, repeatedly, by Beryl's tenacity, and her ability to see a job through. In fact, the overarching message from Beryl and her peers, from the 1940s and 1950s is surely – more than 'keep calm and carry on' – one of being as greedy for life experience as for anything smacking of the word *career*. Yes, she was champing at the bit to travel to somewhere new and face new tasks and demands, but there was never a plan. We may discern three elements in her nature: first, under sheer necessity, that of hard work to a set target; then came the need she had for the satisfaction of visible achievement, and finally, as we see in everything she did, there was her deep hunger for proving in herself the presence of the basic human virtues.

CONCLUSIONS

Those virtues the tabloids and popular histories today often see as sacrifice and denial – the ability to put off individual plans to another day. My opinion would be that there was in her generation an understanding of the pleasure and satisfaction of having succeeded in a life that openly showed companionship, sharing, honest communication and most of all that placing of work as noble, worthy and most slippery of all, fulfilling in itself. I am always reminded of a Victorian painting when I read about the generation that faced the Second World War. It is called 'Work' by Ford Madox Brown, in which a sturdy labourer is digging in the street as Victorian thinkers and writers look on approvingly.

Beryl may not have liked it, but when her friends looked at her, what they saw first was a dedicated worker, the keystone in the arch.

There must have been a high level of frustration when things appeared to have been settled. In July 1953, the press ran the information that the truce had been violated several times. The news was announced for readers at the Korean centres, explaining the allegations: 'When the Military Armistice Commission met again today the chief Communist delegate alleged that UN troops have violated the terms of the truce on eight separate occasions. He said that UN artillery and a machine gun had opened fire, and that three UB aircraft had flown over the Demilitarised Zone.' Decades went by, and the stand-off remained. In 2003, the *National Geographic Magazine* focused on that same uneasy stalemate: 'the truce has survived another night in the DMZ and morning brings a sense of peace. But don't be fooled by the quiet, cautions Major Kim Bong Su, a senior Korean officer, "The North Koreans are the same blood as us but they are the enemy."'

Meanwhile, the war in which Beryl and her workmates served the fighting men in every way they could, though officially ended, has a latent hostility that reads like a lull in the fighting rather than a resolution, though people in Korea have to carry on as if there was normality and peace.

163

The Korean War still resides in a dark back room in the great mansion of modern military history. Occasionally, people and events provoke reminders about the seemingly endless truce and the actual nature of that nasty and brutal conflict. The general public were reminded of the war when it was told that Neil Armstrong served in it, or maybe when they watched Frank Sinatra figure as a supposed communist mind-control victim in *The Manchurian Candidate*. But still, in a strange way, that war figures in history very much like the 'little wars' of Victorian Britain – the many conflicts that went on, overshadowed by the Crimea, the Indian Mutiny and the Anglo-Boer Wars.

There is still such a static situation in Korea today, and in terms of our general knowledge of the country, the sources have been few and very restricted. There have been brief impressions and descriptions, as from James Robbins in his essay 'Parallel Universe' summarising what he sees very powerfully: 'The whole country, or all that we were able to see, looked as if it had broken down with no prospect of repair.' Erika Fatland, in *The Border*, gives a solid profile of the land, and stresses some alarming paradoxes, such as the vast spending on museums while Korean farmers still use spade and hoe. She also points out one of the most staggering facts: 'In 1945... more than one million North Koreans, primarily Christians and opponents, defected south during the first years of Kim Il-Sung's reign.'

The internet has meant that it is now easier for readers to get closer to the war, as they may read a forum or statements made by veterans on oral history projects. There are a few memoirs and group biographies in print. Yet, as always, those who 'stand and wait' are generally overlooked. Readers of history tend to go straight to the headlines and take an interest in the man shooting the rifle, not the man who has cleaned the weapon.

One other major outcome of my research relates to the constant shortcomings inherent in writing about the past: the limitation of a viewpoint and the blinkered view. In the context of this particular war, the obvious element here is the lack of a Chinese or North Korean standpoint, or even of a minor testimony. By this I mean in terms of books and articles that are widely known, not simply scholarly writing in the academic journals. There are rare examples of such alternative insights, such as from the bestseller published in 1991, *Wild Swans* by Jung Chang. One harrowing reference she gives is this, relating to the death of a young colonel called Hui-ge, who had been executed by firing squad:

> *For the Chinese, one of the most terrible things that could happen was not to have a proper burial. They believed that only when the body was covered and placed deep in the earth could the dead find peace... My grandmother had gone herself to the execution ground. Hui-ge's body had been left lying on the ground, riddled with bullets, one of a row of corpses.*

Summing up the nature and impact of the WVS, it is perhaps best to use the words of an officer, and when I asked him to sum up, he wrote: 'The WVS was a force for good and were never afraid to dispute with the C in C [Commander-in-Chief] and his staff. My final memory of the WVS was at a London bombing... in the midst of organised chaos, smoke, rubble and the deceased who were covered but left where they had fallen (for forensic purposes), arrives at the outer cordon a green van with WVS canteen emblazoned on the side. Within minutes they were serving tea, coffee and bacon sandwiches. Two hours later the police catering team arrived!'

I was always aware, in researching this book, that there were claims on my imagination to make this the story of all three sisters. After all, group biographies have their own attractions, and I had the thought of the Brontë sisters in mind at one stage. However, an attempt to bring all three into a narrative would have meant far too much reliance on correspondence alone.

My generation of working class Brits have a strong imaginative affinity with Beryl and her peers. This comes in part from the 1950s world of media and education; as I grew up towards my teens in that decade, I was surrounded by images and narratives of militarism and Empire. As well as the B movies featuring wartime heroism, there were the tales of male imperial adventure such as *The Four Feathers,* and magazines featuring male exploration and derring-do in far-off climes. Older relatives talked about their experiences in the war. My Uncle Bill had been a Chindit in Burma. How could my childish imagination grasp and understand such things? The answer is that it didn't. I and my fellow working class northerners either went to a secondary modern technical school, or (if the 11+ was passed) we would attended a grammar school, but regardless of which path we took, we were aware of soldiers, parades, bands, TV stories of heroism, and of older brothers or cousins who did national service across the world.

Part of this affinity comes from the strange awareness that there was a home front – family members receiving all these thousands of letters. There are so few return letters available that one has to imagine the events and reaction at home as Beryl's letters dropped through the letterbox. What one tends to forget is the family experiences of simple events, such as the impact of rationing. In one of the most highly rated memoirs of the time, simply called *Memoir,* has an enlightening instance of this: 'I hadn't seen a white loaf in years and took it home in high excitement to show it to Katie... That evening we were all given a slice and we ate it in wonder.'

Whereas Beryl and her sisters knew from the start, in 1939, that they were destined to serve – in all kinds of ways – for the good cause of the war and simply for other people who needed their strength and dedication, I and my school friends were fired with a desire to be heroic, to show the courage of all those heroes in the films and comics. Much of this ideology came from the films from *Pathe News* at the cinema. My family had no television until 1959.

Then, again with national service in Korea and elsewhere in mind, there was the general image and range of related stereotypes of Far Eastern people. The learned historian of modern times, Dominic

Sandbrook, summarises neatly the context of these stereotypes: 'The phrase "East of Suez" irresistibly reminiscent of the high days of empire, is from Kipling's "Mandalay". Although the British presence in the Far East had declined considerably... when Labour took office in 1964 there were still more British troops east of Suez than in Germany.' One of the first shocks I recall with this in mind, focused on the stereotypes of Japanese and Chinese people, was when I saw, and later read Willis Hall's play, *The Long and the Short and the Tall*, filmed in 1961 with Richard Todd. The Japanese prisoner in that play was depicted in a repugnant way, constantly done by belittling the man and making him seem less than human.

Films such as that, along with the popular male-centred tales in the cheap comics such as *The Victor* and *Hotspur*, carried on the tradition of making the ideology we absorbed to be something summed up by 'might is right' and to this was added the notion that all was well with the world if Britain was in charge. The *Carry On* films also reinforced all this, of course, with films such as *Carry On Up the Khyber* depicting Indian people in purely stereotypical ways. This is why Beryl's documented experience provides such a liberating education to modern readers who perhaps missed out on the enlightened revisionary historical media presentations of later times. Beryl's open-minded cultural tastes and understanding came from somewhere else, opposed to my own schooling and brainwashing. Her education was normal working class and she left school aged 15, but she set about immediately 'improving' herself. Something in her family ethos pushed her (along with her sisters and cousins) into welcoming and embracing that enlightened attitude to the world that is saturated in her writing and thinking.

One has to feel that, if there were more memoirs about the Korean War and about life in post-war Germany, perhaps more would filter down into school history. But is has to be said that on the major cable channels dealing with the Second World War and the 1950s – and there are hundreds of programmes made – the absence of features on the Korean War is striking. Yet, as time goes on, and the wars thought of as 'small' or even 'secondary' by the media machine recede even further into obscurity, one might argue that the scandalous, celebrity-based and dramatic-personal in life will always take precedence in the papers and on screens over the real, genuine close-contact war stories.

This explains, for instance, the intense interest taken by the press and by reviewers of the socialite diarist Henry 'Chips' Channon in 2021-2022 as his massive diaries made it into print. As Chris Mullin commented, in an effort to redress the balance between the genuine participants of war and the dilettante time-wasters: '... the Channon diaries are in the end an entertainment, and after 3,000 pages of wining, dining and self-indulgence, their spell starts to wear off.' As Channon was at the Ritz and sunbathing a few hundred yards from a D-Day preparation beach, Beryl and her peers were mending clothes, plotting aircraft movements and learning everything they could in order to help the fight for the survival of our civilization.

As explained at the opening of Beryl's story, this book has grown also from my own family's lives during this period. Everything that lies inside the social life of Beryl's world is familiar to me, from the need to attend to medical matters with one's own resources, to the education gleaned from older relatives. I began by stressing that the Baxters and Drivers, in Beryl's family tree, had fought in the First World War hence there was never a doubt or question regarding the call to arms in 1939. When I reached the age of around 7 or 8 I was acutely aware of my own family's efforts and contributions, and my own native village was closely akin to the Cleethorpes of some of Beryl's family. Consequently, this story has been a parallel one to that of the Baxter sisters, dispersed across the globe at a time of horrific conflict, when death could be coming tomorrow and all relationships could be transient.

Though Beryl Baxter was probably not aware of it, she was writing her lengthy and detailed letters at a time when literary folk and publishers in particular were turning their attention to documentary and the need to monitor what was happening among the 'labouring classes' who had hardly been prominent in the mainstream literature of the land. Her documenting of the daily social life of men and women out in the distant quarters of a world war adds richly to the general archive of what we have on the war that happened way beyond the ken of ordinary people back home.

In her later life, nothing was ever going to match the staggering experience she had known across the world, and she must have been full of yarns and sagas when it came to family assemblies. Her life of service was to go on after 1955, but for now, there she was, taking stock of things, tempted by another spell abroad where there was trouble stirring. One might imagine her, with her mind stacked full of memories of war and its effects, while her imagination longed for a return to somewhere feeling the effects of social upheaval. Such memories as she had would surely trouble her in equal measure to a degree of pleasure, gained from all those friendships and a level of affection that few people come to know.

When I wrote about her family in my book *Grimsby in the Great War*, I recall that a young Beryl wrote to an uncle who was in the army in the 1930s, and she also had a relative who sailed on the *Mauritania*. From this, it is plain that we do not have to look so far for the inspiration behind her longing to travel, and her profound need to live a life of service. A body of material had also been preserved in her heap of lifetime experience concerning her relatives who took part in the First World War. There is no doubt that both sides of her family – Baxters and Drivers – were exemplary people in the area of the committed individual. They needed causes and objectives, and this had filtered through to Beryl in 1939 when this story began of her life in war.

A Postscript on the Archive

As I continued to delve into Beryl's archive, sorting out material and using the arduous process of selection and rejection, I was forced to reflect that I was dealing with something special. On the surface it was no more than a huge hoard of letters and ephemera; but further reflection impressed on me the fact that this was social history wrapping around one sensitive soul who was giving testimony from one little standpoint in the turmoil of a world at war.

That fact filtered into every stage of the narrative; there was never any escape from the fascinating tendency of Beryl to offer sharp perceptions as evocative and dramatic as the best diarist in our history. On the surface she was a young woman garnering evidence of a life lived to the full; all experience was valuable to her, and repeatedly, she forced herself to see places, to reflect on them, and to monitor in words and photographs everything in material life that floated past her.

The material goes on; the archive record covers further postings and then very different work she did in later life. She never married, and as I noted at the beginning, her archive was only just saved from oblivion.

I feel a pressure, in completing this first phase of her life, to try to define the importance of the Beryl Baxter testimony to theatres of war between 1940 and 1955. It is no small effort to supply such a summary, but my conclusion is that personal archives desperately try to freeze time; the material culture she grabbed and saved reflects her attempt to halt the relentless pulse of change and destruction all around her. In short, her effort was one familiar to all creative writers: to believe with King Cnut, that it is worth trying to hold back the waves, be they part of the North Sea, or part of that great dynamo that drives time on, and eats up everything we hold dear. For Beryl Baxter, there was much she held dear – mainly the exotic sights, which were just as enticing as the faces of true friends. I have come to see that, with Lord Tennyson, always in her mind was the thought that 'Some work of noble note may yet be done.'

In one sense, an archive like this, which was never written with publication in mind, has a rare quality. It doesn't sell style. It has a genuine feel about it, a raw closeness to lived experience; Beryl's world comes before our eyes without guile or concoction. She never thought about it, as far as we know, but the truth is that she was a natural storyteller as well as the sister who bothered to write home. I often thought, on first reading her letters, that if her peers ever saw the texts before they were posted, they would have seen that there was their very own version of Samuel Pepys in their ranks. She never thought of herself as a 'writer' but in the written word she truly came alive.

From the first time I set eyes on this material, I had a sense that there were multiple stories here. After all, there were three sisters who took part in the Second World War, together with numerous male members of Baxters and Drivers who fought in the First World War. Not one scrap of material was wasted, as Beryl gathered every fragment of evidence from her experiences. Then, ploughing through the mass of written sources, I had a continuous feeling that this was primarily one person's view of a complicated, global world, in utter turmoil. Once I had realised that, what happened next was that I became more and more impressed by the fact that here was clear evidence of that spirit the popular media always tell us about Beryl's generation: the 'keep calm and carry on' spirit. What the archive material shows, above all else, is her focus on the immediate, above the greater questions where there are politics and strategies involved. The more I read, the more I started to sift the immediate from the eternal. That is, although I was faced with one individual's perspective, I could see her efforts to understand what was causing all the fear and terror around her.

One other very significant topic impressed upon me: national service. Korea was a national service war in many respects. Here was a situation where regulars and conscripts were mixed, but it was one in which the conscripts had to 'grow up fast' as one memoir puts it, or perish. In her Korean phase, Beryl was confronted by the issues around national service every day, and on a very wide scale. Her realisation that the young men in front of her, wanting some reminders of the comforts of home, were a very special case in a context of caring. One way for me to describe this is to make a comparison with a visit to HMP Dartmoor I made around 2005. On that visit, I was shown a made-up sitting room, complete with armchairs and hearth. I asked why that was in a jail, and of course, the answer was that many prisoners need to be reminded that there is such a thing as a 'normal' home with the stereotypes of a typical family life. In a sense, Beryl and her peers provided that sitting room. In their mess and common room, where they arranged darts and snooker competitions or held dances and sing-songs, they were presenting pieces of a dream – the dream of home that many men thought they would never see again.

The archive belongs in a place such as the Imperial War Museum, and that will be its destination. Meanwhile, I hope that this mix of her words and mine have brought to life some of that real feel of the past – that 'foreign country' that L.P. Hartley wrote about. Some archives (and I have researched military history in many) offer only statistics and plans, data on losses and advances and so on; but this one consistently gave me the human perspective on a number of theatres of war. As Beryl adopted the mindset and language of people caught up in a massive conflict, she changed inside, and that became a deep change, shifting her sensibility to the world and to others permanently. The experience realigned her values. This is a rare thing in archival study. Once I studied letters from Natal just before the Zulu War in 1878–9 and in one of the notes there was a pressed flower and some soil from Africa, as I sat there in a Lincolnshire archive. The flower and soil were the symbolic representation of the human presence in great world events; Beryl's testimony was like that flower – something that was growing and changing as experience grew. Her life was like the answer given to Petruchio in Shakespeare's *The Taming of the Shrew* when he explains where he is going and why: he wants to go 'with such winds as scatter young men through the world to seek their fortunes farther than at home where small experience grows'.

The Korean War in particular, still appears as a show in the background of other narratives, and so when I saw that such was the case, notably with regard to Britain as opposed to US history, an added value seemed to be placed on Beryl's letters and photograph collection. So often in my historical research I have not perceived it at the time of discovery but only later, that there is a rarity and special value in some evidence from past life as contrasted with others. A clear instance of this is the photo. Beryl took hundreds, and many are very small and sometimes spoiled by sunlight. But in such images as troops enjoying a concert or men relaxing in groups out in the sun, there is a valuable insight gained. A similar point may be made on the material nature of where Beryl and her colleagues worked. So many mentions of 'our mess' and 'the common room' often give no physical description, but one photo says everything in that context. An example is one shot of an office in Iraq – on the surface just an assembly of chairs and tables, but the view is a rare thing.

Finally, I have to say that yes, there is more of this archive. Beryl Baxter went on to travel still more, and just as bravely. She switched from welfare worker in war to house mother in peace. But all the time, I feel certain, in her busy life, she thought of the men, young and old, whom she had guided, supported and sustained, through fear and dread in distant foreign places, where Britain and home were far, far away, and reassurance was hard to find. The material for her later life is more of the same, except that her charges were children, not soldiers; but our subject could not exist without some kind of responsibility for other people. When I read my last Beryl letter I thought again of Beatrice Webb's celebrated statement: 'In the nineteenth century the idea of service was transferred from God to man.' This could not have been a new credo for Beryl, but in substance it could have been written on her notepaper.

Acknowledgements

Obviously, for records relating to the 1940s and 1950s the oral history is relied on, but for Korea, as opposed to the Second World War, only a limited amount of material is available, and very few people from that war are still around to offer reminiscences. Fortunately, there is some literature in print offering most valuable witness testimony.

Thanks go to fellow writers Brian Elliott, Kate Walker and others for constructive conversations. Also, for military matters, Marc Westbrook, an officer once based in West Germany. I would like to thank him for a very useful contribution to our understanding of the WVS work and how it was perceived by army personnel. Thanks also to my brother, Andrew Wade, for suggestions and background discussions.

Special mention should be given to Richard Vinen, whose book, *National Service,* provides an invaluable source to statistics about the conscripts, as well as to the experience of conscription from participants. Also, without Stephen Kelly's invaluable collection of first-hand memories from the war, by serving men, it would have been difficult to offer any substantial testimony from the other side of Beryl's life – her charges whom she cared for.

Bibliography and Sources

Note: Letters cited in the text are all from my own collection, given to me from a contact who was preserving Beryl Baxter's letters. They were destined for the tip. Everything in her collection other than the letters is defined as ephemera, with no copyright or given source. The ephemera of documentation in some of the records mean that references are vague. This is because so much of the material was created on and for occasions that were intended to be transient and insubstantial. Beryl herself retained a number of ephemeral items, but most are not directly concerned with her important experience. These include catalogues, play and musical brochures and postcards.

Books

Cited in text
Agate, James, *A Shorter Ego* (Harrap, 1947)
Agate, James, *Ego 9* (Harrap, 1948)
Brett, Simon, (Ed.) *The Faber Book of Diaries* (Faber, 1987)
Chang, Jung, *Wild Swans* (Flamingo, 1993)
Conrad, Joseph, *Lord Jim: A Tale* (Penguin, 1971)
Cumings, Bruce, *The Korean War: A History* (Modern Library, 2010)
Day Lewis (Ed.), *The Collected Poems of Wilfred Owen* (Chatto and Windus, 1978)
Farrington, Karen, *The Angels of Englemere Wood* (Michael Joseph, 2022)
Fatland, Erika, *The Border* (Maclehose Press, 2020)

Freedman, Lawrence, *Command* (Allen Lane, 2022)

Grant, Tony (Ed.), *From Our Own Correspondent* (Profile Books, 2006)

Hall, A.W., *Woman: On the Diseases of Married Women* (Manchester, 1910)

Harding, Thomas, *The House by the Lake* (Windmill Books, 2015)

Hourani, Albert, *A History of the Arab Peoples* (Faber and Faber, 1991)

Kelly, Stephen F., *British Soldiers of the Korean War in their own words* (The History Press, 2013)

Kerr, Philip, *The One from the Other* (Quercus, 2007)

Lewis, Alun, *In the Green Tree* (Allen and Unwin, 1948)

Lewis-Stempel, John, *England: The Autobiography* (Penguin, 2010)

Lovell, Mary S., *The Mitford Girls* (Abacus, 2002)

MacFarlane, Robert, *The Wild Places* (Granta Books, 2007)

McGahern, John, *Memoir* (Faber and Faber, 2005)

MacGregor, Neil, *A History of the World in 100 Objects* (Allen Lane, 2010)

Mah Yen, Adeline, *Falling Leaves* (Penguin, 1977)

Maugham, Somerset, *A Writer's Notebook* (Penguin, 1967)

Morton, H.V., *In Search of England* (Penguin, 1961)

Morton, H.V., *I Saw Two Englands* (Methuen, 1943)

Murray, Janet Horowitz, *Strong-Minded Women* (Penguin, 1984)

Norwich, John Julius, *Christmas Crackers* (Penguin, 1979)

Pinkham, Lydia E., *Lydia Pinkham's Private Text-Book upon Ailments Peculiar To Women* (Pinkham Medicine Co., 1920)

Ray, John, *The Battle of Britain* (Cassell, 1994)

Rees, Nigel, *The Cassell Dictionary of Anecdotes* (Cassell, 1999)

Sandbrook, Dominic, *White Heat* (Abacus, 2006)

Smith, Robert Barr, *To the Last Cartridge* (Robinson, 1996)

Thomas, Donald, *Villains' Paradise* (John Murray, 2005)

Vinen, Richard, *National Service: Conscription in Britain 1945-1963* (Allen Lane, 2014)

Waterhouse, Keith, *City Lights: A Street Life* (Sceptre, 1994)

BIBLIOGRAPHY AND SOURCES

Reference

Bennett, Alan, *Writing Home* (Faber and Faber, 1994)

Brittain, Vera, *Testament of Friendship* (Fontana, 1980)

Chang, Jung, *Wild Swans: Three daughters of China* (Flamingo, 1993)

Cooper, Diana, *The Rainbow Comes and Goes* (Penguin, 1958)

Husain, Ed, *The House of Islam – A Global History* (Bloomsbury, 2019)

Kerr, Philip, *If the Dead Rise Not* (Quercus, 2009)

Kerr, Philip, *The One from the Other* (Quercus, 2007)

Kynaston, David, *Family Britain 1951–1957* (Bloomsbury, 2009)

Lamont-Brown, Raymond, *Kamikaze: Japan's Suicide Samurai* (Cassell, 1999)

Orwell, George, *The Collected Essays, Journalism and Letters of George Orwell - Vol. 4: In Front of Your Nose, 1945–1950* (Penguin, 1968)

Spicer, Charles, *Coffee with Hitler* (Oneworld, 2022)

Tallack, Malachy, *60 Degrees North* (Polygon, 2016)

Journals, Newspapers and Anthologies

Anon. 'One Woman – Alone – Among 600 Men' *The Sunday Express*, 4 November 1952 pp. 8-9

Davenport-Hines, Richard, 'Engaging with the Enemy' *Times Literary Supplement* 16 September 2022 p. 25

Editorial, 'Faces of the 'Fifties' Down Your Way' (Dalesman, April 2015) pp. 22-3

Fact edited by Raymond Postgate *et alia* July 1937

'Freed British Soldiers Reach Malta' *Times Digital Archive* 1 May 1953 p. 4

Heffer, Simon, 'Hinterland' *Daily Telegraph* 1 October 2022 p. 10

Heffer, Simon, 'When Generals Get Drunk on Power' *Daily Telegraph* 20 August 2022 p. 11

Hemp, Hetty, 'Deafening on Bomber 'Dromes' *Down Your Way* (Dalesman, July, 2015) p. 22

Ignota, 'Ladies at the Front' *Harmsworth Magazine* Vol. 4 1901 pp. 68-72

'Korea – The Forgotten War' Times Digital Archive 13 October 2022 p. 13

Life, international edition 'Reds Shove First into the Big Debate' pp. 13-5

'Military Occupation Can't Succeed' A member of the RAF *Reader's Digest.* February 1946 pp.17-20

Mullin, Chris, 'Partying amid the Ruins' *Times Literary Supplement* 7 October 2022 p. 8

'Murder on Koje Island' *Times Digital Archive* 31 January 1953 p. 6

O'Neill, Tom, 'Dangerous Divide' *National Geographic Magazine* Vol. 204 No.1 July 2003 pp. 2-27

'Reunited' Harry Unsworth, letter to *The Star* 8 January 1987 p. 37

'Secretive Sex, Political Spats and a World at War' diary extracts from Sir Henry Channon *Daily Telegraph Magazine* 3 September 2022 pp. 20-5

'Still Better Cruises for 1934' *The Listener,* 2 May 1934 cover.

The Times Obituary, 'Stella 'Jaye' Edwards 30 August 2022 p. 34

'Transfer of Air Base in Iraq', *The Times* 3 May 1955 p. 8

'What's Wrong with the German People?' *Schweizer Spiegel*, *Reader's Digest* September 1948 pp. 41-5

Online Sources

https://gwulo.com/node/11290 The New Territories: memoir by Bill Griffiths.

www.oldframlinghamian.com 'Ian Denys Peek'

Ephemera

Korean Base Gazette Vol. 3 Number 330 July 30 1953
Overseas with WVS (WVS, 1950)
Pacific Stars and Stripes – Korea Edition June 8 1953
WVS Bulletin (October, 1953 No. 166)
WVS Bulletin (November, 1953, No. 167)

WVS

For WVS events and for most of the documents relating to such things as balls and parties, references are impossible, as information was merely on small cards or on thin, fragile paper. Still, Beryl kept many of these items, and they come under these categories:

Staff
Disposition of WVS in the Middle East 7.12.1957 WVS Administration, Episkopi 2793
Ditto: 20 August 1955
Ditto: 20 October 1955
Ditto: 1 November 1956
Ditto: 1 April 1957

Letters
Letters from WVS NAAFI Headquarters July 1957
Ditto for 27 November 1957

Index